A MISSION
FROM GOD

A MISSION FROM GOD

*A Memoir and Challenge
for America*

JAMES MEREDITH

with WILLIAM DOYLE

ATRIA BOOKS

NEW YORK LONDON TORONTO SYDNEY NEW DELHI

ATRIA BOOKS

A Division of Simon & Schuster, Inc.
1230 Avenue of the Americas
New York, NY 10020

First Atria Books hardcover edition August 2012

ATRIA BOOKS and colophon are trademarks of Simon & Schuster, Inc.

Excerpt on pages 132–36 is from *An American Insurrection: The Battle of Oxford,
Mississippi, 1962* by William Doyle, copyright © 2001 by William Doyle. Used by
permission of Doubleday, a division of Random House, Inc.

For information about special discounts for bulk purchases,
please contact Simon & Schuster Special Sales at 1-866-506-1949
or business@simonandschuster.com.

The Simon & Schuster Speakers Bureau can bring authors to your live event.
For more information or to book an event, contact the Simon & Schuster Speakers
Bureau at 1-866-248-3049 or visit our website at www.simonspeakers.com.

Designed by Kyoko Watanabe

Manufactured in the United States of America

10   9   8   7   6   5   4   3   2

Library of Congress Cataloging-in-Publication Data

Meredith, James, 1933–
  A mission from God : a memoir and challenge for America / James Meredith with
William Doyle.
      p. cm.
  1. Meredith, James, 1933– 2. University of Mississippi—Students—Biography.
3. African American college students—Mississippi—Biography. 4. University of
Mississippi—History—20th century. 5. African Americans—Civil rights—Southern
States—History—20th century. 6. Civil rights movements—Southern States—
History—20th century. 7. United States—Race relations. I. Doyle, William, 1957– II.
Title.
  LD3412.9M47 2012
  378.762'83—dc23
                                                                          2012022963
  ISBN 978-1-4516-7472-9
  ISBN 978-1-4516-7474-3 (ebook)

To my family,
and the generations of Americans yet to be born

To Brendan and Naomi

You and I have a divine responsibility to transform America.

—James Meredith

One day the South will recognize its real heroes. They will be the James Merediths, courageously and with a majestic sense of purpose facing jeering and hostile mobs and the agonizing loneliness that characterizes the life of the pioneer.

—Martin Luther King, Jr.

Contents

Dawn of a New Era: on October 1, 1962, I stormed the holiest temple of white supremacy in America—the University of Mississippi—with the help of 30,000 American combat troops, federal marshals, and two of the bravest men I have ever known—Justice Department official John Doar (left) and James McShane, Chief of the U.S. Marshals Service (right). I was not a civil rights activist. I was a warrior. And I was on a mission from God. *Photo: Library of Congress*

Prologue

"**F**UCK YOU, NIGGER!"

"You're gonna die, nigger piece of shit!"

"We're going to string you up and set you on fire, you fucking nigger!"

It is October 1962.

I am walking across the campus of the University of Mississippi, surrounded by a crowd of screaming young white men.

They are sometimes joined by young white women, freshly scrubbed, lipsticked, and powdered paragons of southern beauty, who run up to me and scream the most filthy combinations of curses you could ever imagine, their faces contorted in paroxysms of rage.

The men surround me in teams by day and spend their nights trying to torment me out of my sleep with noise and threats that continue all night, every night.

I am Public Enemy Number One for every racist in America. I

will soon be at the top of a widely circulated "death list" of twelve Americans scheduled for assassination in Mississippi. Death threats are pouring in from across the United States, nearly one thousand so far, many detailing the gruesome ways I will be killed.

Rocks start to fly in my direction, the screaming intensifies, and the crowd surges closer. I am unarmed and wear no protective gear.

But I have no fear, not a molecule of it. The screaming is now a few feet from me, but I hear nothing, only silence. I see no faces. I am traveling in my own world. I am thinking of history, of America's and my own, of black kings and Indian queens, of vanished ages and empires. I am thinking of generations long dead and far in the future.

I have a slight smile of serenity on my face. I have no fear.

I have no fear because I am a black man in Mississippi and to be so means I am already dead. And a dead man has nothing to fear.

I have no fear because my father sent me on this journey. He guides and inspires my every thought and step. He is invincible, and therefore so am I.

I have no fear because I am an American citizen, heir to a sacred covenant of citizenship bestowed on me by George Washington and the Founding Fathers and Mothers of the nation. Thanks to this covenant, U.S. Army soldiers and federal marshals are traveling right behind me. They are carrying guns. They are supported by a vast arsenal of thousands more guns, jeeps, helicopters, communications gear, and military personnel plugged into the most awesome instrument of physical force the world has ever seen—the American military machine.

I am literally the baddest dude on Planet Earth, more heavily guarded than the president of the United States. I am the biblical David armed with the physical force of thirty thousand Goliaths.

The mob pushes closer. I am serene, completely at peace, focused like a laser on the destination of my journey, a classroom a few hundred yards in the distance.

I am a Zen samurai. I am invincible. Nothing can harm me.

I have been put on Earth for a reason, to restore the power and glory to my bloodline, and to all Americans.

I am not a civil rights activist, I am not a protester, and I am not a pacifist. I am not a Republican and I am not a Democrat. My political affiliation is Black.

I am an American citizen, and a son of Mississippi.

I am a warrior.

And I am on a mission from God.

A MISSION
FROM GOD

CHAPTER ONE

Beast on the Highway

I WAS SUPPOSED TO BE ASSASSINATED ON JUNE 6, 1966.
It happened in late afternoon, on a roadside two miles south of Hernando, Mississippi.

It rained early that morning and the trees were still damp, and the fresh, earthy smell of the countryside was everywhere.

The first signal of danger came softly out of a thicket of water lilies and honeysuckle vines lining the highway, an ice-cool voice that said, "Jaaa-mes."

"James, he's got a gun!" someone yelled.

Heads snapped.

My intended assassin popped up from a clump of bushes. He was a chubby-looking white man wearing sunglasses and a white shirt, and he toted a fully loaded 16 gauge automatic Remington shotgun.

I caught a glint of afternoon sunlight shining off the gun barrel.

After walking through open farm country, I was moving down into a long hollow with thick, junglelike foliage on either side. It was an ideal ambush point.

"James," said the man. "I only want James Meredith."

He called it sort of cold, like he couldn't bear to have my name in his throat for more than a second.

Then he came right out and shouted: "Meredith—I only want James Meredith! All the rest of you stand aside!"

I've seen a lot of movies, but no Hollywood director could have made a man look as cold-blooded as this one. This was the white face the southern black man had been staring at through 350 years of history: the hard eyes; the fleshy face; the hard line of mouth; the supremely confident, homicidal arrogance of the Beast of White Supremacy.

It was the face of the deputy sheriff, the face of the man freed by an all-white jury after murdering a black man, the face of vicious young men carrying Confederate flags who hit civil rights workers with ax handles.

"Just James Meredith," he said, moving up from the bushes and toward the shoulder of the road. I wished suddenly that I had brought a gun, that I had prepared better. Things were happening so fast that I had no time for fear.

My first move was to go toward the man with the gun. I was going to take the gun away from him.

I started toward him, at first convinced I could stop him. I had always felt that I could stop a mob with the uplifting of a hand. Because of a divine responsibility I felt to advance human civilization, I believed I could not die.

But something made me change my mind.

When I saw his face, I knew he was not all there. He looked deranged. I stopped because it struck me that the man must be a nut. I decided I could not deal with him and began to turn away.

He raised his gun and took aim.

"Hit the dirt!" a voice called.

People dived for the pavement and into the dust, crawling frantically across the highway trying to find someplace to hide, scrambling for shelter behind some cars parked beside the road.

He opened fire. The gun roared.

I ducked and dived to the pavement, making him miss the first attempt. The shot went skipping across the highway. I went down hard, my arm held out to break the fall. My pith helmet, cane, and sunglasses smashed into the pavement.

The shooter calmly moved up closer, raised the gun, and methodically opened fire again, hitting me with the next two shots.

I caught the biggest blast in my head. Over a hundred pellets hit me in the head, neck, back, and legs. I was knocked flat.

I lay in the middle of Highway 51 south of Hernando, Mississippi, looked around, and saw no human being in sight. Everyone had vanished behind cover or under the grass, seeking refuge from the gunfire.

I wriggled to the other side of the road, aiming for the relative safety of a gully, but collapsed in the shoulder.

Then there was absolute silence.

The shooter vanished in the brush.

Moments passed. I shouted, "Who? Who? What? Is anyone getting help for me? Oh, my God, is anyone going to help me?" It was an obvious question, a plea. Anyone in the same situation might have asked the question.

I could see the blood starting to come, puddling, coloring the rain-softened dust and gravel beneath my head.

I called out, "Ain't nobody gonna get me a car?"

Someone crept over and snapped a picture of me.

"He's shot in the head!" a nearby reporter called into a pay phone to his bureau in Memphis. The man on the other end of the line flashed out an Associated Press bulletin that ricocheted out to hundreds of teletype machines on news desks across America, "JAMES MEREDITH IS DEAD."

My name now joined the grotesque procession of public figures who would be murdered by gunfire in this decade: John F. Kennedy, Malcolm X, and three men whom I knew personally, Robert F. Kennedy, Martin Luther King, Jr., and a towering giant of a man whom I consider to be the founding father of modern Mississippi, Medgar Evers.

My assassin would enter the tormented fraternity of past and future American assassins like Lee Harvey Oswald, James Earl Ray, Byron de la Beckwith, and Sirhan Sirhan. His name was Aubrey James Norvell, and he was a gap-toothed, chubby, forty-year-old unemployed hardware clerk who lived in an upper-middle-class neighborhood in Memphis. He was a Purple Heart veteran of World War II, and a devoted bird hunter.

His neighbors said he was a quiet, Christian man.

I was joining the list of more than five hundred black men lynched in Mississippi in that century.

I was entering the pantheon of "civil rights martyrs," the scores of black and white Americans who sacrificed their lives in the fight to make America live up to the vision of the Founding Fathers.

My wife would now be a widow with three young sons to raise on her own.

The only thing was, I wasn't dead yet.

I was lying facedown in the gravel on the side of a road in northern Mississippi.

Stray impressions bounced around my brain. "That man shot me like a Goddammed rabbit. . . . He took his own good time about it. . . . Why did I come to Mississippi unarmed? . . . A man ain't ever supposed to be helpless. . . . If I'd had a gun I could have got that guy."

On that day I was on summer break from Columbia University Law School in New York City, where I was in my first year of earning my law degree. I was on a mission to get my fellow blacks in the South to exercise their rights as American citizens and register to vote.

On the day I was supposed to die, I had a Bible in one hand, an ivory-tipped walking cane in the other that clucked against the pavement, and I was walking through an earthly paradise called Mississippi, a land I consider the center of the universe.

To me, Mississippi is the most beautiful country in the world, during all seasons. In the spring, all is green and fresh, the air is clean and sweet, and everything is healthy. As a boy I knew that any running stream of water was fit to drink.

The fall of the year is perhaps the most colorful. Nature begins to fade away. The grass dries up and draws closer to the earth. Trees and bushes start to color and a slow deterioration asserts itself. All remaining fruits and nuts come to full maturity. A great feeling of urgency is generated by such abundance. You feel that time is squeezing you and harvest you must. The temptation to gather the falling nuts—acorns, hickory nuts, scaly barks, pecans, chincky berries, and all kinds in abundance—pulls you to them.

Winter is my favorite season for looking at the land. Everything, except for the cedar trees and a few other evergreens, is bare. You can see for miles.

In the summer there is maturity. The grass begins to level off and seed. A feeling of repose overcomes you. You have the urge to pull alongside the road and take a cow path up into the bushes and lie down under a big tree. The effect of the heat shows everywhere. Blackberries begin to ripen; muscadine vines begin to hang from the burden of a good crop; and a blacksnake is likely to cross the road at any moment or shoot back into the bushes. Since the crops are nearly all laid by now, the whole state takes on a relaxed and idle atmosphere.

Summer was also the most suitable season for a lynching.

On this day, I was supposed to be lynched by shotgun.

In those days, not that long ago, the simple fact of being black in Mississippi was enough to get you shot down on the side of the road in broad daylight.

I wish there was some way for me to explain the awful fear that

5

permeated the atmosphere of everyday life for every black person in America then, especially those in the South.

I wish there was a way to explain what it was like to be black, moving down a deserted highway at night behind the wheel of an automobile, and see car lights blink on in the darkened rear of a service station, and see a car bearing strangers pulling out behind you.

I wish I could put into words the sinking feeling in the stomach and the nervous twitching in the face that came over a black American when he confronted a southern lawman.

I wish I could explain the long history of murder and castration and death in the night; explain the humiliation and insult of the theory of white supremacy; explain all those things that were the excess baggage of the black American's mind, whether he lived in Scarsdale, New York, or Philadelphia, Mississippi.

Their root was fear. And in my own way, that day in June 1966, I hoped that by walking down that road I could remove at least some part of that fear.

I was at the northern tip of Mississippi, walking south along Highway 51, the first highway paved in Mississippi and the highway that most blacks who migrated from the mid-South had taken in heading North.

Ahead of me lay a tottering empire of white supremacy, where Americans of African heritage were still prevented from exercising the most basic right of American citizenship, the right to vote, by the lingering threat of state terrorism. For the past ninety years, if you were black and you tried to vote or encouraged others to do so, you easily could get yourself beaten or killed.

But what few people realize is that whites in the South were as unfree as any black, too. White supremacy was official and legal—it was enforced by judges, law enforcement, banks, and community leaders—and a white person who failed to acknowledge and carry out the mandate of white supremacy was as subject to persecution as any black.

Two years earlier, in 1964, two white New Yorkers, Michael Schwerner and Andrew Goodman, were summarily executed along with their black colleague James Chaney. Their killers: a gang of Mississippi law enforcement officers and Klansmen. Their crime: encouraging their fellow Americans to enjoy the rights of citizenship, by registering to vote.

My mission on this march was to inspire black people to overcome their fear, face down the beast of white supremacy, and register. I did not want this to be a mass demonstration, quite the opposite, I wanted the image of a lone unarmed American, protected only by a Bible and his American citizenship, to inspire black people to go down to their county courthouse and demand to be treated as Americans. Ever the perceived outsider, I sought no organized support, and the mainstream civil rights organizations offered me none.

I wanted to prove that one black man could walk free in the South.

President Lyndon B. Johnson had signed the Voting Rights Act in 1965, but the law was meaningless as long as blacks in the rural South remained gripped by fear. That fear was historically ingrained, and no one knew for sure whether it was still justified in the wake of great changes that were beginning to take hold in the South since the Supreme Court school desegregation decision of 1954.

I began the march the day before, Sunday, June 5, in Memphis, a city in Tennessee that was at the same time considered the northern capital of Mississippi and the cotton capital of the world. The march would end in Jackson, the capital of Mississippi, the citadel of white supremacy in America. Early that year, I announced what I was planning to do and my plans were broadcast through the media.

I headed out of the Memphis Sheraton-Peabody Hotel, talked to a few reporters, and covered the twelve-mile first leg to the Mississippi state line. White passersby looked pop-eyed at the little column; a few heckled and waved rebel flags. Little knots of blacks waved at me and called out encouragement: "We're praying for you!"

When I first announced my walk, I welcomed any able-bodied man who wanted to join me. I insisted that I did not want women and children, because I felt deeply that women and children should not have to take the risks we would face. It was for this reason that I did not take my wife, Mary June, or my six-year-old son, John.

I felt it was time for the American Negro to assert his manhood, to take his own chances, to risk his own life to conquer his fear of white supremacy. I also said I wanted no one to accompany me who would become a burden on the Negroes of Mississippi, imposing upon them for lodging or food. Any whites who cared to come along were welcome, and three of the men walking with me were white.

I passed in peace the first day. I was walking, taking it slow, enjoying my notoriety. The journey was to cover 220 miles. I planned it so it would end on June 25, my thirty-third birthday.

On the second day, I passed the giant road sign that read "Welcome to Mississippi, The Magnolia State," a sign that, if you were black, seemed more like a macabre threat than a welcome. I crossed the state line and passed into the beautiful pine hills of the land of my birth. The press, apparently following the lead of mainstream civil rights leaders, had largely ignored the march, but there was a contingent of reporters and policemen trailing the march, just in case, including fifteen Mississippi state troopers, assorted sheriff's deputies, and FBI men.

Strung out behind me were an odd-lot, tiny handful of followers: the young black vice president of a small New York recording company; a white Episcopal priest from Monroe, New York; a dapper Memphis black man who owned a gas station and sundries store; and a Washington radio man who had volunteered to be my press secretary.

I felt like a dazzling figure with my bright white pith helmet and walking cane made of ebony and ivory, which was presented to me by the chief of a Sudanese village with the words "We shall arrive." The cane symbolized strength, and the ultimate reunification of the dispersed black peoples of the world.

I looked like an elfin Don Quixote, a lonely pilgrim barely five feet six inches tall and 130 pounds, wearing a pith helmet set crooked on my head and sunglasses that rode too high on my nose. It was an image in line with *Time* magazine's description of me as "frail and introverted."

I've been accused of having both a "Messiah complex" and a colossal ego, and both are true. As I walked alongside the two-lane blacktop in the scorching Mississippi heat, I could feel the spiritual presence of my late father walking beside me, and along with him were no less than Jesus Christ and the Founding Fathers of America. There was George Washington, Thomas Jefferson, and Frederick Douglass, along with my African and Indian royal ancestors, all marching with me.

There was never a time I didn't feel divinely inspired. All of my life I studied for my role. I feel like God or some force greater than me provided the mission but left it to me to decide how to carry it out. I had no close friends. My most important mentors were Moses, Christ, and Joseph of biblical times and to a lesser extent, Charles de Gaulle and Napoleon.

Leading our procession, I felt, was God. The Bible in my hand was my ultimate protection, its words my guiding wisdom. Surrounded by all these titanic forces, I felt immortal. I could achieve nothing less than total victory.

On that day, as on all the others of my life, I was inspired by God, and by the greatest man I have ever known, my father. I was inspired by a divine responsibility I have felt my entire life to restore my people to the power and the glory they once enjoyed on this Earth. That purpose sprang out of my own mysticism, a sense of mission and of destiny that has always marked me as a loner among blacks as well as whites.

I was fighting for full citizenship for me and my kind. I was at war against fear.

I was on a mission from God.

When I was born, my father was a Methodist, so I was first baptized in the Methodist church and they sprinkled me. Then I listened to the Baptists for a while and I figured I better not take any chances, so I joined the Baptist Church and got submerged. Then I decided to become completely interdenominational, accepting the truth and power of all human religions. As Mahatma Gandhi put it, "I am a Hindu. I am a Muslim. I am a Jew. I am a Christian. I am, after all, a human being, and I am connected to all my fellow human beings."

I've been sprinkled, I've been baptized, and I've joined churches without any initiation at all. When I die, I bet some church will come up and plant me.

On the second day of my march, every so often someone by the roadside wondered aloud words to the effect of, "What the devil are you trying to prove walking 220 miles in the dead of summer?"

I replied that if I could walk unarmed through Mississippi, then I might just soothe the fears of black people and inspire them to get out to the polls and vote for the first time in their lives.

Out of nowhere, someone said, "There's a guy up the road says he wants to kill you."

But I was busy reading newspaper clippings about myself and thinking about the journey I was on, and I disregarded the warning. I hardly blinked. I just shrugged my shoulders and kept on walking.

I'd gotten countless death threats before, and my father had taught me that there was no way to prevent the mishaps of nature, accidents, or the acts of a fool or deranged person. These were the hazards of life. I had learned long before that the two greatest wastes of one's time are regretting the past and worrying about the future. But just in case, I had taken out a large life insurance policy before the march began.

I focused instead on the heavenly land I was traveling through, the sweet fragrance of the pine trees, the crunching of my footsteps in the gravel, and the buzzing of nature all around me.

Mississippi is mine.

And one must love what is his. I love Mississippi like a bee loves honey.

I love Mississippi because of the beauty of the countryside and the old traditions of family affection, and for such small things as flowers bursting in spring and the way you can see for miles from a ridge in winter.

Always, without fail, regardless of the number of times I enter Mississippi, it creates within me feelings that are felt at no other time. I feel love because I have always felt that for Mississippi. Love of the land. There is the feeling of joy. Joy because I once again have lived to enter the land of my fathers, the land of my birth, the only land in which I feel at home. It also inspires a feeling of hope, because where there is life there is also a hope, a chance.

At the same time, there was a feeling of profound sadness. Sadness because I was immediately aware of the special subhuman role that I must play because I was black, or face death. Sadness because it was the home of the greatest number of blacks outside Africa, yet my people suffered from want of everything in a rich land of plenty, and, most of all, they endured the daily obscenity of being stripped of their rights as American citizens.

My most dominant thought was, "If only I had my fair share in the running and managing of the state of Mississippi, what a wonderful land this could be." And I always ended the meditation with an assurance to myself, from myself, that I would have that share in my land or die trying to get it.

Early that second morning of my march, when I walked over a rise, with the harsh Mississippi sun baking the pavement of Highway 51, I beheld the town of Hernando lying before me like some Hollywood director's idea of a small town in the American South: a few small stores, some old decaying mansions, and many, many unpainted board houses where the Negroes lived.

It was the first town I had come to in Mississippi. I saw white faces at windows, and white men standing in front of their shops or staring blankly from the lawns of their homes. I didn't see any blacks. At least, I didn't see them anywhere around the main street. But they were waiting for me when I walked into the main square of the town. Some of them had been there for two hours, standing together on the far side of the square.

There were young black men, children with pure young faces, and old men bent with age. Most were wearing the long blue overalls of cotton-field workers, and they did not seem to know what to do as I approached. Some looked away, some stared at the ground. All of them were aware of the group of whites, silent and sullen, who watched us from the far side of the square. For both the whites and blacks of Hernando, nothing like this had ever happened before.

I walked up to the group of blacks and started shaking hands. I urged them to register to vote, because that was one of the keys to the future, and they said, "We're gonna register, we're gonna register."

I swept through the crowd shaking hands like a politician, and, when I finally left, I was beaming and there was a new spring in my step. I asked someone, "Did you see them? They were *men!*"

We went around to a café to have something to eat. I was enjoying a cheeseburger and a glass of milk when an old black farmer came over and pressed a dollar bill into my hand. He had probably never earned more than three hundred dollars in a single year. "You just keep that," he said. "You just keep that." I still had that dollar bill in my pocket a few hours later when I was shot.

I entered Mississippi on foot with no food, no tent, no sleeping bag, no backpack, and $11.35 in my pocket. That was it. I knew the black people of Mississippi would take care of me.

Our little procession passed the southern edge of Hernando, where Highway 51 narrowed from a four-lane highway to a two-lane road. Carloads of whites wheeled past to goggle and heckle, little knots of blacks waved at us and called encouragement: "We're praying for you, James!" I had made it fourteen miles south from the Mississippi state line.

A few law enforcement officials and reporters tagged along slowly in their vehicles. Jack Thornell, a twenty-six-year-old cub photographer for the Associated Press in New Orleans, rested in a parked car with a friend from United Press International, waiting for a *Life* cameraman to show up with some soda pop.

I remember thinking things were going even better than expected. An old farmer and his family came down to the highway and gave me water, in full view of the white people across the road. I remember a Negro maid in one white home who edged down the clothesline to the road and gave me a little wave.

Then something strange happened. The cars that had been following, or leapfrogging alongside me, moved up the road and parked on the shoulder. Some of the men in the cars walked on to a small soft drinks store. I couldn't see the sheriff's car or the highway patrol. I was left there with a few friends and reporters.

We were an hour out of Hernando, walking south, when Claude Sterrett, a friend from New York, arrived.

"Jay," he said breathlessly, "I met a man down the road who said someone's waiting for you with a gun. He's gonna shoot you."

I ignored the warning.

I got shot.

And now, according to the Associated Press and the NBC *Huntley-Brinkley Report* nightly news broadcast, I was dead.

That year, I would be the most admired black man in America after Martin Luther King, Jr., according to a national poll, so my obituary would be a prominent one. It would run in newspapers around the globe from New York to Tokyo, Peking, Moscow, Paris, and Johannesburg.

And the vast majority of the headlines would be variations on one theme: "James Meredith Is Dead, Integrated the University of Mississippi."

My whole life would be boiled down to a single night in 1962, when I forced my way into the holiest temple of white supremacy in the United States with the help of thirty thousand American combat troops.

All was still.

I lay motionless in the dust as blood trickled out of my wounds.

CHAPTER TWO

An American Rebel

I AM IMMORTAL.

    I live in the pages of American history, after the Little Rock Nine and the Freedom Rides, and just before the Cuban Missile Crisis.

A half century ago, I engineered a constitutional crisis that forced the president, the Supreme Court, and the armed forces of the United States into a direct legal and physical collision with the governor of Mississippi and thousands of his armed forces and civilian volunteers.

The result was a fourteen-day insurrection by the government of Mississippi that climaxed in a battle between a mob of 2,000 white civilians and a force of 400 U.S. deputy marshals and some 30,000 American combat troops, including national guardsmen, military police, and airborne paratroopers. Two people were killed and hundreds were wounded, an American state was disgraced, and a great American university was nearly destroyed.

The state of Mississippi was in a state of open, official, declared physical rebellion against the United States on the issue of race. That is a very difficult story for America to understand, and it's a story you won't find properly told in most history books, but that's precisely what happened.

In this crisis, the president of the United States had to invoke the Insurrection Act to stage a lightning combat invasion of an American state that refused to comply with federal law. *Time* magazine called it "the gravest conflict between federal and state authority since the Civil War," and *U.S. News & World Report* wrote that the event "came close to being a small-scale civil war."

It was the climax of a year-and-a-half-long legal struggle in which I forced the federal government to honor my right as an American citizen to attend the public college of my choice in my home state.

For eighty years, Mississippi had enforced white supremacy with fear, terror, physical violence, torture, and murder, administered by its own police forces. Black people were treated as subhuman, subject to arbitrary arrest, beatings, and extrajudicial execution at the whim of the governor, sheriffs, deputies, and any white man or woman.

I am a military man and I saw this entire episode as a military exercise.

This was a combat operation. My mission was not to "integrate" the university, which I saw as a minor and relatively timid objective. My mission was to physically and psychologically shatter the system of white supremacy in Mississippi and eventually all of America, with the awesome physical force of the United States military machine.

I had returned to Mississippi because I had developed a master plan to replace what I considered the black American's worst enemy: the principles and doctrines of white supremacy. I had no desire to destroy the customs and systems of the South; instead, I intended to build a better system and to replace the old unsuitable customs with more desirable ones. The first step in the master plan was to return to Mississippi.

That the black American was to become legally and officially free and equal was no longer a question in my mind. I was sure that it would become a reality. Whether the black American would become actually and effectively free and equal was not so certain, and it was for this objective I was prepared to fight. What most blacks and their organizations were fighting for, the principle of equality, the idea that "I am not inferior to you," was to me a foregone conclusion.

Different wars have different goals: defending and repelling, attacking and conquering, forcing an enemy to negotiate a settlement, and, as in the case of the Allies of World War II, demanding unconditional surrender. My objective in this war was total victory: victory over discrimination, oppression, the unequal application of the law, and, most of all, over white supremacy and all of its manifestations.

I wanted to administer a sudden psychological blow that would drive a stake through the heart of one of the most powerful and destructive beasts in the American soul—the poisonous idea that any group of Americans was superior to any other group of Americans.

On the night of September 30, 1962, I entered the most sacred temple of white supremacy in America, the campus of the University of Mississippi at Oxford, Mississippi, and triggered the climax of the most momentous clash between federal and state authority since the Civil War. I started the whole thing.

I am a moment in history.

I am resurrected every year during Black History Month, when I dwell in an exalted stratosphere with giants like Rosa Parks, Sojourner Truth, Mary McCloud Bethune, Harriet Tubman, Fannie Lou Hamer, Marcus Garvey, W. E. B. Du Bois, and Malcolm X.

My praises have been sung by people including Martin Luther

King, Jr., who predicted in his *Letter from a Birmingham Jail*, "One day the South will recognize its real heroes. They will be the James Merediths, courageously and with a majestic sense of purpose facing jeering and hostile mobs and the agonizing loneliness that characterizes the life of the pioneer."

In 2009, *The Nation* magazine put an illustration of me on the cover, an imagined scene showing me and Frederick Douglass standing next to Barack Obama as he was being sworn in as president, surrounded by scores of other human rights heroes.

Sometimes I'm a footnote, sometimes I'm a few paragraphs, and occasionally I'm a whole book. At least four have been written about me, as well as hundreds of newspaper and magazine articles. I've been given awards, certificates, medals, ceremonial banquets, accolades, and honors. I'm a celebrity of sorts, and people stop me on the street almost daily to thank me for what I've done.

I am, in short, a civil rights hero.

But lots of folks think I'm a real odd bird.

I don't behave like a "civil rights hero" at all.

That's because I hate the whole idea of "civil rights" as it is commonly understood and discussed.

You see, I've always found the rhetoric of mainstream civil rights leaders and organizations to be far too timid, accomodationist, and gradualist. It always seemed to me that they behaved like meek and gentle supplicants begging the oppressor for a few crumbs of justice, for a few extra molecules of citizenship rights. I was never a part of the civil rights movement.

Meaningful freedom is rarely gained through the magnanimous benevolence of the predominant powers, but must be won on the field. In the event that I am most known for in history, I chose the University of Mississippi at Oxford, Mississippi, to be my battlefield.

I know that it may strike some people as a kind of historical blasphemy to say this, but the rhetoric and vocabulary of the American civil rights movement has always seemed upside-down and backward to me. In fact, I always found it grossly insulting to me, to you, and to every American citizen, because it always begins with the assumption or concession that some or any of our civil rights are up for negotiation. They are not now and never have been. We were anointed with and guaranteed all of these rights at birth as Americans.

Don't get me wrong—we must address and rectify the violation of any American's citizenship rights anywhere, any time, under any conditions. We must do it if that American citizen is black, white, Latino, Asian, or Native American; if the citizen is Christian, Jewish, Muslim, Hindu, Buddhist, Sikh, or atheist; if he or she is gay or straight; if he or she is descended from the Middle Passage, the voyage of the *Mayflower*, or the Holocaust, or from illegal immigrants who crossed the Mexican border.

But if the discussion of any American citizen's rights does not first acknowledge that all these rights are eternal, sacred, inviolate, and perfectly equal for every single American citizen, and that the very idea of molesting or negotiating for any of those rights is an obscene process, then it is in my opinion an incomplete, and therefore useless, discussion.

When it comes to my rights as an American citizen, and yours, I am a triumphalist and an absolutist. Anything less is an insult. It's all or nothing.

I befuddle people.

People have an awfully hard time trying to figure me out.

I often move in a pattern that is unpredictable and baffling on the surface.

Over the years, I have managed to baffle almost everybody, sometimes myself included. I've backed Democrats and Republicans, and I've criticized black civil rights leaders and white liberals almost as much as I've criticized white supremacists.

People have a real hard time putting me into words. One white Mississippian, veteran journalist Bill Minor, has always found me befuddling. "It's so hard to separate the true James Meredith from what he says for effect," he wrote. "He defies understanding. If blacks should build a monument to someone who did more for them and their cause than anyone, it's him. But for some reason he has never been able to generate a following. He is not and never has been received as a hero in the black community. He does so much to detract from that image. He is highly inconsistent. Sometimes he's a Republican, sometimes he's a Democrat. Somehow he manages to alienate anyone who would support him." He added, "I think James Meredith has a strange desire to confuse both his enemies and his friends. He's the world's most confusing maverick. He doesn't want to be categorized, no matter what it is. I think he's a strange person, a loner. He prefers to isolate himself. I don't think he ever wanted to assume the role of being a leader."

I speak in code, in historical puzzles and pathways that are often impenetrable to other people. In 2008, Australian journalist Geoff Elliott wrote this after meeting with me: "Speaking with a rich southern accent, Meredith leans forward and intones like a preacher at times, slapping my leg at one point for exclamation, and weaving between biblical, European and U.S. history and then melding them with current events, in a way that is implausible, yet the work of a genius." But he added, "At other times Meredith wanders down historical paths that seem to come to dead ends. He is one of the strangest people I have met."

A historian at the University of Memphis named Aram Goud-souzian called me "perhaps the most peculiar hero of the African American freedom struggle." He strained to put my persona into words, writing, "He espoused a political philosophy rooted in his particular vision of black manhood: self-reliance, courage, patriarchy, self-defense, full citizenship rights. Though facets of his ideology connected to a broad range of civil rights activists and allies, he was *sui generis*, both popularly resonant and singularly odd."

The historian wrote that I "could be brilliant, engaging, and heroic, but he also had a quick temper, nervous stomach, and tendency to crash from emotional exhaustion." But he came close to capturing the essence of my message when he wrote, "His conception of manhood shaped his politics of self-determination: to exercise their citizenship rights, black men needed to exhibit courage, shape their own destiny, defend themselves and their families, and assert patriarchical authority."

You see, I am a civil rights hero who is not a professional civil rights figure and never has been.

I am not your mama's civil rights hero.

For one thing, I am not a good speaker. If you're looking for someone to regale your annual fundraising breakfast with inspiring tales of the civil rights movement, I am not your man. My speaking style has been called disjointed, disconnected, rambling, perplexing, and even insulting.

I once reduced black members of an audience at the University of Mississippi to anger and tears when I criticized the poor English skills of young blacks. I started off the lecture by dancing to some Elmore James tunes, then I sat down and told them the truth— that without acquiring proper English skills, which I explicitly defined as not including so-called "black English," they had little chance of succeeding in American society. Studying "black English," I said, was a waste of time.

I was delighted at the friction, debate, and consternation I caused among the students, because to me it meant we were having a real discussion about a crucial taboo subject.

But the students seemed bewildered and furious. One of them demanded to know if I'd ever read Toni Morrison. "No," I replied. Quite frankly, I'm not that interested in "black culture." I'm interested in human culture and American culture, both of which were built in part on spectacular achievements by people of African blood. But I see no reason to ghettoize and diminish and infantilize those achievements by forcing them into some special subcategory of "diversity" studies or "black studies," any more than I see a reason to relegate the spectacular achievements of great Americans like Jackie Robinson, Martin Luther King, Jr., Rosa Parks, and George Washington Carver to the forced Siberian exile of some "Black History Month."

When the students invited me to speak with them that day, I guess they expected a civil rights hero.

Instead, they got James Meredith.

I've been called bumbling, disorganized, unprofessional, rude, temperamental, erratic, brilliant, courageous, a man with no limits on his future, and a loner.

I am not a team player, I'm my own team. Hell, I'm practically my own sport. I am an unpredictable maverick, indeed, an outright enigma to many people.

My ego is so enormous, and I talk about myself so much, that someone once wisecracked that my name should be changed to "I, James Meredith."

I am a tree farmer. I grow, harvest, and sell lumber that grows on the family property I bought from my father in 1960. That's how I've earned much of my adult living. I've never held down a "real" job. Somehow, God has always provided for me. I am also a conservative, a sometime businessman, sometime political candidate, a soldier, a globalist, husband, father and grandfather, and a survivor. An inordinately solitary man, I show all of these faces and often present another one at my critics that puzzles and occasionally angers them.

I once considered myself invincible. I always had the idea that nothing could ever harm me. That feeling was tempered by the death at age thirty-nine of my first wife, Mary June, who suffered a massive heart attack in 1979 and left me the sole parent of three boys. And it is tempered by age, as I enter the eighth decade of my life.

I puzzle people and occasionally anger them.

I am the man who once stood to many as the very symbol of integration, yet I have vehemently rejected integration as it is traditionally defined, along with "busing for racial balance" and affirmative action programs with fixed quotas and many modern social reforms promulgated by the liberal elite.

I am a civil rights hero who spent a year on the U.S. Senate staff of archconservative senator Jesse Helms as a domestic policy advisor. Helms was formerly a longtime segregationist, and was the most powerful conservative in Congress when I went to work for him. I did it because I agreed with him on opposing racial quotas, opposing welfare abuses, and a wide range of other social issues. I also sensed that he had the potential to achieve something great for mankind.

Years after I left his staff, thanks in part of the efforts of rock star Paul David "Bono" Hewson, Helms successfully championed legislation authorizing $600 million for international AIDS relief efforts, and he confessed he was "ashamed" he had done so little in his life to help combat the global spread of AIDS. I wrote him a letter to tell him how proud I was of him.

Lots of people think I was completely out of my mind to have worked for Jesse Helms.

I'll tell you something.

It seemed like exactly the right thing to do at the time.

I'd do it again.

I am a civil rights hero who once endorsed David Duke, a former Ku Klux Klan leader, in his campaign for governor of Louisiana.

I did it for three reasons. First, he had very clearly repudiated and disavowed both the Klan and racism at this point, and had never been convicted of any violent act. Second, I agreed with many of his positions in the campaign, which were mainstream conservative. And third, he was a better man than his main opponent, who was a criminal. Duke lost. He also appears to have later re-embraced much of his racist ideology.

Many people think I was absolutely, certifiably insane to have briefly befriended and supported David Duke.

Well, it made perfect sense to me at the time, like a risk worth taking.

And I'd probably do it again.

I have always considered white liberals just as capable of racism and racial hypocrisy as white conservatives.

I object to being labeled primarily as an "African-American," because all other Americans are not simultaneously described as Caucasian-American, Irish-American, German-American, and so on, nor should they be. I reject the idea of any American being identified primarily as a hyphenated American. A hyphenated American usually implies second-class citizenship. There is no such thing in my America.

I am just as American as anyone else. I refuse to be forced into a special category where I am expected to behave in certain ways and hold certain beliefs.

I am a black man who refuses to be labeled as an ethnically hyphenated American. I am an American with African, European, and Native American ancestors.

I am a black man who has the audacity to often be an out-spoken conservative, and to criticize conservatives whenever I see fit.

I am a civil rights hero who absolutely hates to talk about civil rights.

In other words, I am a free American citizen.

At the same time, you'll never find a man who is prouder of being black than I am.

I was born black.

This fact turned out to be the most important thing in my life.

I was born on June 25, 1933, on a small farm in Mississippi's Attala County, near the town of Kosciusko. I was the seventh of thirteen children. Three died before reaching age one.

As a boy I walked four miles to school in the morning, four miles back in the evening.

My great-grandfather was not only a white man, but the founding father of white supremacy in Mississippi.

He was Mississippi Chief Justice J. A. P. Campbell. He was my father's mother's father. At seventeen he became the youngest lawyer in Mississippi, at twenty-one he was elected to the Mississippi House, and when he was still in his twenties he became Speaker of the House. At the age of twenty-nine, he led the Mississippi delegation to the Confederate Secession Convention. After secession, he organized a military group and was wounded twice in early battles of the Civil War. President Jefferson Davis chose him to be the chief legal officer for the Confederate army, where he served until the end of the war.

Campbell returned to Attala County after the war and was elected circuit judge in which position he served until the United States required all high-ranking Confederate officers to take an oath of allegiance to the United States. He refused and was forced out of office. He was already the richest man in Attala County, and he established the law firm of Campbell and Calhoun, which became the biggest and most powerful law firm in Mississippi. More important, he organized the group of one hundred former Confederate colonels that staged an armed coup d'état and overthrow of the Reconstruction government in Mississippi in 1875. In 1876 he was appointed to the Mississippi Supreme Court, in which he became chief justice and served for eighteen years until 1894.

My great-grandfather J. A. P. Campbell wrote the Mississippi Codes of Law and Constitution of 1890, which established legal and official white supremacy for the first time in the Western world. He resigned because he was not pleased with what the white supremacists in Mississippi were doing. Like many white aristocrats in that era, he had both a white family and a black family. He believed that whites were superior, but that blacks should have the right to vote. He lived twenty-seven years after leaving the Mis-

Confederate official and Mississippi Supreme Court justice J. A. P. Campbell, a founding father of white supremacy in America. He was also my great-grandfather. He helped raise my father. *Photo courtesy of the James Meredith collection*

sissippi Supreme Court and spent most of those remaining years with his black family. He mostly raised my father.

Another great-grandfather of mine, my father's paternal grandfather, was not only a pure-blood Native American, but the last national leader of the Choctaw Nation in 1830 when the United States and the state of Mississippi seized our 25 million acres of land and dissolved our nation. According to our family's oral history, he was a direct descendant of the founders of the Choctaw Nation. He was General Sam Cobb. He fought in every major battle against the other Indian nations alongside General Andrew Jackson. General Cobb never dreamed that his ally and good friend General Jackson, after over a quarter century of fighting side by side with him, would turn his army against him, and demand every acre of his land as well. Sam Cobb led the Choctaw Nation for forty years in the wilderness of our former territory, and he died a landless, heartbroken old Indian.

I always wanted to be a general in the American military, because I heard so much about the exploits of my great-grandfather General Sam Cobb while I was growing up. Also according to family oral history, my black ancestry traced back to a long line of kings of the African empire of Dahomey.

By far the greatest power and influence in my life came from my father, Moses Arthur Meredith.

My father was named after Moses of the Bible and King Arthur of Camelot.

The names fit him perfectly.

He was an intensely proud, dignified, regal man with the carriage of a king and the wisdom of a prophet. He was also always very funny. He was a natural comedian and a wonderful storyteller.

With my father, everything in life was a joy and a pleasure. He made it so.

My father owned eighty-four acres of land and raised all variety of crops. He was the first member of his family ever to own a piece of land. He was a self-sustaining farmer. He produced everything that was needed for our family to live a good life. Like most people black and white, I always called him "Cap," short for "captain." He was the captain of my life.

Cap Meredith was an independent farmer, and a living model of the proper man. He didn't drink alcohol, didn't smoke cigarettes, didn't chase women, never got in trouble with the law, and always paid his debts. No one could remember ever having heard Cap use a curse word. He went to church regularly, sent his children to school, and was known as the hardest-working and most dependable man in the county.

My father, Moses Arthur Meredith, was named after Moses from the Bible and King Arthur of Camelot. The names fit him perfectly. He carried himself like a king and had the wisdom of a prophet. When I was a boy, he told me of my mission from God. *Photo courtesy of the James Meredith collection*

He was a very well-informed man, and he listened closely to world news on the radio. He knew every story of the Holy Bible by memory. Twice a day without exception at breakfast and supper, every member of the family sat down at the dining table for prayer and discussion of family business. Cap always talked about the events happening in the world as well as the weather forecast. All activities on the farm were planned according to the weather.

He was also without challenge the best-dressed man in the county. All of his clothes from head to foot were tailor-made exclusively for him from the very best materials that could be had. He spent a fortune on clothes and shoes.

In his house I learned the true meaning of life. Here I learned that death was to be preferred to indignity. His farm, about three miles from Kosciusko in central Mississippi, was in the hills. The soil was poor, studded with rocks.

Although he had owned the farm since the 1920s, it wasn't until the 1960s that Cap had an indoor toilet. Until the day he died in 1965, my father never made enough money to file an income tax return.

My mother, Roxie Meredith, whom we called "Miss Roxie," was a strong, highly determined and supportive woman, who, like my father, was a great inspiration to me in everything I have ever done. Consistent with the Gothic horror that invades the history of many black families in the South, my mother was the granddaughter of a powerful white man who raped her grandmother when she was thirteen years old. The white man never gave Roxie's grandmother or mother a penny of support her whole life, but when Roxie was born, the man sent word to her mother to take her out to the side of the road so he could drive by and see what she looked like. Roxie's mother replied that she would never allow him to see the child as long as he lived, and if he tried to visit them they would vanish into the great southern forest.

My mother, Roxie Patterson Meredith, a fearless woman who inspired my passion for education. Her past contained a horrible secret. Right before she met my father, she saw a sign in the heavens. *Photo courtesy of the James Meredith collection*

After my father's first wife died, he heard about a young woman named Roxie who was reportedly the most beautiful girl in the county. Many years later my mother wrote an account of their courtship, which tells you everything you need to know about my mother.

I remember one February morning, I looked out of the window and saw a big beautiful star in the sky. I called my sister to behold its beauty. I told Sis that the star had great news for me. On the very same day, I received a letter from the man I was to marry. I didn't know who the letter was from, it was signed Mr. Meredith, asking if he could call on me the following third Sunday. I answered in agreement. Mr. Meredith arrived about two o'clock.

It was a cold fair day, but when I saw this tall, handsome hunk of man, my heart was warmed, for I knew then, he would be mine. I learned on our first meeting that Mr. Meredith was a widower and the father of five children, ages ranging from three to thirteen years. In a period of three months we were married and I was the happiest woman in the world.

I loved my husband and the children very much, but

there was the natural desire to have children of my own, so on the twenty-fifth of June 1933, God blessed us with a son, James H. Meredith who was destined to become an integral part of a great social revolution in this country. I am the mother of seven children.

Among my great desires, education ranks among the top. Poor schools and unqualified teachers along with my father's illness forced me to stop school at the age of fifteen. My desire for learning has never abated. When an adult class opened up in Kosciusko Mississippi, I would walk nine miles the round-trip to school each night until it closed. Even now I wish it were possible for me to further my formal education.

I have been commended by many for my contribution to society, but I still feel that there is much I can do if I only had the chance.

I was more fortunate than most blacks in Mississippi.

For one thing, my father owned his own subsistence farm, which kept us alive no matter how bad the times might be. It was also an isolated place. My father kept it that way. My father built his fences a few feet back from his property lines, declining to use a border line with a common fence. This way, the white man owning the adjoining land would never have any reason to invade Cap's property.

When I left Mississippi in 1950 I had never seen the inside of a white person's house, chiefly because a Negro had to enter by the back door. I was taught to believe that the most dishonorable thing that a Meredith could do was to work in a white woman's kitchen and take care of a white man's child. I know that I would starve to death rather than do either. I am sure that the blacks with the greatest sense of pride come from the farms, because working in the fields never carried the disgraceful connotations that working in the white folks' kitchens did.

Cap Meredith organized a school for blacks in the county before I was born, mortgaging forty acres and thirteen head of cattle to build it.

He had been the only citizen of the black race to remain on the voting list in Attala County, Mississippi, from the day he registered in 1925 till the day he died.

To him, Mississippi was the original land of his forefathers, and he could trace his heritage many generations in the very spot where he was born, back hundreds of years through oral history. He deeply loved this land, which was in a desperate need of change, and he chose me as one to do something about it, and to pass a better world on to his descendants.

In the state of Mississippi, race had always been a central factor. But in Cap Meredith's house, character was the defining factor. In Attala County there were white people of every category from the highest to the lowest, from the richest to the poorest. There were black people, good ones and sorry ones, and then there were the Merediths. We were a separate world.

Our family was powerful and not to be trifled with. For example, two white men cut my grandfather's throat when he was nineteen years old and left him for dead. A few days later, the two men disappeared and were never heard from again.

I can still take you to the exact spot where their bones are buried.

When my siblings and I had to walk to school, white students threw rocks at us out the windows of their school bus. I threw a rock back one day, hitting a boy who was a neighbor of ours. His father came over to discuss it with my father. My father told him simply, "Stop bothering my children." The rock throwing stopped.

Another time, a local law enforcement officer started snooping around our property for no apparent reason. My brothers and sisters watched from behind a tree as my father stood out in the open, leveled a shotgun at him, and waved him away. The lawman retreated. We were awestruck.

On one occasion, Cap and I sat in a wagon for two hours waiting for a white man to come out of a house and meet us, because Cap refused to go to the back door as the man expected of a black man.

If anyone was a king in his own domain, it was Cap. It was as if our eighty-four acres constituted a sovereign state and we neither recognized nor had any diplomatic relations with our neighboring states. The house of a white family was within one hundred yards of the back side of our place, yet I never saw it. Because of his desire to shield us, my father forbade us even to go to that area of our farm. Some black families lived on the white man's farm, and their children were our best friends. Since we were not allowed to visit them, they had to come over to our side of the fence to play with us.

The beginning of knowing what it was to be black came when I was a little boy on my father's farm. My father was buying a cow, and he and my brother and I set off in our wagon to a farm where the deal was going to be made. Cap parked the wagon about a hundred yards from the farmhouse and we all got off the wagon. But I had to go to the bathroom, and without saying anything I went behind a tree to do what I always did on the farm.

The next thing I knew my father was screaming at me, "Don't do that! Don't you ever do that again!" in a pitch of voice I had never heard before. It was a pitch that signaled to me great danger, a life-or-death warning. The message was "never do that in front of these people's house." "These people," of course, were white folks.

This is my first recollection of how a black mental pattern was being set, a pattern that was trying to tell me that I was something less than someone else.

I was a little older when a second but similar experience occurred. I was walking downtown in Kosciusko, the county seat of Attala, with a friend, Samuel Hugh George. We were no more than twelve or thirteen at the time. Samuel knew more about white folks than I did. His mother worked for a white family in town.

So when I put my head down and started walking with my eyes on my shoes, Samuel let out a shout, his voice filled with the same kind of anxiety and warning my father's voice had contained years before on that white man's farm.

"You'd better not walk with your head down—you might accidentally bump into a white woman and there'll be hell to pay!" Basically, I learned very early that a black man's life from birth to death consisted of being told what to do and what not to do in relation to white superiority, not reality.

My father was the greatest man I have ever known, and ever since I was a little boy he had told me it was my divine responsibility to save the black race; to unify the black, white, and Native American peoples; and to lead our nation to the position of power and glory that is rightfully ours, under the Constitution of the United States and the principles of the Holy Bible. I took this responsibility very seriously.

My father, quite literally, put me on a mission from God.

"You must bring together the best of the white and the best of the black and save the world," he explained to me. "The black race caused its own downfall many years ago through its excesses and now the white race is well on its way to doing the same thing. God wants to preserve the best from both worlds and build a new reality. We are the passageway for the best of both worlds. It's God's will and nothing can stand in the way of God's purpose.

"We are the future of the human race. We are the channel through which the future of the black race is destined to pass. We are the chosen family. Mississippi is the incubator and we are the conduit. It is your duty and responsibility to lead our people to their proper place in the world."

My father taught me that I was descended from white, African, and Native American royalty and aristocracy. The worst thing ever to have happened to Mississippi, he said, was the ascendancy to power of white supremacists, or as we called them, "poor white trash." Not because they were bad people, necessarily, but because they didn't know how to govern. Their control had become complete by the 1890s, and it was my divine responsibility to take it away from them and restore everything to its proper order, where enlightened people were leaders and all citizens were free and equal in the eyes of God and under the laws of man.

My father taught me that ever since 1798 when Mississippi became a territory, the white man's greatest fear had been the black man, but in all of these years the black man had always proven to be a friend. The primary goal had been to profit from his strong muscle and keep him tame and in fear. During the first three hundred years of chattel slavery, capture, lockdown, and severe beating were used to keep the black man in line.

I was fifteen when I first fully appreciated the personal impact of white supremacy. My brother and I were riding the train home from Chicago on the famous train called the City of New Orleans. At Memphis, we were ordered to vacate our seats and move to the "colored car," as we were about to enter Mississippi. It was overcrowded, and we had to stand. Tears rolled down my cheeks for the rest of the trip, and in that moment I swore to myself that I would devote my life to changing the degraded position of black people in the world. Ever since then I have been self-consciously aware that I am black. Of course, I had known that I belonged to a group that was distinctly different from at least one other group, but until I was fifteen I didn't fully appreciate that my group was supposed to be the inferior one.

I was luckier than most young blacks, because I got less of it than anyone else I knew, thanks to the autonomous life my father carved out for our family. I think this enabled me to be immune from some of the fears that many black people were affected by. Years later, during the emotional days when I was trying to enroll at the University of Mississippi, blacks would ask me, "How can you stand up to Governor Ross Barnett and all those white people and their guns and their power?"

To me it was the other way around. For me, it was almost an

insult for anyone to ask me how it was that I could stand up to Barnett. It is a suggestion that he was someone to be feared. It was always a foregone conclusion for me that "I am not inferior to you."

When I was seventeen years old, my father sent me to live with an uncle in St. Petersburg, Florida, where the high school was supposed to be better than the one I had attended in Kosciusko. I immediately sought to gain power over my classmates. To prove that I was the toughest kid in the school, I beat up the two school bullies, the first using a stick studded with nails, the second with my bare-knuckled fists.

I entered an American Legion essay-writing contest on "Why I Am Proud to Be an American." Instead, my theme was: "I am proud to be an American not because of what it is but because of what it can become." The essay was rejected by my own teachers, who said it wasn't good enough to represent the school. I went over their heads and submitted it. I won the contest.

At a student assembly, the school principal raised a hand, pointed to me sitting in the audience, and asked the students, "How could you let that little nigger come down here and embarrass us?" This was an important moment for me, perhaps a turning point.

Whenever anyone asked me what I wanted to be, I replied: "I want to be a man, run for governor of the state of Mississippi, and get a degree from the University of Mississippi, in reverse order." I would then explain that by "to be a man" I meant in contrast to being a "Negro man" or a "colored man." The stress in "run for governor" should be placed on "run." I never wanted to be elected, I simply wanted to run and get the vote of every Negro in Mississippi. With this power the Negro could name the governor. To "get a degree from the University of Mississippi" was a necessary prerequisite to the other two ambitions.

This three-point goal gave me a psychological sense of continuity, and it gave the more cautious blacks an opportunity to express themselves on the race issue. They could treat it as a joke, and could then jokingly speak their sober mind.

I joined the United States Air Force in 1951, right out of high school, at the age of eighteen.

I chose that branch of the military because it had the best reputation for treating blacks as full American citizens, at least in the lower ranks, though black commissioned officers were still rare in all the services. I passed all the tests for admission to flight school as an air force pilot, but when I got to Colorado to begin the training, the medical experts said that although my eyes were perfect then, with 20/20 vision, they would go bad sometime in the future. Nearly sixty years later, they are still almost 20/20.

I was in the first experiment in boot-camp training in the United States in which blacks and whites trained together in large numbers. In 1952, my first permanent military assignment was to Topeka Air Force Base, Kansas. My first job was with a B-29 bomber squadron. I was the first black in the outfit. I was assigned a room on the second floor of an old barracks. When I returned from work the first day not only had my roommate moved, every airman on the second floor had moved off the floor so they wouldn't have to endure the experience of living near a black man.

My first duty assignment was as a records clerk for the B-29 bombers. My workplace was on the flight line, where the airplanes are kept and operated. Before I came, blacks were not even allowed to go on the flight line.

After three years, I was eligible for a promotion. The U.S. Supreme Court's 1954 *Brown* decision had recently come down, outlawing segregation in schools, and the promotion board questioned me at length about it. I told the board I thought it was an epic event that would transform America.

At the end of the interview, the commanding officer of the B-29 outfit, a Colonel Busby, dismissed the other two colonels and asked to speak with me in private. He was from an aristocratic white family from the Mississippi Delta.

"The whites of Mississippi will never allow integration," he explained with brutal frankness. "They will kill all of the niggers and half of the white folk before they allow it to happen."

Then Colonel Busby said something that changed my life.

"We're for you. I'm for you. But it's up to you. *You have to make it happen.*"

In that moment, my destiny became clear.

It felt as if the U.S. military, through Colonel Busby's voice, was giving me a direct order to fulfill the mission from God that my father had sent me on. He was saying I would be the instrument in doing something he and many others wanted to do, but didn't have the courage or the power to do.

"It's up to you." Those four words were like a Godsend to me. I knew that some day, I had to go back to Mississippi and fulfill my destiny.

When I was promoted to sergeant, some white airmen were placed under me. One day in 1956, during the heat of Martin Luther King's Montgomery bus boycott, when I was stationed at Peru Air Force Base in Indiana, one of my best troops came in and said: "Sergeant Meredith, sir! You are all right with me. But I just can't work for no nigger!" The airman left the military with a dishonorable discharge rather than continue to serve under the command of a black man.

Discrimination against blacks at Peru Air Force Base in Indiana was so bad both on and off the base that I decided to stage a protest and demand change. I refused to get out of my bed for over two weeks. The commander came to my room every day and begged me to come to work because he did not want to punish me. He eventually had me reassigned overseas to Japan.

Much had happened during the years I was in the air force. The integration of the armed forces of the United States had been carried into effect. The United States Supreme Court made its landmark ruling against the "separate but equal" doctrine that was the legal underpinning of the southern system of dual education facilities for white and black. President Eisenhower had ordered troops into Little Rock, Arkansas. Change was in the air. Black expectations were running high, particularly those of a black man viewing the American scene from a country as distant as Japan.

Those expectations were not too high, however. A black GI still dreaded his return home and the humiliation he faced in traveling with his family across the continent. A black traveling across country faced nights where he might have to sleep in his car, days where he might have to go hungry because a restaurant wouldn't serve him or his family food.

This was a particularly hard reality for me after nine years in an integrated air force. I had been in the military for the purpose of defending the freedom and democracy of my nation, preserving something that I knew I didn't enjoy and my kind didn't enjoy.

My nine years in the air force were valuable ones. The air force gave me my first taste of college, my first chance to settle down in various parts of the United States, my first chance to travel abroad. It was while I was in the air force that I met Mary June Wiggins, a girl from Gary, Indiana, who became my wife in 1956.

It was also in the air force that I began to first lay the plans for an assault on white supremacy in Mississippi. I decided not only what I wanted to do, which I had known for a long time in a vague way, but how to go about doing it. I would have to say the process matured in Japan, where I spent the last three years of my hitch as a sergeant, from 1957 to 1960, based at Tachikawa Air Force Base near Tokyo, the largest air force base in the world.

My years in Japan changed my life.

Japan is where I became a man.

Being in Japan was an absolutely amazing experience for me. For three years, when I was off duty, I traveled the cities and small towns of Japan, I walked its country lanes, visited its museums, climbed its mountains, breathed its air, ate its food, and savored the company of its people. I felt a personal kinship with many aspects of Japanese culture, with values instilled in me by my parents: pride, stoicism, reverence for nature, industriousness, and the sanctity of the family.

It was in Japan that I got to fully realize that white supremacy and the inferior position of blacks in America was a man-made construct, not a natural construct. I never felt inferior as a human being in Japan. It was the only place where I have not felt the air of difference at being black. It was an entirely different universe, a nonwhite, thousand-year-old civilization where I was treated with respect and equality. The concept of "white supremacy" in such a civilization was so nonexistent as to seem completely absurd.

Part of it was no doubt the natural courtesy ingrained in Japanese culture, and the remote but polite deference shown to American servicemen in the years immediately following World War II. But my time in Japan fully convinced me that the relationships between men were man-made and consequently, by my being a man, I had the capability of changing them.

One day, while walking along a Japanese country road flanked by luxuriant pine trees and crystal-cool streams, I was gripped with the startling feeling that I was back in Mississippi. The air smelled just as sweet, and the black crows reminded me exactly of the ones we had back home.

A Japanese boy started walking with me, eager to practice his English. He was amazed that I was from the South, which he had heard was a terrible place for black people. I in turn was shocked by his awareness of the distorted racial equilibrium in the United States, and stunned that a little Japanese boy could be so familiar with the stories of the Little Rock Nine and Emmett Till.

I felt ashamed by it, by the stain and disgrace white supremacy cast on my country and on me personally, and almost in that moment I resolved to return to Mississippi to change things for the better.

I knew then that I had to leave the air force, come back to Mississippi, and go to war.

CHAPTER THREE

A Declaration of War

IN 1960, I CAME BACK TO MISSISSIPPI TO CONQUER WHITE supremacy.

I was at war.

And I was prepared to fight to the death.

I chose as my target the University of Mississippi, which in 1960 was the holiest temple of white supremacy in America, next to the U.S. Capitol and the White House, both of which were under the control of segregationists and their collaborators.

I reasoned that if I could enter the University of Mississippi as its first known black student, I would fracture the system of state-enforced white supremacy in Mississippi. It would drive a stake through the heart of the beast. If I managed to not get killed or chased off, I could create an earth-shaking precedent in Mississippi, a moment in the apocalypse of white supremacy. There would be no turning back.

I had spent every year of my adult life and the three years before my twenty-first birthday in the U.S. Air Force; in other words, I grew up in the military. A soldier must at all times be ready, without hesitation or question, to die for his country and his cause.

My philosophy was that under the conditions that existed in Mississippi, I was a dead man. The only thing I had to gain was life, freedom.

During all those years I was conscious of my purpose in being a soldier: to secure my country and its principles against any enemy. I saw white supremacy as one of the most powerful enemies the United States faced. I considered myself first and foremost an American soldier, not a black soldier, though I was always highly aware and proud of my black heritage.

My objective in this war was total victory. Victory over discrimination, oppression, the unequal application of the law, and, most of all, over white supremacy and all of its manifestations. I knew my enemy would use every legal, social, political, educational, and economic institution in Mississippi to perpetuate and fortify white supremacy.

I did not believe in turning the other cheek. I thought that anyone trying "civil disobedience" in Mississippi was crazy, because state-sponsored white supremacy was so powerful and so violent that it had nearly crushed the civil rights movement in the state. I thought that the traditional discussion of integration and civil rights was a total insult. The fundamental question was whether I was an American citizen.

For me, the issue was not civil rights, but American citizenship. I considered my rights as an American citizen, all of them, to be non-negotiable.

I considered myself an active-duty soldier.

I was at war, and everything I did I considered an act of war.

It is an ugly reality that Americans have never fully owned

up to, but the people who actively or passively collaborated with segregation and racism, the people who did not combat these scourges—in other words, the vast majority of white Americans in the North and South at the time—were just as powerful in supporting the pillars of white supremacy as were the openly racist whites. Without the vast legions of such collaborators, the openly racist white supremacists could not hold on to power. And in 1960, despite some cracks in the wall and moves toward desegregation in the armed forces and some American towns and schools, make no mistake about it, white supremacy had a stranglehold on America.

In 1960, the University of Mississippi was a multiracial, multiethnic institution that welcomed students from every corner of the earth, every color and every ethnic group—except Americans of African descent.

I decided that I would attempt to register as a student at the University of Mississippi to complete a bachelor's degree in political science. I'd already accumulated most of the credits I needed to get a degree, through college courses I'd taken at various schools while I was in the air force.

I first thought of going to the University of Mississippi when I was around twelve years old, when I visited a white doctor who had attended the school and I asked him about the diplomas on his wall. He told me about the university, its rich history and exalted position in Mississippi culture, and the legendary prowess of its football team, the "Ole Miss Rebels." This sounded like exactly the school I should attend.

The University of Mississippi's nickname is "Ole Miss," which was the colloquial expression for the white mistress of the plantation, who was the de facto ruler of the feudal society of Mississippi from the 1700s until the 1950s.

The "Ole Miss" of the plantation was by far the most important person in Mississippi. She made the plantation system run smoothly. She was in total control of all domestic affairs. She held the keys to every lock on the plantation. She controlled the daily lives of every person on the plantation from birth to death. She was the monitor of culture, the developer of Christian virtue, the matchmaker, and the director of education and training. Above all she was the queen of white supremacy.

The University of Mississippi played all these roles for the state. She was truly the Ole Miss of the plantation state. It is a fitting nickname, for Ole Miss was and is the dominant, most powerful institution in the state. It was the Ivy League of the state, the place where the state's white leaders were groomed, where lawyers were minted and automatically admitted to the bar, where marriages were born, lifelong networks of friends and cronies established. This is still largely the case today.

It was the breeding ground for white aristocracy, where girls met their husbands-to-be, where sons walked in the footsteps of their fathers and grandfathers into law school and medical school. Sixty percent of all political leaders in Mississippi were graduates of Ole Miss and 80 percent of the lawyers were graduates of Ole Miss.

Mississippi, you see, is the center of America's racial universe, and the University of Mississippi runs Mississippi.

By 1960, most southern states had seen at least token racial integration on the university level, except Mississippi. Integration at the University of Alabama hadn't lasted long before Autherine Lucy was chased off the campus by white rioters in 1956, but at least she'd managed to enter the university, backed by a U.S. Supreme Court decision. But Mississippi was still totally segregated in its public institutions, and Ole Miss was the Queen Bee of segregation.

In a real sense, the University of Mississippi *was* Mississippi. From the moment the university was established in the north Mississippi hill town of Oxford in 1848, the assumption was that it would be forever closed to black Americans.

The university was not only closed to blacks, it excluded 95 percent of Mississippi whites also, those who were not part of the aristocratic elite. The rest, who were poor or unconnected, had to go to other segregated white schools, such as Mississippi State University, Mississippi Southern University, Delta State University, or Mississippi University for Women.

But the University of Mississippi wasn't my main target. My target was the state of Mississippi. The university turned out to be the most vulnerable spot to attack the enemy. I was going after the enemy's most sacred and revered stronghold. My application to Ole Miss had little to do with "integration" but was made to enjoy the rights of citizenship, and by doing that, to put a symbolic bullet in the head of the beast of white supremacy. Through this solitary action, I thought I could address the whole problem of social, economic, and political advancement of the black race in Mississippi.

I knew this action would put my life on the line, as it had long been the practice of the Mississippi leadership to eliminate any person who posed a threat to white supremacy.

I went ahead because I had everything to gain, including life itself.

I also knew that my success in this war depended upon a power struggle between the state of Mississippi and the federal government. The state of Mississippi was certain to use the armed forces of the state to prevent my attendance at Ole Miss. Only the armed force of the U.S. government could overpower the state of Mississippi.

Temporary or partial victory and relative advancement had no place in my thinking. I was prepared to retreat from every battle if doing so would improve my chances of winning the war. Most great wars have been lost because the generals, blinded by the glories of temporary victories, were advancing when they should have been retreating. I could not jeopardize the prospects of establishing a new order in Mississippi by compromising with evil in order to allow America to say to the world that we have a Negro in the University of Mississippi.

Mississippi in 1960 was a terrorist American police state.

White supremacy and racism was a widespread form of undiagnosed national mental illness that dominated the entire United States, and it is very hard for younger Americans to understand the bestial depths to which white supremacy had submerged most of America not that long ago.

And Mississippi was the capital of this madness.

If you think I'm exaggerating, consider these facts.

Mississippi was the scene of more lynchings of black Americans than any other state—532 from 1882 to 1952.

The use of raw, demonstrative violence had become a religion to whites; its ceremonial and ritualistic aspects were a vital part of the Mississippi way of life. The very existence of the white society required periodic doses of this violent religious lunacy. Without sacrificial violence to bind it together, the white world would completely fall apart.

Fear is the natural reaction to violence, and the threat of violence. Although the black community was constantly in a state of siege by the white community, the ultimate enforcement of the principles of white supremacy among the blacks was done indirectly by the whites. The direct aspects were carried out by the black community itself. The less frequent manifestations, such as lynching, served mostly as symbolic acts to impress the Negro community. Usually when the white community wanted someone or something in the Negro community, it simply said, "Produce whatever it is we want or you will suffer." Although violence was a definite part of Mississippi life, it was resorted to only periodically. Some communities went for generations with only the threat of violence, but the threat was so powerful there was no need for direct action.

If you were black in Mississippi, you were stripped of almost every vestige of American citizenship. The odds were overwhelming that you were not allowed to vote. You could not hold public office. You could not even run for public office. You could not be

a police officer, highway patrolman, sheriff, deputy, or national guardsman. You could not use facilities designated for white people only. You could not serve on a jury. You did not have the right to public freedom of speech. You were likely condemned to a life of poverty, ignorance, and premature death due to grossly inferior education and virtually nonexistent medical care.

Despite the fact that you paid taxes to run them, if you were black you could not attend any state school or university, except vastly inferior ones designated for blacks only. White schools in Mississippi were thoroughly poisoned by the forced indoctrination of children in the vilest forms of racist propaganda in all Mississippi public classrooms. The state sponsored scholarship competitions for the most eloquent racist essays.

The statewide mass media were controlled by radical white supremacists who blocked and censored national TV network feeds and used newspapers as propaganda tools to preach the glories of segregation as an American tradition and the genetic deformities of black Americans.

You could not organize to protest these conditions without fear of unlawful arrest or assassination by Mississippi state police officers.

Like many southern states, Mississippi had been a one-party Democratic segregationist state for over eighty years. In 1960, Mississippi was co-ruled by a shadow government run by William Simmons, chief of the Citizens Councils of America, a rabidly racist white supremacist network of community leaders across the American Deep South, whose headquarters in downtown Jackson looked down upon the governor's office from a nearby office building.

In 1956, the Mississippi state legislature declared the U.S. Supreme Court's *Brown* decision outlawing segregation in public education to be "invalid" and enacted a "Resolution of Interposition" requiring state officials to prevent any attempt to enforce the decisions of the nation's highest court.

Mississippi state law was propelled on a direct collision course with federal law and the federal courts.

It was a recipe for utter chaos.

Also in 1956, the state established a secret police agency called the Sovereignty Commission, whose mission was to spy on white and black citizens to prevent any flickering of independent thought and action against white supremacy and segregation. It has been called an "American KGB" and an "American Gestapo." Make no mistake about it, that's exactly what it was. In conjunction with the Citizens Councils and local law enforcement, Sovereignty Commission thugs in black suits and fedoras roamed the state, poked into people's bank records and personnel files, ruined some people's lives and ran others out of town, all in the name of keeping black Americans under the jackboot of segregation and white supremacy.

White supremacy was official and legal—it was enforced by judges and law enforcement—and a white citizen who failed to acknowledge and carry out the mandate of white supremacy was just as subject to persecution as any black.

Mississippi was the spiritual capital of what I call the Resurrected Confederate States of America, the counter-revolutionary empire of white supremacy that largely reversed the outcome of the American Civil War, overthrew democratically elected state governments, and reconquered the South in the late 1870s through terrorism and political maneuvering. This alternative American empire flourished for some eighty years.

On March 28, 1961, the Resurrected Confederacy exploded in joyous delirium with a six-mile-long parade and military demonstration that wound through the streets of the capital city of Jackson, Mississippi, as tens of thousands of white Mississippians marked the centennial of Mississippi's secession and the start of the Civil War.

On this day, wrote the local newspaper, the South "rose again, in all its Confederate splendor." It was billed as the largest public event in Mississippi history and featured the world's largest Confederate flag.

The pounding strains of "Dixie" echoed off the buildings, onlookers shouted rebel combat yells, and six thousand fully costumed Confederate rebel cavalry and infantrymen passed in review before the governor of Mississippi, himself resplendent in a Confederate general's uniform. He was said to have been happy that his "boys could battle the Yankees on even terms if they had to." The *New York Times* reported that "among the marching and mounted gray-clad troops were most of the state's officials and members of the legislature."

Every so often, according to a witness, "to the delight of the crowd, a mounted cavalryman would stop his horse, point to a member of the crowd, and shout, 'There's a Yankee; shoot him!'"

By 1960, the struggle for full citizenship for black Americans had begun to threaten the stronghold of white supremacy in the South. Blacks and whites devoted and sometimes lost their lives in their struggle for freedom and equality. Lynchings and lunch-counter sit-ins became front-page news, and the nation stood on edge as the black race began to voice the frustration of a people too long oppressed.

By 1960, the state of Mississippi was fully prepared for a showdown on the question of integration. The state government had decided to draw the line and retreat not one inch more, and strange as it may seem, the best minds in Mississippi were absolutely convinced that they could win their case before the full judgment of the people, the courts, and the government of the United States.

Amid the racial unrest of the time, Mississippi remained mostly outside the crossfire. It was in many ways the forbidden territory, the epitome of white domination. It was also home to more citizens of the black race than any other state. The Mississippi system of segregation and white supremacy had gone virtually unchallenged since it was enshrined after Reconstruction.

And I was convinced that nothing less than overwhelming

physical force, legally delivered by American combat troops, could conquer it.

In September 1960, my wife and I enrolled as full-time students in Jackson State University, an all-black, state-supported institution. For me, it was only an interim stop.

I attended classes at Jackson State from 1960 to 1962, at the same time I unleashed a legal struggle against the state by applying to the University of Mississippi.

The first thing I did after enrolling at Jackson State was to secretly organize a small group of students who I hoped would ultimately become the backbone of a Mississippi movement against white supremacy.

Secrecy was necessary because of the terror of the times. Blacks in Mississippi in 1960 were even afraid to talk about their rights, let alone move actively toward getting them. Somehow, we got organized into a group we called the Mississippi Improvement Association of Students, or MIAS.

We had our own underground *samizdat* press, and we circulated secretly mimeographed pamphlets. We came up with a slogan, "MIAS vs. Bias." The slogan popped up on blackboards in classrooms and scrawled on store windows and was a powerful organizing tool in those days. It was like the ubiquitous "Kilroy was here" graffiti of the 1940s. The slogan showed up everywhere. And my colleagues in the MIAS group strategized and planned with me as I made my first moves to enter the University of Mississippi.

It was a statement by President Theodore Roosevelt that helped propel me on a collision course with the white supremacists and the state of Mississippi.

I first read it in the base newspaper at Forbes Air Force Base in Topeka, Kansas, in January 1952. I cut the entire quotation from the paper and learned it by memory and said it to myself every day for many years. One paragraph especially captured my undying determination to defeat white supremacy at any cost:

> The credit belongs to the man who is actually in the arena, whose face is marred by dust and sweat and blood, who at the best, knows in the end, the triumph of high achievement, and who at the worst, if he fails, at least fails while daring greatly, so that his place will never be with those cold and timid souls who know neither victory nor defeat.

No matter what happened, I knew I would not be one of "those timid souls." No matter what I would have to face in the end, I would know either victory or defeat.

For a philosophy class at Jackson State, I was assigned to write a paper on "My Philosophy of Life." I summarized my thoughts on political action: "Why are men afraid to speak, in a society whose very existence is based on freedom of expression? Why are men afraid to meet, when the law says that freedom of assembly is an undeniable right? Why do men call good bad and right wrong, when they know its true nature? Is this freedom? My answer is *no*. . . . Unless *we* do something ourselves nothing of value will be done."

I reported to class each day wearing an army uniform and a black leather biker jacket and a leather cap and carrying a bamboo cane. I wanted to look like a bad dude, mainly because I had an agenda: to take over the school. The president of the university, I decided after conducting a quick evaluation, had less power on campus than the football coach, so I devised a plan to intimidate the coach and let him know who was in charge.

I did this by beating up the coach's biggest player, who was nicknamed Lotsa-Poppa. He was twisting a girl's arm and did not stop when I told him to. I put a judo spin on him and he went up into the air and fell like he'd been hit by a car. I walked up to the three-hundred-pounder and proceeded to knock him to his knees with a series of judo blows. While holding him on the ground by one arm, I gently kicked him in his big butt while fifty or more of his teammates looked on and laughed, with his coach watching from the football dormitory balcony.

It was really the coach that I wanted to intimidate, to show him who was boss on campus.

One day in 1960, I gave Martin Luther King, Jr., a ride in my Volkswagen.

The students at all-black Tougaloo College had invited him to speak at their school to support the Tougaloo students who were in jail for trying to use the public library in Jackson, but no one would pick him up at the Jackson airport. Everyone was afraid that King would be attacked on the route from the airport to the school.

So Martin Luther King was stuck out there at the airport.

I heard of this and drove out there with a friend in my VW to volunteer to be his driver.

"Hey, man!" my friend said, "that looks like Martin Luther King standing there."

Dr. King was leaning against a post looking dejected, and only one person was with him, his aide Hosea Williams. Apparently they had been stranded there a long time. I invited them into my tiny car and King never said one word the whole trip. It was about fifteen miles. He just looked out the window, lost in thought.

I had seen him once a few years before, at a church rally in Oklahoma City supporting the boycott of the downtown commercial district. Dr. King was the guest speaker. What struck me wasn't his speech, which I could barely hear, but the looks of pure joy, hope, and jubilation I saw on the faces of the throngs of black people in the audience. They were in a state of spiritual excitement I'd never seen before. I was amazed.

That night in Jackson I attended Dr. King's rally at the Tougaloo College chapel. The place was jam-packed, with not even standing room left. After finishing his speech, Dr. King held a question-and-answer session.

I stood up and asked a question that challenged Dr. King's most precious belief.

"Dr. King, about this nonviolence business," I said, "are you really serious about that? I don't see how any American can be serious about that."

Well, all hell broke loose in that church hall when they heard that. The audience was in an instant uproar.

But King's idea of "nonviolence" was a totally alien concept to me. I grew up in the military. I had been a soldier all of my adult life. Soldiers are the keepers and users of organized violence, legally applied. The beast of white supremacy was so powerful and strong in America at that time that I saw little chance of its being vanquished by meekness and "turning the other cheek." I thought American combat troops would have to do the job, as they did so effectively in Little Rock in 1957.

At that time, in 1960, I strongly disagreed with the tactic of nonviolent resistance as practiced by Dr. King and his followers. I respected him tremendously, but I felt that the forces of state terror in the Deepest South, especially in Mississippi, were so fiendish and so powerful that it was futile and weak to demean ourselves, especially our women and children, by volunteering to have our heads bashed in by mobs, or our bodies blasted by water cannon, or bullets placed in our heads by law enforcement officials.

I know this idea is a flagrant historical blasphemy, and I must be one of the very few black or white Americans to admit to it, but I disagreed with King's strategy of nonviolent resistance. I still do. I believe it put black Americans in a position of weakness, of lambs subjecting themselves to slaughter, staging media theater to shame our oppressor into behaving like human beings. It demeaned our status as American citizens. I am disgusted and offended by the idea of holding hands and singing "we shall overcome some day." When it comes to my rights, there is no some day, there is only today, there is only *right now.*

The battle for full black citizenship was in large measure a battle of images.

As for me, I did not want to project the image of a stoic member of a group of victims, getting beaten by white police or a mob or having food dumped over my head at a lunch counter by white goons, turning my cheek and refusing to strike back. I don't mean to imply a molecule of disrespect for the black and white and other civil rights heroes over the years who risked their lives for freedom in America. In my opinion they were as courageous as the men who hit the beaches on D-Day or the firefighters who rushed into the World Trade Center on September 11, 2001.

But I strongly disagreed with the images of passive civil disobedience as promulgated by civil rights leaders through the media. I thought they were the wrong tactic.

The image necessary to shatter white supremacy in America, I believed, was guns, thousands of them, locked and loaded, in the hands of black and white American combat troops, marching alongside black Americans enjoying their rights as citizens. I wanted images of triumph and military conquest, not images of weakness and submission.

The concept of American citizenship is sacred and inviolate. You can't be a 33 percent American citizen or a 99 percent American citizen. It's all or nothing. You can't make "gains" when it comes to American citizenship. There's no in between; either a citizen has equal protection or he doesn't. If a man is innocent but unfairly sentenced to one hundred years in jail, you can't say it would represent a gain if he had been unfairly sentenced to only ten years.

I was born an American citizen and I was guaranteed all the sacred rights of American citizenship—*all of them*—at birth. The Constitution discussed slavery, but it said nothing about race, about black, white, or brown. Therefore any free black person in American history is a full American citizen and always has been.

The idea of negotiating one or two or three of my "civil rights," or yours, is an obscenity to all Americans. I am greatly offended by the idea and you should be, too. This simple idea is in my opinion the missing link in almost all discussions of civil rights that occurred in American history. Sure, let's confront injustice and racism and discrimination and the violation of civil rights for blacks, Latinos, Native Americans, gays, immigrants, and white Americans, anywhere, any time—but unless we acknowledge first, at the beginning of the discussion, up front, that the very idea of one American's civil rights being threatened in any way is an outrage to all Americans, then the idea of citizenship has no meaning for any of us and we are engaging in a bogus, invalid argument. That's the whole point of America.

If I opposed Dr. King's exalted tactic of nonviolence, then what better idea could I possibly have? It's simple. I believed in overwhelming physical force and the threat of organized violence, legally applied by the federal government.

I believed that black Americans should stage widespread, massive legal action across the United States, in the form of lawsuits, to force the federal government to protect and enforce all the rights of citizenship for all Americans, with physical force applied legally by federal marshals or federal combat troops if necessary. The Legal Defense Fund of the National Association for the Advancement of Colored People (NAACP), the U.S. Justice Department, and others were already engaged in legal action in Mississippi and elsewhere, but I believed we needed much more of it. In fact, I believed that all our energy should be applied to legal action, not to flooding the streets with bodies to be sacrificed to brutality, but to flooding the courts with lawsuits, which would trigger American troops to move in and enforce federal court orders.

The Little Rock Nine to me presented a perfect case history of this. The students sued, they won, the state of Arkansas refused to obey the law, and the president of the United States was compelled to send in over one thousand crack combat troops of the 101st Airborne to force the students into Central High School. The issue was settled by guns, in the hands of American soldiers. This display of overwhelming physical force settled the matter of desegregation completely and decisively in Arkansas. This, I thought, is what we should be doing anywhere in the North or South that was not honoring our rights as American citizens—not mass marches or sit-ins, but legal action to trigger the threat of federal firepower.

At Tougaloo College, Dr. King was willing to discuss the matter with me when I challenged him about how he could believe in nonviolence, but the audience sure didn't want to hear it.

"Thank you, young man," said King. "Let me try to answer that."

The black audience was in chaos, enraged at me. They wouldn't let Dr. King answer.

"Kick that nigger's ass!"

In those days, many blacks in Mississippi used the "N-word" among themselves, both as a term of friendly teasing and as an insult. People in my own family used the word, and I still sometimes use it today among friends as a kind of irreverent shorthand when I want to criticize a black person. I know plenty of black folks who still kick the word around in friendly conversation. It is obviously an extremely offensive term to many, then and now, but I'm just telling you the way things were, and are.

The chorus rang out, "Throw that nigger out of here!"

Dr. King protested loudly, trying to calm the audience down and insisting that he wanted to answer my question, but to no avail.

I was picked up by members of the crowd and literally thrown out of the chapel.

I got to know Dr. King much better in the years ahead, and the thing that impressed me most was how eager and willing he was to listen to other people's ideas. He loved words, the music and poetry of human conversation, discussion, and debate. He had a mind in which all the windows were open and a clear light was shining through.

He loved to hear other people's ideas.

Even my own.

On January 21, 1961, the day after John F. Kennedy was inaugurated president of the United States, I wrote to Ole Miss requesting an application for admission.

Why did I do it? I wrote in my journal at the time, "My greatest single reason to act is my son. He is only one year old, and yet I have already spent countless sleepless nights, trying to answer this question of my conscience—When he grows up and sees all of the injustices and learns the illogical justifications upon which they are built, he will ask me, What have you done to correct these conditions? What will I give as an answer?"

I was not inspired by John F. Kennedy as a potential civil rights savior, quite the contrary.

I knew that so far in his career JFK had done virtually nothing to help the cause of black Americans. Like the vast majority of Americans, he was a segregationist collaborator, and a millionaire power politician who I knew had to be forced to do the right thing.

At that moment, one of the strongest weapons black Americans had was the relatively strong civil rights platform that John F. Kennedy had insisted upon at the Democratic National Convention that nominated him for president. Since the election was one of the closest in the history of the United States and the black vote had been widely reported as being the decisive factor, the new Democratic administration was on the spot and would be forced to act if put under pressure.

I believed that now that John Kennedy had been elected president, black Americans could force him to honor his platform commitments, or be exposed as a man who wouldn't keep his promises. The time was right for me to move.

The University of Mississippi soon responded favorably to my first request for an application. In their form letter sent to all students, I was routinely welcomed and told when to report for registration and to please fill out and return the formal application for admission that was enclosed.

I filled out the application, which had a space for my picture. I attached one.

It clearly revealed the fact that I was black.

I attached a cover note to the application:

> To The Registrar—University of Mississippi
>
> I am very pleased with your letter that you recently sent to me. I sincerely hope that your attitude toward me does not change upon learning that I am not a white applicant. I am an American-Mississippi-Black Citizen. I will not be able to furnish you with the names of six University Alumni because I am a black citizen and all graduates of the school are white. However, as a substitute for this requirement, I am submitting certificates regarding my moral character from black citizens of my state. I am requesting that immediate action be taken on my application and that I be notified of its status, as registration begins on February 6, 1961, and I am hoping to enroll at this time.

The official response of the state of Mississippi over the next eighteen months can be summed up in the words of state senator E. K. Collins, who declared as the crisis reached its peak: "We must win the fight, regardless of the cost in human lives. Meredith cannot be enrolled in the university as long as there are red corpuscles in the bodies of true Mississippians."

Days after receiving my application and picture, the registrar of the University of Mississippi sent me a telegram revoking his earlier invitation to apply and denying me any further consideration for admission on the grounds that the deadline for applications was the day before they had received my first letter.

> Western Union Telegram Dated: Feb 4, 1961, 2:05 PM
> J H MEREDITH
> FOR YOUR INFORMATION AND GUIDANCE IT HAS BEEN
> FOUND NECESSARY TO DISCONTINUE CONSIDERATION
> OF ALL APPLICATIONS FOR ADMISSION OR REGISTRATION
> FOR THE SECOND SEMESTER WHICH WERE RECEIVED
> AFTER JANUARY 25 1961. YOUR APPLICATION WAS
> RECEIVED SUBSEQUENT TO SUCH DATE AND THUS WE
> MUST ADVISE YOU NOT TO APPEAR FOR REGISTRATION.
> ROBERT B ELLIS
> REGISTRAR

This was a bogus move, as no application deadline had been mentioned in previous correspondence. The rejection was no surprise, however, and the battle would now move to the courts. Interpreting the telegram as a stalling tactic, I realized I would have to undertake a legal battle to gain admission to the school. I wrote to the United States Department of Justice stating that the "power and influence of the federal government should be used where necessary to insure compliance with the laws."

At the start of 1961, Robert F. Kennedy was an unknown quantity to me. All I knew was he was the president's brother, the United States attorney general, and head of the Justice Department, and a white politician who had ignored the rights of citizenship for black Americans his entire life. But he also symbolized to me the power of the federal government, power that I knew had to be brought to bear if I was going to be successful in my mission to enter the University of Mississippi.

I wrote to Robert Kennedy shortly after I submitted my application to the university. I had another motive in writing to Attorney General Kennedy beyond the obvious political one. I realized that the period after my application was received would prove to be the most dangerous for me personally. In terms of my personal security and safety, this was a most critical time. Clearly at this point in time my greatest concern was not to be exterminated.

I knew the state of Mississippi would stop at nothing to stop my campaign, including killing me.

How to engage in this operation without becoming a casualty was of prime importance once I made the decision to invade the enemy's most sacred and revered stronghold.

Some sinister precedents had occurred in recent Mississippi history, while James P. Coleman was governor. Clennon King, an eccentric black teacher at the black Alcorn A&M College in Mississippi who attempted to enroll at the University of Mississippi, had been hustled off the university campus in 1958, kidnapped by Mississippi law enforcement officers, forcibly taken to a mental institution, and later driven from the state.

Coleman, who later became a federal judge, bragged about how he kept blacks out of the University of Mississippi. Later, when I was a student at Ole Miss, he came to the campus to make a campaign speech in his bid for re-election as governor of Mississippi. I listened in the crowd as he jokingly retold the story of how he had personally had Clennon King arrested and committed to the insane asylum the day he appeared to register as a student at Ole Miss.

The punch line to his speech was, "Any nigger attempting to enroll at Ole Miss is automatically crazy!" The audience roared with laughter.

The traditional practice in Mississippi was to eliminate potential troublemakers before they got a chance to cause trouble. Far more Negroes had been lynched for having a bad or wrong attitude than for committing a particular crime. Whenever a Negro questioned the status quo in Mississippi he just simply disappeared. Knowing

this about my home state, I naturally was concerned for my life.

The case of Clyde Kennard was a sadistic recent example of the homicidal blood lust of the Mississippi state government.

Kennard was a gentle, humble farmer and U.S. Army veteran who wanted a good education and should have been the first black citizen to attend a previously segregated Mississippi state university. He proceeded in quiet obscurity, with little publicity or fanfare, and was arrested as he tried to enroll at all-white Mississippi Southern University at Hattiesburg.

In 1959, Clyde Kennard was kidnapped by local Mississippi lawmen, framed and convicted on bogus theft charges, and then condemned to the brutal state penitentiary at Parchman, where he would remain until being released by the governor shortly before his death in 1963. At Parchman, where conditions rivaled those of the Soviet *gulag*, the fatally ill Kennard was literally thrown onto brutal work details against the advice of the medical staff. He eventually died shortly after his release, from medical neglect, cancer, and tuberculosis he suffered in prison.

A few days before he died, he wrote a poem called "Ode to the Death Angel":

> *Oh here you come again*
> *Old chilly death of Ol'*
> *To plot out life*
> *And test immortal soul*
> *I saw you fall against the raging sea*
> *I cheated you then and now you'll not catch me . . .*
> *But here you are again*
> *I see you paused upon that forward pew*
> *When you think I'm asleep*
> *I'm watching you*
> *Why must you hound me so everywhere I go?*
> *It's true my eyes are dim*
> *My hands are growing cold*

Well take me on then, that
I might at last become my soul

Clyde Kennard was kidnapped, tortured, and crucified by the state of Mississippi. He was murdered because he tried to behave like an American citizen. He was posthumously cleared of the charges and declared innocent by a Forrest County, Mississippi, circuit court judge on May 16, 2006.

Clyde Kennard. Remember the name. He died for you and your children.

I was familiar with the kidnappings of both Clennon King and Clyde Kennard when I moved to apply to the University of Mississippi, and had no intention being eliminated by the state if I could help it.

The lesson I learned from these cases was to make myself a public figure from the start. Visibility would be a key part of my offensive strategy. It would be much harder for the state to dispose of me if I was known to journalists and police forces.

So I wrote to Attorney General Kennedy to start a paper trail at the federal level, knowing that this would gain immediate attention in the Justice Department, where a file would be opened up on me and officials would now have to track my progress.

I also visited the local FBI field agent in Jackson, to start another defensive paper trail.

Another one of my first moves was to contact Medgar Evers, the Mississippi field secretary for the NAACP. Medgar had his office down the street from Jackson State University in the Masonic Temple building. I had met him shortly after I enrolled at Jackson State, and he was already becoming well-known locally as a crusader for justice.

I was immediately impressed by Medgar Evers. He was a very likeable man and a man of total dedication. He was an enthusiastic, daring strategist for human rights, a paratrooper in World War II, and literally a great action hero and detective. He spent the last several years as the point man for the civil rights group that was the most hated organization to white supremacists in Mississippi, the NAACP, or as one Mississippi judge put it, "Niggers, Apes, Alligators, Coons, and Possums." He dashed around the state on his own, unarmed, as he investigated atrocities against black Americans, using his day job as an insurance salesman as cover, while being tailed, tracked, and secretly investigated by state law enforcement officials. A few years earlier he had even briefly staged an abortive attempt of his own to enter the University of Mississippi Law School, before concluding the timing just wasn't right for such a revolutionary act.

Medgar would drop in daily at the Smackover Restaurant, the student hangout at Jackson State. He'd have his lunch and chat with anyone who approached him. Everybody knew Medgar and he seemed to know everybody. I talked to him in general about my plans. He asked me to drop by his office and talk to him about them in more detail.

Medgar suggested I write to the NAACP head office in New York to ask for legal assistance. My letter read:

January 29th, 1961

Mr. Thurgood Marshall
Legal Defense and Educational Fund
10 COLUMBUS CIRCLE
NEW YORK, NEW YORK

Dear Sir:

I am submitting an application for admission to the University of Mississippi. I am seeking entrance for the second semester which begins the 6th of February, 1961. I anticipate encountering some type of difficulty with the various agencies here in the state which are against my gaining entrance in the school. I discussed this matter with Mr. Evers, the Mississippi Field Secretary for the NAACP, and he suggested that I contact you and request legal assistance from your organization in the event it is needed for I am not financially able to fight a legal battle against the state of Mississippi. I hope your decision on this request will be favorable. Below is a brief history of my background which might help you in reaching a decision.

I am a native Mississippian. All my elementary and secondary education was received in this state, except my last year of high school, which was completed in Florida. I spent nine years in the United States Air Force (1951–60), all of which were honorable. I have always been a "conscientious objector" to my "oppressed status" as long as I can remember. My long-cherished ambition has been to break the monopoly on rights and privileges held by the whites of the state of Mississippi.

My academic qualifications, I believe, are adequate. While in the Air Force, I successfully completed courses at four different schools conducting night classes. As an example, I completed 34 semester hours of work with the University of Maryland's Overseas Program. Of the twelve courses completed I made three A's and nine B's. I am presently enrolled at Jackson State College, here in Jackson. I have completed one quarter of work and I am now enrolled in a second quarter at Jackson. For the work completed I received one A, three B's and one C.

Finally, I am making this move in what I consider the interest of and for the benefit of: (1) my country, (2) my race, (3) my family, and (4) myself. I am familiar with the probable difficulties involved in such a move as I am undertaking and I am fully prepared to pursue it all the way to a degree from the University of Mississippi.

Sincerely yours,
J H MEREDITH

One day Medgar Evers took me to his house with my wife and young son. He wanted to telephone his New York office but didn't want to do it from his NAACP office telephone in Jackson, which he assumed was tapped. The next thing I knew I was on the phone with the legendary attorney Thurgood Marshall himself, head of the NAACP Legal Defense Fund and later to become a U.S. Supreme Court justice.

Thurgood Marshall was a titanic figure in the struggle for black freedom. He had won a long string of tactical legal victories, culminating in the epic 1954 and 1955 *Brown* decisions striking down racial discrimination in higher education.

But Thurgood Marshall and I didn't hit it off. Here's how our conversation went:

"How do you do sir?" I asked the venerable Marshall.

Medgar Evers was listening in on an extension in the next room.

"I got your letter," Marshall said, "but we need some documents to prove that you are legitimate."

"Legitimate?" I thought. I was instantly infuriated by the idea of anyone challenging my "legitimacy," whatever that was. If Medgar Evers vouching for me wasn't enough to start our relationship amicably, we were getting off on the wrong foot.

"Mr. Marshall, sir," I explained, "I included everything in my letter to you over my signature."

"Yes, we got all of that," said Marshall, "but we don't know whether you are telling the truth or not."

Now he was practically accusing me of being a liar. Marshall wanted me to send him proof of my authenticity. He wanted my honorable discharge from the military, and the records of my grades.

I slammed the phone down on Thurgood Marshall without so much as a "good-bye," and walked out of the room.

Some people later told me they thought this was an arrogant move, but the one thing I could never deal with was anyone questioning my integrity. I just didn't do business with anyone to whom my word wasn't good enough.

Medgar Evers chased after me, pleading, "James, please don't go. Let's talk this thing over."

"I'm through with it," I told Medgar, "they can do whatever they want to do."

I urgently needed the powerful resources of the NAACP Legal Defense Fund to complete my mission, but I was about to throw them all away over a point of pride.

Medgar Evers stayed on the line, placated Marshall, and unbeknownst to me, arranged through his contacts at Jackson State University to send Marshall my school records without my knowledge. Medgar wasn't going to let my pride stop him. He persisted. And he completely rescued my mission.

Several weeks later I found in my mailbox a letter advising me that the NAACP Legal Defense Fund was interested in my case. The letter said that Mrs. Constance Baker Motley had been assigned to handle the matter and would be in touch with me.

The letter was signed by Thurgood Marshall.

My lawyer, Constance Baker Motley, was a tall, commanding black woman with a regal bearing and a brilliant legal mind, and she already had a big reputation in Mississippi. Back in 1949, she had argued the case for equal pay for black teachers in the state. She lost the case but gained a reputation.

In our first meeting she told me, "I think we should appeal to the university officials and to the Board of Higher Education to reconsider their decision to deny your application."

"No," I said, "we don't have time for that. It will delay everything for months."

Motley replied, "But we have lost a number of cases around the country because we did not exhaust our administrative remedies. We don't want to take a chance of losing your case on technicalities."

"In Mississippi we lose cases because we lose the clients," I explained. "They are eliminated by the state. They hauled Clennon King off to an insane asylum. They threw Clyde Kennard in the state penitentiary. If we give these Mississippi white folks too much time, they will eliminate any opposition. I have no desire to be eliminated."

So she came up with a surprise attack.

The secret plan Motley eventually came up with was to catch prosegregation U.S. District Judge Sidney Mize completely by surprise in his morning session in Meridian, Mississippi, and spring our lawsuit against the state with no advance publicity, to give the state no time to prepare a counterstrategy. We had to find a lawyer in Mississippi to file the case and then get the papers notarized, and the locally renowned Jess Brown agreed to handle the case. Jess was one of only four black lawyers in the whole state of Mississippi and was credited with filing the first civil rights suit in Mississippi.

At one of our first strategy sessions with Medgar Evers and Jess Brown, Motley said, "James, we believe that projecting the proper image is important for the black race."

I asked, "What do you mean?"

Actually, I knew exactly what she meant.

I looked like a Marxist revolutionary.

I was wearing an army khaki uniform, black leather cap, had a full-grown beard, and was carrying a bamboo cane. No one acted as if they had noticed, but this was the problem of the hour.

"We discussed it," Motley declared, "and we think you should shave."

"What's wrong with a beard?" I countered. "Abraham Lincoln had a beard. Jesus Christ had a beard!"

"Yes, I know," she granted. "But Fidel Castro is the only one wearing a beard these days. Except for you, of course. We just think it would be better if you shaved."

"I will think about it," I offered, "but I won't promise you anything." Eventually, I complied.

Then Motley asked Jess Brown, "Are you going to wear that suit?" He was wearing a super-loud orange-maroon suit.

"Constance," protested Jess, "don't you like my pretty suit? My wife loves it. This is the suit that I've tried all of my big cases in. It's my lucky suit."

"They may run us out of the courtroom," grumbled Motley, perhaps now regretting she'd ever come down to Mississippi to team up with such a strange-looking group of Negroes.

In the meantime, I reapplied for admission, this time to the University of Mississippi's summer session. On May 25, 1961, the registrar rejected my application, citing two ludicrous reasons: one, that Jackson State was not a member of the all-white Southern Association of Secondary Schools; and two, that I did not have letters of recommendation from five alumni of the University of Mississippi.

By the time I had filed the application to Ole Miss, I had become more or less settled in my courses at Jackson State College. I had no intention of stopping my education there while attempting to gain admission to the university, and the relationships that I enjoyed with my instructors were important to me as a morale factor. Tacitly, and often openly, there was great support and even much enthusiasm, particularly among those whom I knew well.

On May 31, 1961, we filed suit against state officials and the University of Mississippi in the U.S. District Court in Meridian, Mississippi, under Judge Mize, alleging that my admission had been denied on the basis of race. Judge Mize, the federal district judge in Mississippi, had previously made his position clear in an earlier school case, saying that "differences between Caucasians and Negroes are genetically determined and cannot be changed materially by environment."

Our surprise appearance in court sent out a shock wave. The local Meridian newspaper put out a special edition that was on the street before we left town the same day:

James H. Meredith, Kosciusko Negro, has filed in federal court to enter the University of Mississippi for the summer session. Fortunately, his case can't be heard until June 12th in Biloxi. This gives grounds for hope that he won't really become a serious problem. Some misguided people ask what difference it makes if only a few Negroes go to a white school. Integration will mean future intermarriage. Intermarriage in the South means the end of both races as such, and the emergence of a tribe of mongrels. If you value your racial heritage, we must lock shields. We must fight for our race and for the South to the last bitter ditch. We can triumph—we will triumph—we must triumph.

Under federal court procedures, lawyers for Mississippi officials were entitled to take a deposition from me, both to discover what evidence I had against them and to probe any other areas that the judge would permit. Mississippi placed its case in the hands of the deputy attorney general of Mississippi, Dugas Shands, one of the state's leading white supremacy strategists. He was from the white aristocracy of Mississippi and had a deformed hand from birth, which he used artfully to his advantage in court. His chief assistant was Assistant Attorney General Ed Cates, who came from a poor white origin and was later convicted of fraud and sent to prison.

Ten minutes after the deposition started on June 8, 1961, I knew I could outmaneuver Shands any day of the week. Shands tried to give me the "nigger treatment" tactic, which was widely used in Mississippi for generations in courtrooms in dealing with cases involving blacks. The tactic was to provoke the black, to frighten him, then to break the black down and cross him up. The aim was to imply that the black was dishonest, immoral, a thief by nature, and in general unworthy of being considered fully human. The outcome of the trial was a foregone conclusion, and the excerpts from the deposition and trial proceedings show how it sometimes veered in farcical directions:

BAILIFF: "Everybody rise. The Honorable Judge Sidney Mize, United States Federal Court Southern District of Mississippi."

JUDGE MIZE: "Y'all be seated."

STATE LAWYER: "I move that this baseless case be dismissed."

JUDGE MIZE: "We will hear the case and decide on its merits."

MY ATTORNEY, CONSTANCE MOTLEY: "We move that a temporary injunction be issued ordering the University of Mississippi to admit James H. Meredith immediately as a student."

JUDGE MIZE: "Motion denied. Call your first witness."

MOTLEY: "Your Honor! We call the University of Mississippi registrar Robert H. Ellis. Mr. Ellis, do you know what this case is about?"

ELLIS: "No. I have no idea."

MOTLEY: "Mr. Ellis, are you familiar with the application of James H. Meredith for admission as a student to the University of Mississippi."

ELLIS: "No. I never heard of a James H. Meredith."

MOTLEY: "Mr. Ellis, are you telling this court that you do not know why we are here today?"

STATE LAWYER: "Objection, your honor! She is badgering the witness."

JUDGE MIZE: "Sustained. He has already answered the question. He said he didn't know."

STATE LAWYER: "Have you been on any military base since you were discharged?"

MEREDITH: "Brookley Air Force base in Mobile, Alabama."

STATE LAWYER: "What were you doing there?"

MEREDITH: "Visiting a friend."

STATE LAWYER: "Visiting a friend; who was that friend?"

MOTLEY: "We object to this."

STATE LAWYER: "This is testing his recollection."

MOTLEY: "No, you can't test his recollection by asking him irrelevant questions. His friend at some military base has nothing to do with this lawsuit and the issue in it, and we object and instruct him not to answer these irrelevant questions."

STATE LAWYER: "Do you own a typewriter?"

MEREDITH: "Yes, sir."

STATE LAWYER: "Where did you get it?"

MOTLEY: "We object to that on the ground that it is not relevant and we instruct him not answer."

STATE LAWYER: "You won't answer where you got your typewriter? Is that the typewriter you used to type those recommendations on?"

MEREDITH: "Yes, sir."

STATE LAWYER: "Where did you get the paper you typed it on?"

MOTLEY: "We object to that on the ground it is not relevant."

STATE LAWYER: "How do you spell notary public?"

MEREDITH: "N-o-t-a-r-y p-u-b-l-i-c."

As my legal struggle began, I confided in my father as I would no one else.

I told him that I had come home to begin to fulfill my divine responsibility to break the system of white supremacy in Mississippi.

"I came here to fight a war. I am a soldier," I told him. "Mississippi is the battlefield. White supremacy is the enemy. I am a citizen of this country. I want to enjoy every right or I don't want to be around to enjoy any of them. My objective is total victory over white supremacy."

"I knew this time would come," said my father. From that moment on he was the mentor, inspiration, and chief strategist for my campaign. In this and other conversations we had in the months ahead, my father guided every important step I made.

71

"I knew it may get rough on everybody," I noted.

"You don't have to worry about us," Cap replied unhesitatingly. "We are with you all the way."

"There are three main groups that we have to watch," he explained. "First, the white Citizens Council—these are the rich and powerful white folks who mostly want to keep control of everything. Second are the little white folks who recently got out of the po' white trash class, like small office holders, law officers, and such. And finally, the bottom of the barrel, crazy fools like the Ku Klux Klan and the misfits.

"They have been working this plan now for fifty years," he said. "That is why I'm so glad to see you trying to get into Ole Miss. It can change the whole power structure. It can change everything."

"It is our divine responsibility to rule," I said.

My father replied, "That's why God is sending us through this wilderness of suffering and pain. It is part of the preparation. We must prepare first."

"It seems more like a punishment," I observed.

"It is that, too. Our forefathers indulged in excesses and greed. That's why they sold us to slavery."

My father continued, "My time left on this earth is not long. I have passed on all the knowledge and wisdom that I possess to every member of the family. I must now pass on to you the mantle of the divine responsibility."

I could only reply, "I don't know if I can fill your shoes."

"You are not supposed to fill my shoes," he explained. "You are required to meet your own responsibility."

"What have you been hearing around town?" I asked him one day in 1961, after I had completed the application forms for the University of Mississippi.

"The whites are putting a lot of pressure on the blacks who signed statements in your support," said Cap. "The rich white folks are coming up to me more than ever now, asking me about you."

"What do you tell them?" I asked him.

"I don't tell them nothing. Whenever they ask me about you, I tell them I don't know nothing about what you are doing. Rich white folks are always sending me messages by their 'niggers' telling me I'd better make you do this or do that. I just tell them, 'You know I ain't never been able to do nothing with that boy!' They just laugh and go on."

"Are they planning anything violent yet?" I asked.

My father said, "The rich white folks still got pretty good control. Po' white folks are talking real mean, though, and having several meetings where they are doing a lot of threatening."

I told him what I'd been hearing: "I've been getting a lot of secondhand rumors about how the Sovereignty Commission people or white Citizens Council folks told this nigger to tell that nigger to tell the Jackson State College president to throw me out of school.

"The poor rednecks are real dangerous because they think that their whole way of life is being threatened," I told him. "A fellow told me the other day that some white men were in the community asking people where I lived. Two white men in a big Cadillac. One of the men got out, a great big mean-looking cracker in his forties. He had an army .45 pistol stuck in his belt."

He said to my friend, "You that nigger trying to go to Ole Miss?"

"No!" he replied.

"Where do that nigger live?"

"I don't know."

"Well, you tell that nigger we are going to kill him."

Then he got into the Cadillac and drove off.

My father smiled, shook his head, and told me, "You don't have to worry about them. That's just an old scare tactic. White folks been using that tactic for years to cause the black community to put pressure on whoever they want to change something. They won't be back. They did what they set out to do. Scare the blacks in the community."

"Well, it sure worked," I noted. "My neighbors have been taking turns watching our place. They even have a special parking pattern."

Cap explained, "Rich white folks send their 'head niggers' to warn you when they are going to do something. And them po' crackers talk it up all over the country before they act."

"I see."

"You just go on and act like ain't nothing unusual happened. That will throw them off. Whites don't know how to deal with a black person that ain't scared."

"They sure don't know how to deal with me then," I said.

"Some of my friends want to put an armed guard around me," I told him.

"No!" replied my father. "You don't ever want to do anything like that. That's a sign of fear. You can't let whites or blacks think you are afraid.

"Power respects power," he continued. "When a man stands up, other men respect him. When I was a young man I always carried a gun, sometimes two. I've never gone to bed a night in my life when I didn't have a loaded shotgun in the rack above my head and everybody in the county, white and black, knew that I would use it."

My father advised me, "The main thing is for you to act quietly and quickly once you decide what to do, so you can outflank the enemy and capitalize on public opinion. Move secretly, move fast, and then make the headlines."

"My objective," I agreed, "is to make myself more valuable alive than dead."

"Just keep on living, J-Boy," said my father. "Power respects power. Only the strong survive."

There was much debate about my safety among the people close to me. The majority maintained that an armed guard should be posted at my house and that I should never go anywhere alone.

They insisted that I always travel with at least two cars and that the one without me should be armed.

I rejected these precautions. I believed that the proceedings would be long, and the security measures would only tend to suggest to the opposition that they were obligated to kill me. I knew that these security measures would only last for a while, because the people keeping watch would soon tire of the extra burden and drop the guard just when it would really be needed. And I was convinced that one should never waste his energy where there is no "clear and present danger." Furthermore, I knew that the very best possible protection against my particular enemy was the enemy himself.

I took personal precautions to make sure that I remained under the eye of the Jackson police, who were the most professional law enforcement people in Mississippi and the least corrupt, when compared with the highway patrol and local sheriffs and deputies, who were on the whole rabidly racist and a law unto themselves when it came to abusing black people. I had no feeling that the Jackson police as a department would have any official interest in eliminating me, unlike the Mississippi Highway Patrol, the plain-clothes goons of the state spy agency, the "Sovereignty Commission," and the local sheriffs and deputies.

I found a way to make the Jackson police my bodyguards. I would drive my car a little too slow, a little too fast, or operate with the wrong tags, just to make sure they were on my trail and watching me. By watching me, they would also have to keep their eyes on anyone else who might be tailing me. I always made it my object to stay near the borderline of the law. I would sometimes try to look mean or suspicious to the law officers on patrol.

Aware of the zeal with which Mississippi cops look after their Negro assignments, I endeavored to make sure that they were kept on my trail. Mississippi society is very legalistic, and no injustice is committed against a Negro without some semblance of an excuse. The excuse can be real or imaginary.

Mississippi law enforcement officers were jealous of their prerogatives, and once they were assigned to do the job of "taking care of a nigger," their prey then became their prized possession and they were duty-bound to make sure that he did not fall into the hands of others. Police surveillance could serve both as harassment and as protection. Since harassment is a part of the Negroes' way of life in Mississippi, it was not a really significant consideration, but the protection aspect was.

I always drove very slowly past the police station in order to make sure that all the policemen got a chance to take a good look at me. This may seem strange, but it is perhaps the main reason why I was seldom trailed or bothered by the police during my many visits home while I was in the air force.

If there was anything that a Mississippi cop hated, it was for someone to know something about a Negro that he didn't know first. By giving the police the first look, a black person relieved them of the necessity of finding the "nigger" and "getting the goods on him." When a Mississippi policeman had to suffer the embarrassment of looking for a "nigger," he was likely to make the trip worth his while.

I always took great care not to give a "peckerwood" a chance to put his hands on me. No white man in Mississippi had ever put his hands on me.

My greatest concern was for the safety of my family and parents. The problem was how to draw attention to myself and keep the focus always on me, and thereby lessen the chances of an assault on my family and parents.

The initial reaction to my application to the university was in my family's home town of Kosciusko and followed the time-tested formula for weeding out the attackers of the system. The first step was for the police to go around the black neighborhood, asking questions about me and my family. As a rule, this act was usually enough to trigger panic in the Negro community.

The idea was to let the social pressure from the community and the neighborhood force the nonconformer to conform. The last resort of the white community, before taking direct action, was to call upon "Negro leaders" to use their personal influence to bring about conformity.

I was well aware of these tactics and had previously briefed my parents, although they already knew even better than I what was to come. The last resort was to be the burden of the high school principal. It must have been a terribly painful experience for him. He was a member of the church in which I had been baptized, and every Sunday morning he and my mother went to the same church.

The white "powers that be" called on him to give my family what amounted to an ultimatum. The ultimatum was for my parents to tell me to withdraw or face the understood consequences.

The principal went to the home of my parents and gave them the ultimatum. "James has to withdraw or he will face the consequences. He will get himself killed."

"If someone has to die," my mother replied defiantly, "who is my child more than anyone else's child to die?" My father added simply, "He was born to die." The principal left in sorrow. There was no rest in my father's house that night.

About three o'clock the next morning, I heard my doorbell ring. I peered out the window to see my mother and father, looking alarmed and shaken. My sister Willie Lou was with them.

Many thoughts ran through my mind. Had they been run away from their home? What did this unexpected visit mean?

They had driven from their home in Kosciusko eighty miles down to Jackson to wish me luck, and give me a warning.

They came in and my father would not even pull off his hat. He did not intend to linger; he only wanted me to know what was going on. Although he was obviously excited, my father spoke slowly and unemotionally. He told me what had taken place during the last couple of days and asked me to be careful and not to worry about them.

"You've got to stay out of Kosciusko for a while," my father warned me.

My family began to receive threatening mail and phone calls; their home was vandalized, and they were refused service in local businesses.

My mother was furious at the "scary niggers" in Kosciusko, and my sister appeared ready to take them all on by herself in hand-to-hand combat, the white folks and their "niggers."

In less than five minutes my father was ready to go.

"Don't come back to Kosciusko, you'll be killed inside of a day," he said. "Don't use the telephone, I'm sure yours and mine are tapped.

"Now, J-Boy, don't worry about us," he concluded. "Do whatever you think is right, no matter what the cost.

"Keep fighting, J-Boy," he said.

I watched them drive off in the night.

As a way of preparing myself for the extended legal struggle I knew would accompany my enrollment at the University of Mississippi, for weeks at a time I would get out of bed before dawn.

I would walk the streets of Jackson in the early dawn light so I could watch the maids and cleaning women, the hospital workers and other poor black folks leaving their homes in Jackson and heading for work. Seeing the reality of hardship in the lives of these working people strengthened my own sense of mission.

These were the people I was trying to help toward freedom. "These are the people I am fighting for," I thought, "and they deserve nothing less than absolute victory."

Back-and-forth legal maneuvering continued through the end of 1961. On February 3, 1962, Judge Mize ruled as expected, claiming absurdly: "The evidence overwhelmingly showed that the Plaintiff [me] was not denied admission because of his race.

The record shows, and I find as a fact, that the University is not a racially segregated institution."

I appealed to the Fifth U.S. Circuit Court of Appeals in New Orleans, which finally ruled in my favor on June 25, 1962, my birthday. Judge John Minor Wisdom, an eminent Republican jurist appointed by President Dwight Eisenhower, reversed Judge Mize's decision as the product of an "eerie atmosphere of never-never land" and ruled in my favor, stating: "James H. Meredith was turned down solely because he is black.

"A full review of the record," Judge Wisdom wrote, "leads the Court inescapably to the conclusion that from the moment the defendants discovered that Meredith was a Negro they engaged in a carefully calculated campaign of delay, harassment, and masterly inactivity. It was a defense designed to discourage and to defeat by evasive tactics which would have been a credit to Quintus Fabius Maximus."

Judge Wisdom further ridiculed the state of Mississippi for wrongful delays for bogus reasons, other than race, to keep me from being admitted to the university, such as bogus charges of falsification of voting registration and for using a report from a U.S. Air Force psychiatrist that described me in 1960 as "a twenty-six year old negro Sergeant, who complained of tension and nervousness, and occasional nervous stomach. Patient is extremely concerned with racial problems, and his symptoms are intensified whenever there is heightened tempo in the racial problems in the United States and Africa. . . . He loses his temper at times over minor incidents both at home and elsewhere."

To this, Judge Wisdom described me approvingly as "just about the type of Negro who might be expected to try to crack the racial barrier at the University of Mississippi: a man with a mission and with a nervous stomach." My air force record was spotless: I received both an honorable discharge and a good-conduct medal.

Despite the ruling, celebrations were not yet in order, however, for other roadblocks ensued, none greater than a proclamation from Mississippi governor Ross Barnett instructing state education and university officials to ignore the court orders. Mississippi had declared itself in effect no longer subject to the laws of the United States.

And incredibly, in a bizarre judicial implosion, another Fifth Circuit Appeals judge, Ben F. Cameron, issued an order nullifying his fellow justice Judge Wisdom's order.

I was interviewed by *New York Post* columnist James A. Wechsler, and his July 24, 1962, article included these passages:

> By all our conventional standards, James H. Meredith, the son of a dirt farmer, should be recognized as the embodiment of the American story and saluted as young-man-of-the-year by the Junior Chamber of Commerce.
>
> Graduated from high school in 1951, he patiently and stolidly served as a clerk-typist in the Air Force for nine years, finally accumulating sufficient funds to finance himself through the University of Mississippi and then perhaps through law school. Along the way, he met and married a girl who was working on an Air Force post in Indiana.
>
> When he decided he had amassed adequate resources to realize his dream, there was, of course, only one trouble with the life plan. He was a Negro, and the state of Mississippi has now for many months mobilized all its legal resources to thwart his aspiration. Three full semesters and four summer sessions have passed since he began his fight to break the educational color line in that state, but victory still eludes him.
>
> Meredith coincidentally resembles a thinner image of Martin Luther King. Like King, neither his voice nor manner exhibits any surface scars of martyrdom, nor does he, by the way, affirm any doctrinaire allegiance to King or anyone else.
>
> He remains convinced that "the politicians" are responsible for the backward racism of the state, and that, if he

gained admission to the University, he would be treated decently by faculty and students alike. He insists he has no fears about being the first to cross that line.

The question of whether I should accept my degree from Jackson State College became increasingly more pressing. I had already earned enough credits for a degree from Jackson State. Of course, it would probably make me ineligible for admission to the University of Mississippi as an undergraduate, thereby making the pending case moot, even if we won. But the best use of my time was involved: How much should one give up to prove a point? Many interested groups asked me not to graduate, including the NAACP Legal Defense Fund, the Justice Department, and the Federal Appeals Court, which had suggested in its opinion that I procrastinate. Another crucial factor was that I was living primarily on my savings, and, above all, I could never allow my family to suffer from a lack of the necessities of life.

By the spring of 1962, my graduation was long past due and I could no longer keep my name off the list of graduates. My diploma was ordered, along with the yellow tassel to indicate that I was graduating with honors. The only way that I could prevent myself from receiving my degree was to decline to pay the $4.50 fee, a final requirement for graduation. I didn't pay it. It was a great disappointment to see my classmates leave me behind. It was a difficult decision to make.

Meanwhile, I had been accepted for admission to Howard University Law School and had been admitted to the Atlanta University Graduate School with a scholarship to study political science. Atlanta's director of admissions was probably decisive in making it possible for me to continue my efforts. He had assured me that I would be permitted to enroll at Atlanta at any time that I felt it no longer feasible to try to enter the University of Mississippi. Without this assurance, I would probably have chosen to get my degree from Jackson State College and go on to graduate study.

To escape the constant pressure of my legal struggles, I often went out to savor the nightlife of black Mississippi.

I pulled up to Mr. P's after midnight on a Saturday. It was a juke joint on Sunset Strip out in Hinds County.

It was a good time to arrive because the band, composed of two guitars and one drummer with a two-piece drum contraption, was just hitting its pace after the first intermission. The cooks and nursemaids who had to work in the white woman's kitchen and take care of the white man's baby were out on the town by this time. By 1:30 a.m. everybody was high and fallen into the groove.

The talk was loud, bad, and nasty, and the women were just as free and foul-mouthed as the men. There was a girl sitting up on the front end of a car with her legs crossed high, holding on to her boyfriend's shirt. She had him pinned in her legs. "Mother*fucker*," she declared, "what are you doing fucking with that bitch?"

The boyfriend replied, "Whore! Turn me loose before I knock you on your ass."

His girl countered, "Nigger! If I catch you fucking with that bitch again, I'm gonna kill your motherfucking ass!"

I slipped inside the crowded door. The heat and odor hit me at the same time. The place was packed solid with black men and women. Their dress ranged all the way from expensive furs to maid uniforms. The men wore everything from seventy-dollar shoes and three-hundred-dollar suits to four-colored shirts and purple trousers to musty, sweaty, sawdust-filled overalls that they worked in all week. In the back room, slot machines lined the wall. One roped-off section contained the dice games and another was devoted to the card games. The big game in Mississippi was a card game called "skin." You'd hardly see so much money in a Las Vegas casino.

On any night at Mr. P's you would see a show that could be seen in very few other places: shake dancing, belly-rolling, stunt-cutting, trick dancing, and the sexiest kind of sexy dances. One

man had on a loud-colored, tight-fitting pair of pants and wore a pair of pointed-toe imitation alligator shoes. He was really "cutting a rug," jumping all over the place and executing some very difficult and tricky steps. Booze flowed freely. Mississippi was officially a "dry" state where serving alcohol was illegal, but Mr. P's, like lots of black and white joints in the state, skirted the prohibition at the price of sporadic token enforcement by the authorities.

The band was playing "Shake Your Money Maker," a sure satisfier for this crowd. It had a fast, sensuous beat and was loud and moving. Sometimes the band would play it for thirty minutes or longer without stopping, and the crowd would still beg for more when it was over.

There on the stage was the legendary blues guitarist and singer Elmore James, king of the slide guitar. The kind of music he played was known by many names—gut-bucket, down in the alley, back in the woods—but to me it is folk music of the highest order. It tells the story of the black man and woman: the history of slavery, segregation, discrimination, prejudice, poverty, and hope. I've learned more about the black experience in America from listening to and digesting this music than from any other source. Elmore James loved to hear the crowd beg, and the audience knew that he had to be treated with tender care, because the least thing might upset him and he would refuse to play a note.

I edged my way up toward the stage. There was no dance floor as such, the dance floor was everywhere, in the aisles, between the tables, on the tables, or anywhere you could find a little space.

A beautiful girl dressed in a fake fur dress took center stage. Everybody formed a circle to watch her dance.

"Look at that!" said the emcee, "Go 'head girl, show it all!"

She went down toward the floor and her dress would come up over her pretty thighs and it looked like she didn't have on anything under the dress. Just when it looked like she was to reveal everything, she would push the dress down and start the heart-taxing process all over again.

The crowd roared and begged for more. A fan called out, "That bitch is just showing off. Thinks she's something cause she been up North!" More laughter and all-around hollering.

Elmore James turned the guitar picking over to his understudy and slid up to the microphone to sing my favorite song, "Dust My Broom."

"I believe! I be-lieve! I'll dust my broom. I say raise your window, Baby, I say raise your window, Baby, And let me ease out real slow, I hear somebody knocking; it may be your husband, I don't know."

At this point, four white men in uniform appeared on the dance floor. It was the local sheriff and his deputies. The music stopped.

I had seen blacks fighting in a juke joint, standing man to man and knocking each other in the head with chairs. I've seen them go get sawed-off shotguns and pistols, shoot into the ceiling, and occasionally shoot at somebody. Then I've seen one white man come in and completely paralyze the whole room. Why? Pure, unadulterated fear, the kind that gripped Mr. P.'s at this moment.

"Which one of these niggers you want me to take tonight?" the sheriff announced.

The owner shrugged his shoulders. "Whatever you say, man."

"Play that song!" the sheriff ordered the drummer.

"Yes sir, boss man!" relied the drummer, "Git right on it!"

"Okay!" said the sheriff, pointing around randomly with his five-battery flashlight, "I want that nigger, and this nigger, and that nigger over there."

Deputies grabbed the ones pointed out, cuffed them, took them on out to the cars, and drove away. Nothing else ever stopped in the joint. Everyone kept on having a good time. It was just like it hadn't happened.

Thinking about Mississippi is one thing.

But *being* in Mississippi is quite another.

On September 10, 1962, my legal struggle reached its apparent climax when United States Supreme Court Justice Hugo L. Black, a former Ku Klux Klansman, overruled Judge Cameron's order and ordered the University of Mississippi to admit me immediately, on the same terms as any other student. The Supreme Court was not in session, but Justice Black consulted with his fellow judges on the nation's highest court and they all concurred with his decision.

Now there evidently were no further legal blocks that Mississippi could throw in my path to keep me from enrolling as a student at the University of Mississippi. Consequently, the U.S. district court, acting under the various court of appeals mandates and Justice Black's mandate of September 10, issued an injunction on September 13 against University of Mississippi officials, ordering them to admit me to the university and enjoining them from excluding me from admission and continuing attendance at the university or discriminating against me in any way whatsoever because of my race.

The U.S. Supreme Court had spoken, and I had won. Case closed. Crisis over.

Or so you would think, in any rational universe.

But this was Mississippi, and it floated in a perverted fantasy-land all its own, a world far outside the borders of the United States.

Mississippi, it turned out, was not a part of the United States on the issue of race.

Mississippi was its own universe.

And instead of obeying the law, the white rulers of Mississippi decided to launch an insurrection and shove the state toward the abyss of absolute chaos.

CHAPTER FOUR

The South Rises Again

F OR THE FIRST TIME IN MY LIFE, I WAS FACE TO FACE WITH
my arch-enemy.

We smiled at each other.

Ross Robert Barnett, Jr., was the governor of the Great State of
Mississippi, the son and grandson of combat-hardened Confederate army soldiers, and a man called by *Time* magazine "as bitter a
racist as inhabits the nation."

He had ten thousand National Guard soldiers at his command,
many thousands of guns, a small air force, and more than two
hundred armed state troopers. And he was ready to turn all those
troops and weapons against me.

I first saw him on September 20, 1962, in an administration
building on the campus of the University of Mississippi, at my first
attempt to register. He looked like a kindly, elderly funeral direc-

tor, and he was stepping into his supreme moment in history. He was playing his part so magnificently he reminded me of the actor Charlton Heston playing Moses in *The Ten Commandments.*

For two weeks in history, thanks to me, Ross Barnett blazed a trail of superhuman glory across the firmament of white supremacy in America.

On September 13, the same day the federal courts issued what looked to be their absolute final order on the matter of my admission to Ole Miss, Barnett threw down the gauntlet and made a hare-brained, apocalyptic radio and TV speech to the people of Mississippi, a speech handwritten by his boss, William Simmons, chief of the Citizens' Councils of America.

They were, in effect, the words of the president of the Resurrected Confederate States of America. Excerpted passages from Ross Barnett's speech give you a flavor of how incendiary the moment was, and how explosive the stakes were to the overlords of white supremacy.

> I speak to you as your Governor in a solemn hour in the history of our great state, in a solemn hour, indeed, in our nation's history. I speak to you now in the moment of our greatest crisis since the War Between the States.
>
> In the absence of constitutional authority and without legislative action, an ambitious federal government, employing naked and arbitrary power, has decided to deny us the right of self-determination in the conduct of the affairs of our sovereign state.
>
> Having long since failed in their efforts to conquer the indomitable spirit of the people of Mississippi and their unshakable will to preserve the sovereignty and majesty of our commonwealth, they now seek to break us physically with the power of force.
>
> We must either submit to the unlawful dictates of the federal government or stand up like men and tell them

"NEVER!" The day of reckoning has been delayed as long as possible. It is now upon us. This is the day, and this is the hour. Knowing you as I do, there is no doubt in my mind what the overwhelming majority of loyal Mississippians will do. They will never submit to the moral degradation, to the shame and the ruin which have faced all others who have lacked the courage to defend their beliefs.

I have made my position in this matter crystal clear. I have said in every county in Mississippi that no school in our state will be integrated while I am your Governor. I repeat to you tonight: NO SCHOOL IN OUR STATE WILL BE INTEGRATED WHILE I AM YOUR GOVERNOR!

There is no case in history where the Caucasian race has survived social integration.

We will not drink from the cup of genocide. Mississippi, as a sovereign state, has the right under the Federal Constitution to determine for itself what the Federal Government has reserved to it.

Therefore, in obedience to legislative and constitutional sanction, I do hereby interpose the rights of the Sovereign State of Mississippi to enforce its laws and to regulate its internal affairs without interference on the part of the Federal Government or its officers.

With the help of Almighty God, we shall be invincible, and we shall keep the faith!

With this open declaration of rebellion against the federal government, Ross Barnett channeled a national surge of white resentment to so-called "forced integration," and he transformed himself from a bumbling politician on the downswing of a mediocre term as the state's chief executive into the sacred incarnation of Robert E. Lee himself. "Ross is standing like Gibraltar," went the popular saying, "he shall never falter." He became a southern superhero, and he was savoring every moment of it.

Lord of Chaos: Governor Ross Barnett launched an insurrection against the federal government over me. He was chief of a terrorist police state that stripped black Americans of the rights of American citizenship, and his father and grandfather were Confederate Army combat veterans. Here he surveys a mob of thousands of white civilians and police at Oxford on September 28, 1962, ready to blockade me and my federal caravan from entering the campus. The mob was getting out of control, guns were appearing, and Barnett suddenly realized that scores of white people were about to be slaughtered. He got on the phone to plead with Attorney General Robert Kennedy to turn my motorcade around and retreat. RFK capitulated. The mob rejoiced in triumph, and Barnett was hailed as a Southern Superman. *Photo courtesy of Donald Proehl*

Earlier in the day on September 20, the day I first encountered him in person at the University of Mississippi, the Mississippi state legislature, called into special session over the crisis, passed a new law at Barnett's behest, which specified that "no person shall be eligible for admission to any state institution of higher learning if he has a criminal charge pending against him in any Mississippi state court." This was a desperate attempt to defeat me by a manufactured technicality, referring to the bogus false-voter-registration charge that was filed against me in absentia by state officials in a Jackson court, a charge for which I was arrested one morning, placed in a Hinds County courthouse, and inexplicably released the same afternoon.

As an attorney in private practice and a master courtroom showman, Barnett, who earned his law degree at Ole Miss, had earned a reputation for championing personal-injury cases for poor whites and blacks in Mississippi. When an elderly black man was injured in a traffic accident and was asked what doctor should be called, the story went, the man said, "I want you to call Doctor Ross Barnett!" But to win the 1958 gubernatorial election, he made a deal with the Devil, in the person of Citizens Council boss William Simmons, in swearing to never allow integration of any school in the state. Given the tides of history in America at the time, it was a promise he should have known he could not keep.

Now Ross Barnett was riding a tidal wave of white popular jubilation. How many white Mississippians and Americans sympathized with Barnett at the time is impossible to say. I think it was an overall minority but it was still a powerful minority, probably numbering in the millions.

And right now, several thousand of these white people had me surrounded in a building in Oxford, Mississippi.

An hour earlier, I was in a U.S. border patrol car racing down from our federal command post at the Millington Naval Air Station in Memphis, Tennessee. When we crossed the state line and passed the giant green "Welcome to Mississippi" sign, Chief U.S. Marshal James McShane, who was assigned by Attorney General Robert Kennedy to be my bodyguard, asked me, "How does it feel, Jim, to see that sign?"

"Well, I always have mixed emotions," I told him, "but to me Mississippi is the most beautiful country in the world—in natural beauty." That seemed to have disarmed McShane for a few miles as he silently studied the countryside.

I thought, as we drove along the highway, how utterly ridiculous this was, what a terrible waste of time and money and energy to iron out some rough spots in our civilization. But realistically I knew that this action was necessary. I knew change was a threat to people, that they would fight it, and that this probably was the only way it could be accomplished.

Batesville to Oxford was the final leg of the trip. It was a long drive for me. For the first time in my life I knowingly surrendered complete control of my fate. As previously arranged, our cars were surrounded and escorted in a caravan of Mississippi State Highway Patrol cars personally directed by the force's chief, Colonel T. B. Birdsong, who left no doubt in anybody's mind that Mississippi was in command. Two state troopers' cars were in front, Colonel Birdsong was directly in front of our car, and a state troopers' car was directly behind us; the other federal government car and more highway patrol cars followed.

We were prisoners of Mississippi.

Now this was a spectacle that Mississippi had never seen before—a black man was the star of an official government motorcade! All the other traffic had to pull over and stop and let me have the road. For a moment I felt like the governor, or the president of the United States.

I thought about the purpose of all this, about the mission from God my father had sent me on. The dilapidated Negro shanties along the route, with an occasional mansion to emphasize the contrast, gave me a perfect view of what I was fighting for: the people in those never-painted shacks, and the half-naked children playing in the dirt.

This was my first visit to the bucolic university city of Oxford. I had traveled extensively throughout the state but Oxford was off the main route to anywhere, and I had never been there. It seemed the entire town was out to see history turn upside down. As we

entered the university campus, I could see scores of state highway patrolmen lined up shoulder to shoulder, and a crowd of what looked like thousands of white people, many of them students.

To the humming of the crowd we emerged from the car and walked briskly toward the building. As soon as I got out of my car, the crowd booed and chanted: "Two, four, six, eight, we don't want to integrate!" I smiled and waved at them and then entered the Center for Continuation Studies with my entourage to enroll. The center was not technically considered a part of the university because it belonged to a private group.

The heckling never ceased: "Go home, nigger!" the mob chanted outside. A Mississippi lawman angrily declared the sentiment of the crowd to a reporter: "I don't give a damn whether they got United States marshals or not, the nigger ain't goin' to the University of Mississippi, period. It'll take federal troops to keep him alive."

Inside, I was confronted by the first representative of the huge welcoming committee. A mean-looking man told me he was the sheriff, and he sternly served me with a set of summonses. I thanked him, handed the papers to the Justice Department lawyer, and that was all I ever heard about them.

There was a lot of talking and shaking hands between the Mississippi and federal officers. There was Governor Barnett, relishing the spotlight. He asked people how good business was, asked someone if they were "kin" to someone he knew, shook hands (except mine), and invited them to "come see me some time."

I stepped forward and announced, "I would like to register."

I came face to face with Barnett. He seemed to wink at me, unsuccessfully suppressing a smile, and asked, "Which one of you is James Meredith?" Mississippi officials stifled belly laughs. I almost laughed myself. It was a funny line. The federal officials, all of whom were white, seemed stunned. They didn't understand the Mississippi game, but Barnett and I sure did.

That afternoon, Governor Barnett had himself appointed temporary registrar of students at Ole Miss by a special meeting of the board of trustees. I handed the governor a copy of the federal court order directing the registrar to register me as a student. He took it and laid it aside and with a theatrical flourish he produced and read from a grand proclamation of states' rights gobbledygook that concluded, "Therefore, you, James H. Meredith, are hereby refused admission as a student to the University of Mississippi. Take due notice thereof and govern yourself accordingly." He handed me the personal signed and sealed proclamation as a historic souvenir.

"Governor, you are in violation of a federal court order," said a U.S. Justice Department lawyer. The governor did not respond. The lawyer briefly protested, but soon seemed to sense that the most logical thing to do was for us to get out of there.

I thanked the governor and we hastened out to our waiting car, which sped away with hordes of shouting, rock-throwing students hot on the chase. The state troopers led us on our way north to the Tennessee line as fast as one could imagine.

The first registration attempt was over.

———

The next day, Barnett was hit with a roundhouse legal punch when the U.S. Fifth Circuit Federal Court of Appeals charged him with contempt and issued a restraining order against him and state officials attempting to block my entrance to the university. His codefendants, the state Board of Trustees of Institutions of Higher Learning, collapsed like a house of cards and promised the court they would assist in my enrollment.

But Barnett tried to stay a step or two in front, by issuing a proclamation on September 24 that declared that "the arrest or attempts to arrest, or the fining or the attempts to fine, of any state official in the performance of his official duties, by any representative of the Federal Government, is illegal and such representative or representatives of said federal Government are to be summarily arrested and jailed."

The edict empowered state officials to throw federal officials in jail if they tried to force me into the university, and was read aloud to the cheering Mississippi state legislature. Barnett had rejected the Court's ruling and essentially dared the Kennedys to enforce the federal court order. Incredibly, the same day, Mississippi State Senator Jack Pace introduced in the Mississippi state legislature "a petition to the United States Congress to sever relations between the Union and the state of Mississippi." His colleagues rushed him out to lunch to calm him down.

The U.S. government could not tolerate this defiance, and at 8:30 a.m. on September 25, the Court of Appeals for the Fifth Circuit entered another temporary restraining order against state officials' interfering with my entering the university.

White Mississippi was being whipped to a fever pitch by a state media apparatus that was controlled by diehard segregationists who controlled the newspapers, radio, and television, and mobilized to support the governor in this hair-raising, extremely dangerous, and illegal revolt. This was in keeping, however, with both prevailing white opinion of the time in Mississippi, and the feelings of a good many white Americans across the North and the South who felt that so-called forced integration was a bad idea. Ross Barnett was elected with a majority of white Mississippians for the express purpose of stopping it, and that's exactly what he was doing in his confrontation with me.

At New Orleans on the morning of September 25, I boarded a plush federal-government-operated Cessna 220 aircraft, which would be my primary mode of travel during the crisis, and set off for my second attempt to register, this time in the state capital of Jackson.

The pilot was a top-notch flyer from Florida and a very friendly person. Chief U.S. Marshal James McShane sat beside him in the front seat and U.S. Justice Department Civil Rights Division attorney John Doar and I were on the backseats. For the next three weeks or so almost every time I appeared in public I was flanked by McShane and Doar, two of the bravest men I have ever known. I never saw either of them weaken under any condition of danger. The only three people who showed no fear during the entire time were myself, Jim McShane, and John Doar. Every Mississippi person was scared to death.

We taxied out to the airstrip and then waited while a faked flight was being staged. To fool the newsmen, and frustrate the state of Mississippi, another plane took off at the time we were scheduled to leave. It flew around for a few minutes and returned to indicate that we had changed our minds and returned to New Orleans. Then we took off and headed for Jackson.

I had my first long talk with John Doar on this trip. He was a tall, lanky, laconic Republican from Minnesota who had been a successful small-town lawyer and was almost totally uninvolved in the Negro situation before he had been appointed to the Civil Rights Division by President Eisenhower. Once he had become engaged in the effort to insure the civil rights of the Negro, his dedication to this cause seemed genuine. I probed into his reasons and his ideas concerning his involvement, because I wondered what a white man thought and how he justified devoting a major portion of his life to the battle for civil rights. He was at my side everywhere I went by car and by airplane. He actually wound up sleeping in my room at Ole Miss for several weeks.

The thing I remember most about John Doar was the fact that he really believed that every American should enjoy full, first-class citizenship rights and complete equality. There was not a molecule of deception, guile, or hesitation and nothing tricky or shifty about Doar. He truly believed in what he was doing. Doar had a commanding, soft-spoken authority to him, a classic salt-of-the-earth American strength that reminded me a great deal of movie stars like Gary Cooper, Jimmy Stewart, or Gregory Peck.

I told Doar that I considered such maneuvers as we were going through an utter waste of human manpower and intelligence.

As we crossed into Mississippi airspace and I looked out on

all sides at the natural beauty of the land of my birth, I thought again, as I had for many years, what a wonderful place Mississippi could be.

Suddenly, a squad of Mississippi National Guard aircraft began to circle and cut across us from every direction.

At first our pilot was upset and made some unscheduled maneuvers and turns, but the Guard planes settled down at a reasonable distance from us and just kept us under observation. Evidently they had decided to obey the Geneva Convention's rules of international warfare and were not going to fire on an unarmed enemy plane.

A large crowd had assembled at a state office building adjacent to the Mississippi State Capitol in Jackson that was to be the scene of the showdown. The Mississippi Board of Trustees for Institutions of Higher Learning had promised the Court that they would personally register me at this office. State troopers cleared a path through the hostile crowd, which was shouting, "Nigger, go home," and which already had many of the characteristics of a mob. We went up several floors to the meeting place.

The secret script agreed to among Mississippi officials went something like this. The board and university officials had told the Court that they would comply with its orders and they had met to execute the agreement. However, while they were meeting, the governor and the state legislature, which had been called into special session to deal with the crisis, had come and were physically restraining them from performing their task. The governor was to block the representatives of the federal government and me from meeting with the board and university officials, theoretically ready and waiting to register me.

Every inch of available space inside and outside the building was taken up by hundreds of whites.

When my federal escorts and I arrived at the office on the sixth floor, there was Governor Barnett literally standing in the doorway blocking our entrance to the office with his own flesh, backed up by a mob of members of the state legislature, many of them whooping and hollering.

As live TV cameras rolled, Barnett winked at me again, once more trying to hold back a smile, and I could barely restrain mine. I could guess what was coming next.

"Now, which one of you is James Meredith?" he asked loud and clear, to our group of otherwise all-white faces. The crowd outside listening on transistor radios roared with laughter at the governor's feigned color-blindness.

Playing along with the now familiar wisecrack, I raised my hand; Barnett brought out another of his beloved proclamations and read grandly from it, concluding, "To preserve the peace, dignity, and tranquility of the state, I hereby finally deny you admission to the University of Mississippi."

He handed me a copy of the document and ad-libbed: "My conscience is clear. I am abiding by the Constitution of the United States, the State of Mississippi, and the laws of Mississippi."

My federal party withdrew to our vehicle through the unruly mob and returned to the airport to our government plane, which beat a hasty retreat from enemy-held territory.

It now appeared that a peaceful solution to the problem of my registration was out of the question. The matter was destined to be settled by physical force. I still was not sure that America was ready to go to war with Mississippi over my rights of citizenship, but I had no choice. I had to press on. The battle was now between Mississippi and Washington.

This was getting ridiculous, and extremely dangerous.

———

On September 27, the federal government again tried to escort me to the Oxford campus to register to go to school. We assumed that by now, in a rational universe, the state government would have capitulated and withdrawn any efforts to block us. But we knew we were going into territory that was behaving like a break-away republic on the issue of race, so we had no idea what might happen.

The same crew—the pilot, McShane, Doar, and myself—flew up to Oxford from New Orleans. There was an agreement between the federal government and the state of Mississippi that everybody would be unarmed. Can you imagine a law enforcement officer entering an area where law and order have broken down, without his arms? It happened this day at Oxford.

I thought there was a fair chance I would be dead before the crisis was over, so I wrote out a public statement as a last testament in case I was killed:

> In this time of crisis, I feel it appropriate for me to clarify my position as to my intention, my objectives, my hopes, and my desires. The prime objective is, of course, to receive the educational training necessary to enable me to be a useful citizen of my own home state of Mississippi. The future of the United States of America, the future of the South, the future of Mississippi, and the future of the Black Race rests on the decision of whether or not the Black citizen is to be allowed to receive an education in his own state. If a state is permitted to arbitrarily deny any right that is so basic to the American way of life to any citizen, then democracy is a failure. The price of progress is indeed high, but the price of holding it back is much higher.

At the Oxford airport, local citizens cursed, spat, and threatened us with violence as we transferred to our motorcade. Governor Barnett's plane was grounded in Jackson due to bad weather, and his replacement motorcade was running late, so his lieutenant governor, Paul B. Johnson, who was in Oxford, got his chance to stop me this time, put on a show, and bask in the adoration of a jubilant white mob.

Johnson stood in the middle of the road leading to the entrance of the campus, backed up by three skirmish lines of defense, composed of highway patrolmen, sheriffs, and deputies. There they stood in battle formation. Except for the skinny "Little General," Paul Johnson, everyone else looked like a pack of big, beefy bears. Even McShane, who seemed to be a giant among ordinary men, seemed slight in comparison to these bullies.

It was a wall of human flesh. Some of the Mississippi lawmen opened up their coats to show newsmen they were unarmed.

My federal entourage of U.S. marshals and government lawyers came up head to head with Lieutenant Governor Johnson and the state's wall of flesh. As always, Doar was on my left and McShane on my right.

I stood directly facing Lieutenant Governor Johnson at the center of the scrum.

The entire landscape seemed gripped with fear, as federal and state officials squared off in a football-style showdown of physical force that only one side could win. An extra layer of dread was provided by the possibility that somebody might start shooting from somewhere. I had little doubt that the Mississippi lawmen had probably stashed weapons within easy reach, in their back pockets, strapped to their legs, and otherwise out of sight. Given McShane's girth, Doar's height, and my slight build, if anyone started shooting at us, they were liable to hit Doar or McShane instead.

McShane went through the motions of serving court orders, injunctions, and summonses on Lieutenant Governor Johnson. When he refused to take them, McShane touched Johnson with the papers, a legal technicality, and let them drop at his feet. Johnson replied by reading from a proclamation denying my admission. We tried to walk on through, and a shoving match began as we attempted to penetrate the first line of defense, which included some bulging Mississippi lawmen who looked in the three-hundred-pound range. The scene quickly devolved into a near-comic spectacle resembling a group belly dance and an imminent roadhouse fracas.

The lieutenant governor of Mississippi raised his fist, as if preparing to punch Chief Marshal McShane. McShane shimmied to the left, looking for an opening. A beefy, twinkle-toed Mississippi lawman shimmied sideways to block him. Pushing and shoving ensued.

I got in a few good elbow blows and shoves against the state officials. The crisis subsided as the state lawmen proved that they had no intention of budging. There were too many of them and we were outnumbered.

Our federal formation turned and withdrew.

Mississippi had again triumphed over the federal government.

And again, my rights as an American citizen were trampled upon before the world.

———————

The crisis was getting completely out of control. Thousands of white volunteers from states across the South and as far away as California and Georgia were preparing to descend on Oxford to back up Barnett in repelling any further attempts to get me on campus. In Alabama, the imperial wizard of the Ku Klux Klan, Robert Shelton, put his entire organization on "standby alert," and prepared his followers to move on Oxford with rifles and guns.

The national press was covering every move and countermove of the drama, and as the chief protagonist, my name became known around the world.

In Washington, D.C., Attorney General Kennedy was pulled directly into the crisis.

In New Orleans, the U.S. Fifth Circuit judges attempted vainly to administer a coup de grace to the crisis by setting a deadline of October 2, 1962, for Governor Barnett and Lieutenant Governor Johnson to comply with the order to enroll me at Ole Miss, or face

John F. Kennedy and Robert F. Kennedy were not civil rights heroes to me, but super-rich politicians who spent their lives ignoring the plight of black Americans and had to be forced to do the right thing. But the more I got to know Bobby, the more I respected his honesty and his appreciation of pure power politics. He was the most refreshingly honest white politician I ever met. He told me, "People only get what they are willing to fight for." JFK installed a secret recording system through this desk that recorded his secret negotiations with Governor Barnett over the crisis I triggered. *Photo: John F. Kennedy Library*

a compulsory personal fine of ten thousand dollars and five thousand dollars per day, respectively, for contempt of court. I was later told that this struck pure terror into the heart of Governor Barnett, who had previously been a successful trial lawyer but had limited financial resources and would quickly be wiped out by such a huge personal fine. But still, Barnett continued the fight.

With all else failing, RFK and his brother, President John F. Kennedy, entered a series of comic-opera telephone negotiations with fellow Democrat Ross Barnett. The Kennedys seemed to be following the line of Ivy League gentlemen, while Barnett was dancing around them like the slippery, swamp-fox negotiator he was.

From the beginning of federal involvement in my case, the Kennedys insisted upon avoiding the use of armed force, hoping to avoid repeating Eisenhower's action in Little Rock in 1957, when Ike sent in the 101st Airborne to force black students into Little Rock's Central High School. The Kennedys were looking to the next election and the vote of the Democratic white South. They thought the key to success was a display of moderation. They hoped to sidestep a disaster where a lot of marshals were killed, or as the president put it to his aides, "James Meredith is strung up."

So the Kennedys decided to try to work things out with Governor Barnett by telephone. Surely a few white Democratic politicians could smooth things out if they spoke in private, man to man.

The result was a series of secret telephone conversations, most of them recorded stenographically by RFK's secretary or electronically by JFK's secret White House taping system, negotiations that were conniving, futile, and quite revealing. The Kennedys bent over backward to try to give Barnett a face-saving "out." Both parties sought to accommodate each other while protecting their own political skins. One line of ludicrous scheming pursued by RFK and Barnett involved staging a show of force by the federal marshals, the choreographed drawing of dozens of guns in public in the middle of an enormous crowd of civilians, and a script of dialogue to procure my admission. Marshals would draw their guns on Barnett to give him a macho photo opportunity of defiance, but the deal broke down over how many guns would be drawn. Bobby wanted one, Barnett wanted dozens.

At another point, an exasperated Attorney General Kennedy rather meekly pointed out to Barnett, "Governor, you are a part of the United States."

Barnett replied, "We have been a part of the United States, but I don't know whether we are or not."

It was rumors of these secret negotiations that bothered me the most during my late September attempts to enroll at Ole Miss. Sometimes I wondered if President Kennedy would not go so far as to deliver me to the noose if it would assure his re-election to the presidency. Many Americans began to wonder about the Kennedy administration and its appearance of weakness and trepidation. The secretly transcribed conversations, made public years later, confirmed my fears.

At this point in his presidency, John F. Kennedy was not a convinced and devoted proponent of civil rights as a policy. He thought it was, in his words, a "Goddamn mess" that embarrassed him on the world stage.

The white supremacist rulers of Mississippi were encouraged by Kennedy's appeasement attempts. They were now fully convinced that all they had to do was show force and the willingness to use it and the Kennedy administration would back down and would not use armed force against them to ensure the citizenship rights of one black American.

But the negotiations were not only inept and ridiculous, they were futile. The stage was finally set for the most dangerous clash between a state and the federal government in nearly a hundred years. The point of no return had been reached by both parties.

The negotiations were doomed from the start. The Kennedys wanted to avoid at all costs the specter of federal troops invading Mississippi with bayonets to force me into the university. But Barnett saw facing down thousands of federal bayonets as the only way he could politically survive this crisis. He could manfully step aside to avoid bloodshed in the face of overwhelming force and continue the struggle in the courts. If word got out he cut a secret deal to admit me, he would be a dead man in Mississippi politics. He might even have to leave the state in disgrace.

On the afternoon of September 27, RFK spoke to Governor Barnett and Lieutenant Governor Johnson, by telephone, to try to choreograph yet another entry of mine to the campus. This time, it looked as if the Mississippi side was capitulating, but that was contingent on an extremely dangerous public showdown.

In one of the most bizarre, muddled conversations I have ever heard of in American political history, the U.S. attorney general tried to stage-manage with state officials a scene in which scores of American law enforcement officials would draw guns on each other, in a scene right out of a Wild West movie. Here's how the conversation went:

RFK: "Governor, how are you?"

BARNETT: "I need a little sleep."

RFK: "I just talked to Mr. Watkins [Barnett advisor] and we were going to make this effort [to enroll me at the university] at 5 o'clock this afternoon your time [the next day]."

BARNETT: "They will be here about 5 o'clock our time?"

RFK: "Is that satisfactory?"

BARNETT: "Yes, sir. That's all right."

RFK: "I will send the marshals that I have available up there in Memphis and there will be about 25 or 30 of them and they will come with Mr. Meredith and they will arrive at wherever the gate is and I will have the head marshal pull a gun and I will have the rest of them have their hands on their guns and their holsters. And then as I understand it, they will go through and get in and you will make sure that law and order is preserved and that no harm will be done to Mr. McShane and Mr. Meredith."

BARNETT: "Oh, yes."

RFK: "And then I think you will see that's accomplished?"

BARNETT [EVIDENTLY RESPONDING TO FACE AND HAND SIGNALS FROM OTHER STATE OFFICIALS LISTENING IN ON EXTENTIONS]: "Yes. Hold just a minute, will you? Hello, General, I was under the impression that they were all going to pull their guns. This could be very embarrassing.

We got a big crowd here and if one pulls his gun and we all turn it would be very embarrassing. Isn't it possible to have them all pull their guns?"

RFK: "I hate to have them all draw their guns, as I think it could create harsh feelings. Isn't it sufficient if I have one man draw his gun and the others keep their hands on their holsters?"

BARNETT: "They must all draw their guns. Then they should point their guns at us and then we could step aside. This could be very embarrassing down here for us. It is necessary."

RFK: "If they all pull their guns—is that all?"

BARNETT: "There will be no shooting."

RFK: "There will be no problem?"

BARNETT: "Everyone pull your guns and point them and we will stand aside and you will go right through."

RFK: "You will make sure not the marshals but the State Police will preserve law and order?"

BARNETT: "There won't be any violence."

RFK: "Then we can get the other people out as soon as possible."

BARNETT: "One second. General, we expect them all to draw their guns. Lt. Governor Johnson is sitting here with me. Will you talk to him?"

LT. GOVERNOR PAUL JOHNSON: "General—"

RFK: "How are you?"

JOHNSON: "It is absolutely necessary that they all draw their guns. There won't be any shooting."

RFK: "Can you speak a little louder?"

JOHNSON: "We are telling them to lay their clubs aside and to leave their guns in their automobiles. But it is necessary to have all your people draw their guns, not just one. And anyone who shoots at all will leave. We appreciate what they have done so far and go back home and that there would be no shooting under any circumstances."

RFK: "The one problem—when we come down there representing the Federal Government and draw guns, it's going to disturb your people, understandably—"

JOHNSON: "As much as it would bother them if they just drew one gun and 350 highway patrolmen—"

RFK: "If they all draw their guns and they go into the university, thereafter, law and order will be preserved by your people?"

JOHNSON: "We are going to attempt to preserve it."

RFK: "They won't leave, will they? What I want to be sure is that it wouldn't be left up to our people."

JOHNSON: "We can possibly leave many people up here today. We will do that."

RFK: "As I understand from Mr. Watkins and from the Governor, law and order will be preserved by the local people. I don't anticipate a great problem but I don't want an angry crowd descending on Oxford this evening. You'll be sure?"

JOHNSON: "Yes."

RFK: "I don't care how you do it just as long as you take that responsibility. So I've got assurances from the Governor that no harm will come to Mr. Meredith and the marshals?"

JOHNSON: "Not as far as we're concerned."

RFK: "We will do anything to preserve law and order."

JOHNSON: "We will do everything to preserve law and order at all times."

RFK: "As long as I have the Governor's assurance and yours."

JOHNSON: "To the best of our ability. I believe that we have sufficient men to take care of it."

RFK: "Let me talk to the Governor again."

BARNETT: "General?"

RFK: "Governor, that's all I wanted. That's the best thing in the long run."

BARNETT: "There won't be any violence. We will control them
  if there are a few there. The other day—there were several
  thousand at the state office building and we didn't have a
  bit of trouble."
RFK: "Just as long as it is left at the local level. They will be
  there at 5 o'clock and draw their guns."
BARNETT: "We are going to step aside if they do that."
RFK: "If there is any problem, you will call me?"
BARNETT: "I will, General."

Bobby Kennedy had just agreed to the recipe for a bloodbath. He
had agreed for twenty-five or thirty federal marshals to travel deep
into hostile territory and try to protect me while pulling their guns
on over two hundred allegedly disarmed Mississippi state troopers
who would be backed up by a screaming mob of several thousand
white civilians ready for battle.

And this vastly outnumbered squad of lawmen would be pulling their guns just as the sun was going down, around five o'clock
at night.

In Mississippi, that's known as "the lynching hour."

The next day, September 28, with this explosive bargain in
place, my beefed-up motorcade set out yet again from Memphis
on our fourth attempt to storm the heavily defended High Temple
of White Supremacy in Oxford.

We flew down the highway at speeds of one hundred miles
an hour, with a federal spotter plane flying above to relay radio
communications back to Attorney General Kennedy's office in
Washington, D.C.

Inside the vehicles, the thirty federal marshals were increasingly
apprehensive; their morale had taken a beating over our repeated
public humiliations. In another dangerous humiliation for law
enforcement officers, they were ordered to remove the bullets from
their pistols. They had to stuff their pockets with bullets, and if we

came under attack, they would have to waste precious time fumbling for ammunition to load their guns.

Meanwhile, the streets of Oxford were flooding with white spectators, and men with shotguns and rifles appeared in sedans and pickup trucks, mingling with the crowd. This was a popular insurrection in the streets, a vast wall of humanity that would have been impossible for my forces to penetrate. An advance party of ready-for-battle plainclothes Klansmen from Alabama had arrived and were blending into the swelling mob. Teams of gunmen were rumored to have taken up positions on the city's outskirts, ready to rake our motorcade with enfilading fire.

The towering, mustachioed specter of Citizens Council boss William Simmons could be seen proudly and quietly surveying the multitude. This was the zenith of his power over the currents of white supremacy. As he studied the legions of white volunteers, he knew that this was it, this was the final battle, he later explained. All his work and all his life came down to this confrontation. If I entered the university as a student, he knew that the pillars of segregation in Mississippi would be toppled and history would take a new course. Black people would eventually storm the ruins of segregation and take their place as American citizens in Mississippi.

Simmons knew that rivers of blood were probably about to flow; in fact, he welcomed it. He figured that if the federals killed white men and boys on the streets of Oxford tonight as they tried to force me onto campus, then he and the Citizens Council would be handed a priceless propaganda victory, a victory he could use to stop integration in its tracks. It was a dark, apocalyptic vision, but Simmons thought that some things were worth fighting and dying for.

But as Governor Barnett and Lieutenant Governor Johnson surveyed the scene they quickly realized that a full-scale disaster was about to happen, and they seemed increasingly horrified that they would be blamed for wholesale slaughter. They realized the situation had become far too volatile to choreograph the heroic photograph they yearned for.

It would have been quite a photo, the two Mississippi men defiantly staring down the barrels of federal guns, and then gallantly stepping aside to prevent bloodshed while vowing to continue the battle in the courts. The photo might have guaranteed their futures in Mississippi politics for years to come.

But instead, the photos would be of chaos, of Americans killing other Americans.

The two politicians got on the phone and literally pleaded with Bobby Kennedy to turn our caravan around before we reached the Oxford city limits, where they were afraid we might get shot to pieces.

"There are liable to be a hundred people killed," Johnson said.

Reluctantly, the attorney general agreed and gave us the order to turn around, retreat, and hightail it out of enemy territory back to the Tennessee border. Many of the marshals in our caravan were relieved at this news.

But since our radio communications with the spotter plane above were choppy, McShane and Doar decided that our single car should peel off alone a few miles ahead to the town of Batesville to confirm the order by phone.

It was a very eerie scene when we got there. It was a ghost town. There were no people. Apparently, everyone had gone to Oxford to witness the drama. We found a pay phone to call Washington, reversed the charges, and confirmed the order. We rejoined the motorcade and blasted off across the border to Tennessee.

Our fourth attempt to enter the campus ended in humiliation. In Oxford, the white mob rejoiced. There was dancing in the streets.

The Resurrected Confederacy was triumphant.

The white mobs were growing with each failed attempt. My rights as an American citizen, and by extension all Americans' rights, were being trampled upon over and over for the world to see.

I told my federal protectors that these public spectacles were an insult to my American citizenship, and a disgrace to the federal government. The United States was being made to look ridiculous in the eyes of the world, and each time we were turned around, the forces of white supremacy were being whipped up into a more dangerous frenzy.

"I am not going anywhere," I told McShane, "until we go in with sufficient force."

I told my federal escorts that unless they moved in with enough force next time, I would pull the plug on the whole operation and refuse to participate. I was in personal command of the entire spectacle and I reserved the right to stop it at any point.

I knew it was now only a matter of time before the government would have to admit defeat or use substantial and fully armed physical force.

The next afternoon, on September 29, both President Kennedy and his brother got on the phone in the Oval Office, called Barnett, and tried to strike a new deal that would enable me to enter the university. Excerpts from the transcripts of the negotiations reveal an exercise in futile shadowboxing.

PRESIDENT KENNEDY: "Hello, Governor? How are you? I'm glad to talk to you, Governor. I am concerned about this situation down there."

GOVERNOR BARNETT: "Oh, I should say I am concerned about it, Mr. President. It's a horrible situation."

JFK: "Well, now, here's my problem, Governor: I didn't put him in the university, but on the other hand, under the Constitution, I have to carry that [court] order out and I don't want to do it in any way that causes difficulty to you or to anyone else. But I've got to do it. Now, I'd like to get your help in doing that."

BARNETT: "You know what I am up against, Mr. President. I took an oath to abide by the laws of this state and our constitution here and the Constitution of the United States. I'm on the spot here, you know. We have a statute that was enacted a couple of weeks ago stating positively that no one who had been convicted of a crime or, uh, whether the criminal action pending against them would not be eligible for any of the institutions of higher learning. And that's our law, and it seemed like the Court of Appeals didn't pay any attention to that."

JFK: "Right. Well, of course, the problem is, Governor, that I got my responsibility, just like you have yours."

BARNETT: "Well, that's true. I realize that, and I appreciate that so much."

JFK: "Well, now here's the thing, Governor, what I want, would like to do is to try to work this out in an amicable way. We don't want a lot of people down there getting hurt."

BARNETT: "Mr. President, let me say this. They're calling, calling me and others from all over the state, wanting to bring a thousand, wanting to bring five hundred, and two hundred, and all such as that. We don't want such as that."

JFK: "I know. Well, we don't want to have a lot of people getting hurt or killed down there."

BARNETT: "I appreciate your interest in our poultry program and all those things. Thank you so much."

JFK: "I know your feeling about the law of Mississippi and the fact that you don't want to carry out that [federal] court order. What we really want to have from you, though, is some understanding about whether the state police will maintain law and order. We understand your feeling about the court order and your disagreement with it. But what we're concerned about is how much violence is going to be and what kind of action we'll have to take to prevent it. And I'd like to get assurances from you that the state police down there will take positive action to maintain law and order. Then we'll know what we have to do."

BARNETT: "They'll take positive action, Mr. President, to maintain law and order *as best we can.* We'll have 220 highway patrolmen and they'll absolutely be unarmed. Not a one of them'll be armed."

JFK: "Well, the problem is, well, what can they do to maintain law and order and prevent the gathering of a mob and action taken by the mob? What can they do? Can they stop that?"

BARNETT: "Well, they'll do their best to. They'll do everything in their power to stop it."

JFK: "Now, what about the suggestions made by the Attorney General in regard to not permitting people to congregate and start a mob?"

BARNETT: "Well, we'll do our best to, to keep them from congregating, but that's hard to do, you know."

JFK: "Well, just tell them to move along."

BARNETT: "When they start moving up on the sidewalks and different sides of the streets, what are you going to do about it?"

JFK: "Well, now, as I understand it, Governor, you would do everything you can to maintain law and order."

BARNETT: "I'll do everything in my power to maintain order and peace. We don't want any shooting down here."

JFK: "I understand. Now, Governor, what about, can you maintain this order?"

BARNETT: "Well, I don't know. That's what I'm worried about you see. I don't know whether I can or not. I couldn't have the other afternoon. There was such a mob there, it would have been impossible. There were men in there with trucks and shotguns, and all such as that. Not a lot of them, but some, we saw, and certain people were just enraged. You just don't understand the situation down here."

JFK: "Well, the only thing is I got is my responsibility."

BARNETT: "I know you do."

JFK: "This is not my order; I just have to carry it out. So I want to get together and try to do it with you in a way, which is the most satisfactory and causes the least chance of damage to people in Mississippi. That's my interest."

BARNETT: "That's right. Would you be willing to wait awhile and let the people cool off on the whole thing?"

JFK: "Until how long?"

BARNETT: "Couldn't you make a statement to the effect, Mr. President, Mr. General, that under the circumstances existing in Mississippi, that, uh, there'll be bloodshed; you want to protect the life of, of, of James Meredith and all other people? And under the circumstances at this time, it just wouldn't be fair to him or others to try to register him at this time."

JFK: "Well, then at what time would it be fair?"

BARNETT: "Well, I don't know. It might be in, uh, two or three weeks, it might cool off a little."

JFK: "Well, would you undertake to register him in two weeks?"

BARNETT: "Well, I, you know I can't undertake to register him myself—but you all might make some progress that way, you know."

More back-and-forth negotiations that afternoon seemed to result in a secret agreement between Barnett and the Kennedys for me to be brought onto the campus in two days.

But that night Governor Barnett attended an Ole Miss football game in Jackson before a sellout crowd of forty-six thousand hysterical fans, and what happened there confirmed that the white people of Mississippi expected him to stand firm.

At halftime the governor marched onto the field and gave a defiant speech. The roaring, feverish response of the mob clearly indicated Barnett had reached the peak of his political career and popularity.

Barnett held his fist in the air and proclaimed, "I love Mississippi! I love her people, her customs! I love and respect our heritage!" Everyone knew what he meant, which was, "I love segregation, I love racism, I love white supremacy!"

The crowd went berserk. He was enveloped in one of the greatest mass raptures in the history of American politics. Barnett was bathed in glory. He was the southern Superman, the incarnation of all the gallant Confederate heroes. At that moment, if he had called for the multitudes to march across the state of Mississippi and burn down every piece of federal property, believe me, they would have done it.

But Ross Barnett was not exactly what he seemed to be in those days. As strong an advocate as he was of white supremacy, Ross Barnett, I believe, did not want violence to be committed against blacks. He was playing on the emotions of the time, basically for the sake of his own political survival and for what he saw as white tranquility. If he had suggested to frustrated whites that they were supposed to deal with the blacks on their own, you would have had a widespread massacre in Mississippi.

Instead, he focused attention on himself, channeling it in a way that it might be controlled and steered toward some outcome that would not trigger violence. So there were no massacres in Mississippi during this time, in fact there was little if any violence toward blacks during the crisis. And that was the result of Ross Barnett's channeling white energy and emotions away from harming blacks.

But by now the rank-and-file white supremacists were encouraged by the Kennedys' appeasement attempts with the aborted attempts to register me. They were now convinced that all they had to do was show force and the willingness to use it and the Kennedy administration would back down.

And as well as I thought I knew Barnett, his game was now beginning to confuse me.

In addition to being a shrewd, pragmatic politician as well as a racist (though no more racist than a great many white Americans in the North and South), it now appeared that Barnett's full allegiance was given over to the white supremacists at the cost of a clash with the federal government. With the virtually unanimous backing of the state legislature and the support, at least tacit, of most of the white citizens of Mississippi, the governor thought he would be able to orchestrate a carefully organized united front of resistance.

It was beginning to look like Barnett was actually starting to believe he could fight the federal government and win, by keeping me out of the University of Mississippi indefinitely.

The point of no return had been reached by both parties.

The stage was finally set for the most dangerous clash between a state and the federal government in a hundred years.

I knew the great battle was now at hand.

And I knew I would win, or die trying to.

CHAPTER FIVE

The Last Battle of
the Civil War

O N September 30, 1962, the stage was set for the last battle of the Civil War.

Mississippi had once again rebelled against the United States.

The state was in a state of full-blown insurrection against the United States, over me, on the issue of race and the rights of citizenship for black Americans.

I wore a blood-red necktie that day, which was my personal statement of solidarity with all the black Americans who had been shot, lynched, castrated, beaten, raped, or otherwise brutalized by white supremacists through history.

Fearing the total collapse of federal authority on a piece of American soil, President John F. Kennedy decided to use force against the state of Mississippi to honor my rights as an American citizen.

I left President Kennedy no choice in the matter. I had compelled the U.S. Supreme Court to uphold the federal court orders mandating my admission to Ole Miss, and JFK was bound by his oath of office to enforce the order. This was a vivid illustration of the fact that the president works for the people of the United States, not the other way around. The president is a public servant, and in this crisis, he was doing my bidding, and through me he was enforcing the citizenship rights of every American.

The president and attorney general decided that the U.S. military would have to help force me onto the campus of the University of Mississippi. They ordered advance elements of combat troops to help federal marshals get me onto the school property, and a vast wave of soldiers to stand by in case they were needed: U.S. Army infantry, military police, paratroopers, pilots, and engineers—a mind-blowing twenty thousand in all, from bases across the United States, plus some ten thousand state national guardsmen.

At midnight that day, President Kennedy took direct action to enforce the federal court orders. He invoked the Insurrection Act and issued an executive order to mobilize the armed forces to force me into the University of Mississippi. The order authorized the secretary of defense to "take all appropriate steps to enforce all orders of the United States Courts," and "call into the active military service of the United States, as he may deem appropriate to carry out the purposes of this order, any or all of the units of the Army National Guard and of the Air National Guard of the State of Mississippi to serve in the active military service of the United States for an indefinite period and until relieved by appropriate orders."

JFK federalized the all-white Mississippi National Guard, few members of which supported the idea of my attending the university. With the stroke of a pen, JFK flipped the over ten-thousand-man force from the command of Governor Barnett to the command of the president of the United States. Suddenly, the order of battle was tipped significantly in my favor, although some federal officials were very afraid that National Guardsmen could mutiny or desert in significant numbers rather than be called into service to support me.

That morning, at the military base that had become my temporary home, I witnessed a military spectacle that would have inspired Julius Caesar. Thousands of American combat troops were emerging from an assembly line of incoming military transports, bristling with weapons and military gear. It was the beginning of a staggering orchestration of physical force being quickly coiled up and ready to strike, the kind of miracle only the U.S. military can pull off.

Watching this amazing ballet of men and machines, I was impressed as only a former air force man can be, as U.S. marshals, navy ground personnel, marine and air force pilots, and army troops surged into Millington Naval Air Station, ready to follow me into battle. And I was especially proud to see how many black army soldiers were coming out of the aircraft, proof of how well the American military was respecting the rights of black citizens to serve their nation in uniform, even as long ago as 1962.

Surveying the scene, I felt a little like Dwight Eisenhower on the eve of D-Day, but unlike Ike I knew I was going to ride at the "tip of the spear," on the very front line. We didn't know when we were going to launch toward our objective, but I knew it would be soon, probably the next day, October 1, which was a Monday.

In Mississippi the day started off just like any typical Sunday. Though they were very aware of the ongoing verbal battle between the state and the federal governments, many citizens seemed convinced that the two sides were engaged in a mere "grandstand play," and that I would go away, or at worst, it would all be worked out in court months or years later. One lifelong Oxford resident, the brother of famed writer William Faulkner, scoffed at a reporter's suggestion of potential violence.

Privately, Governor Barnett was still talking with the White

House, and he was still willing to try to make some kind of deal with the Kennedys, but he didn't tell any of his state officials this, other than the lieutenant governor. It appeared quite likely that a good deal of bloodshed was about to happen, and Barnett would be blamed for it. Barnett seemed to be lurching back and forth tactically in a sea of confusion.

He continued to tell Attorney General Kennedy that federal troops should force his hand, making it appear as though he had no choice. This way his voters would still believe their governor had done his best to keep blacks out of the University of Mississippi, James Meredith could safely enroll, and no blood would be shed. Even a small group of Ole Miss professors who worked in conjunction with the U.S. Justice Department behind the scenes to try to get me enrolled had assured the president that only a show of force would be necessary to make Ross Barnett back down. The Kennedys agreed, and the president decided to allay the nation's fears in a televised speech that night on the crisis.

But by now both the Kennedys and Barnett had grossly underestimated the degree to which the white supremacists would go to "save Mississippi." Thousands of angry whites from all over Mississippi, the South, and as far away as California were preparing to descend on Oxford on Monday, the probable date for my next, and fifth, attempt at enrollment. Some of them had already started off for Oxford.

At 12:45 p.m. Washington time, Barnett called Bobby Kennedy to try to delay everything, and if that failed, to again line up another spectacular Wild West photo opportunity for my arrival the next day.

> GOVERNOR BARNETT: "I am sorry I'm so late calling you. I had to go to the doctor this morning—an injured ear. General, [Barnett aide Tom] Watkins and I are here and no one else. Here is what we think should be done; you should postpone this matter."

ATTORNEY GENERAL KENNEDY: "We can't do that."

BARNETT [ABRUPTLY LAYING OUT HIS PLAN]: "Then you had
better have enough troops to be dead sure that peace and
order will be preserved at the University. I am going to
do everything in my power to preserve peace. We will
have about 175 or 180 highway patrolmen in there—
unarmed; no guns, no sticks of any kind. We will have
quite a number of sheriffs—unarmed—probably 75 or 100
deputy sheriffs. Then they will form this second line. The
highway patrolmen will form the first line; the sheriffs the
next. The sheriffs will have probably 200 or 300 soldiers
[he presumably meant deputies] behind them. No one will
be armed. I will be in the front line and when Meredith
presents himself, I'll do like I did before. I will read a
proclamation denying him entrance. I will tell the people
of Mississippi now that I want peace and we must have no
violence, no bloodshed. When you draw the guns, I will
then tell the people. In other words, we will step aside and
you can walk in."

RFK: "I don't think that will be very pleasant, Governor. I
think you are making a mistake handling it in that fashion.
I suppose that if you feel it is helpful to you politically. It
is not helping the people of Mississippi or the people of
the United States. But I gather that is secondary in your
judgment. I think it is silly going through this whole
facade of your standing there; our people drawing guns;
your stepping aside; to me it is dangerous and I think
this has gone beyond the stage of politics, and you have a
responsibility to the people of that state and to the people
of the United States. This is a real disservice."

BARNETT: "I'm not interested in politics personally. I have said
so many times—we couldn't have integration and I have
got to do something. I can't just walk back."

RFK: "You can say the National Guard has been called up and

you don't want to have people from the State of Mississippi responsible for placing Mr. Meredith in the institution and therefore you are going to step aside on this."

BARNETT: "I'll say words to that effect. But I have to be confronted with your troops."

Once again, the two sides were at an impasse.

Suddenly, Bobby Kennedy had a brainstorm. On a Sunday, the campus was deserted. What if they jump-started the whole operation and launched marshals in to seize and secure the campus now, ahead of schedule, before a mob gathered?

RFK: "What if we came down and the marshals took over this operation this afternoon; if I called you a half hour before they are going to leave. There is no one down there now. I don't want any gun fighting; if they arrived and took it over before you got there. All I want to do is get assurances they won't be fired on. If 300 [marshals] arrived on the campus of the university and took over that entrance."

BARNETT: "You mean have him registered today?"

RFK: "No. Take over the entrance to the university and he can be flown in by helicopter tomorrow."

BARNETT: "You mean 300 armed men?"

RFK: "Right; no one knows about it."

BARNETT: "You have more than 300."

RFK: "We have 400. They are not prepared to get in a pitched battle. They can go in there. You can say the 400 arrived by helicopter."

BARNETT: "They would stay at the entrance until tomorrow and not permit people to go in?"

RFK: "That's correct."

This was a major misjudgment on Kennedy's part. In order to seal off and secure the center of the sprawling campus he needed at least fifteen hundred trained soldiers deployed in a wide circular skirmish line, not three hundred poorly equipped U.S. marshals with no military training.

The attorney general continued, "I'd apprise you of it just when they were ready to leave, and it was too late for you to be there; or just time for you personally to be there. A big crowd wouldn't gather. I'll bring him in tomorrow or today. The situation would be stabilized then. You could announce we came in a different way or whatever you want to announce. The National Guard coming in there tomorrow to put Meredith in and before this overwhelming force you gave way, and you don't want the National Guard to put Meredith in the institution, and that you are calling on the people and everyone to behave themselves."

Governor Barnett seemed to flounder like a fish on a chopping board. He was running out of time and options. "Do this thing tomorrow?" he wondered aloud. "People are coming in here from Alabama and other states; they might have guns."

Finally, RFK had enough of Barnett's wiggling. The fed-up attorney general unsheathed his most powerful weapon—a threat to go public with details of their secret negotiations to get me onto campus, a move he knew would kill Barnett politically in Mississippi. "The President is going on TV tonight," Kennedy declared. "He is going through the statement he had with you last night. He will have to say why he called up the National Guard; that you had an agreement to permit Meredith to go to Jackson to register, and your lawyer, Mr. Watkins, said this was satisfactory; and you would let him fly in by helicopter."

A stunned Barnett exclaimed, "That won't do at all!"

RFK said, "You broke your word to him."

Probably reeling at the prospect of being impeached or run out of Mississippi on a rail, Barnett asked, "You don't mean the President is going to say that tonight?"

RFK: "Of course he is; you broke your word; now you suggest we send in troops, fighting their way through a barricade. You gave your word. Mr. Watkins gave him his word. You didn't keep it."

BARNETT: "Where didn't I keep it, in what particular?"

RFK: "When you said you would make an agreement and that Meredith would come into Jackson; send everybody to Oxford."

BARNETT: "Don't say that. Please don't mention it!"

RFK: "The President has to say that. You said we would fly him into Jackson and register him while you had everyone at Oxford. Then you would say he has been registered and you would permit him to come to Oxford by helicopter on Tuesday and go to school. Mr. Watkins pledged his word to the President; we have it all down [transcribed or recorded]. You talk to Mr. Watkins and reach an agreement between the two of you, and how you are going to handle this."

The game was over. Barnett now surrendered, or so it seemed. "Why don't you fly him in this afternoon," he blurted, adding the plea, "Please let us treat what we say as confidential?"

RFK rubbed salt in Barnett's wounds to make sure he understood the threat: "You made an agreement with the President of the United States and I was on the phone, and the agreement, within an hour and a half, was broken by the Governor. I had an agreement with you on Thursday and it was broken. You are putting the President in an impossible situation. He is going on TV as announced and will tell how all this came about. He has been put in an extremely untenable position."

Aides to both officials came on the line to work out the logistics of getting me onto the campus by aircraft and trying to get the Mississippi State Highway Patrol to assist in the operation.

Barnett came back on the line with the attorney general to plead for his political life: "I am sorry about the misunderstanding last night. I am extremely hurt over it really. I didn't know I was violating any agreement. Please understand me."

> RFK: "If we get it straightened out by 7:30 tonight, the whole matter will be alleviated. He [the president] either won't make his talk [to the nation] or won't mention this [negotiation]. Let's get going."
>
> BARNETT: "What we have said here before won't be . . . ?"
>
> RFK: "That's correct—if we get this thing done."
>
> BARNETT: "If I am surprised, you won't mind or if I raise Cain about it?"
>
> RFK: "I don't mind that; just say law and order will be maintained. Let's get it straightened out. It takes 40 minutes for them to get down there; if I can know as soon as possible when he will be there and have the situation under control."
>
> BARNETT: "Please let's not have a fuss about what we talked about."
>
> RFK: "I don't think that will be necessary."
>
> BARNETT: "Tuesday at 11:00. I hope you will consider my position here."
>
> RFK: "Let's talk about that after tonight; I'll talk to you then."
>
> BARNETT: "You understand about our continuing the legal fight?"
>
> RFK: "I have no objection; I understand."

Two white Democratic politicians poised on the sharpest edge of history were juggling live hand grenades, trying to save their own skins. I had forced the government of the state of Mississippi into a direct physical clash not with me but with the world's most powerful military machine.

In a final, secret, last-minute agreement between Barnett and RFK, the plan was to escort me onto campus that day, quietly enroll me, and present my presence on the campus as a fait accompli on the following day, Monday, October 1, 1962, when thousands of white civilian volunteers were expected to arrive in Oxford from across America.

At the military base in Memphis, I abruptly got word that we were flying down to Oxford. I packed my things and prepared for a confrontation that I assumed would be the final assault.

It looked like the U.S. government was finally committed to applying overwhelming firepower to the collision course we were on.

I was told that hundreds of federal marshals were going down ahead of us to overpower any resistance that might occur, thousands of army combat troops would stand by on rapid alert in case they were needed, and we would try to get school officials to register me that afternoon, Sunday, in hopes of presenting me on campus the next day as an enrolled student.

At 5:30 p.m. I landed at the Oxford University airport in my government plane as dusk fell and press cameras popped.

We drove onto the quiet campus through a side entrance and proceeded to my assigned dormitory, Baxter Hall, where I remained with a force of twenty-four United States marshals as bodyguards. I was assigned to a spartan corner suite in the dormitory.

Now, a series of logistical problems and tactical misjudgments began happening that would combine to unleash a riot and battle in less than three hours. Communications between Barnett, his state highway patrol, and various state officials in Jackson and Oxford broke down completely. No one was clearly in charge and no one was sure if the state lawmen were supposed to fight the federals or help them.

My federal escorts couldn't find anyone at the school to register me. For lack of any other plan, several hundred marshals simply surrounded the university Lyceum building, the administration building and registration office, for a registration attempt that now looked like it would occur the next day, Monday morning. This served as a decoy to make the people think I was in that building

so as to divert any attention and violence from me where I was located, one-quarter of a mile away in my dormitory. The ensuing battle would soon be centralized in the attempt to seize the Lyceum back from the federal forces.

As dusk fell, students returning from a football game in Jackson began gradually crowding around the front of the Lyceum building, attracted by the sudden presence of the United States marshals, foot soldiers of the hated federal government now in their midst. They looked like mismatched gladiators ready for battle, as they wore crash helmets and tear gas weapons over suits, blue jeans, and Hawaiian shirts. Their bizarre appearance inflamed the blossoming crowd, and in the rush to deploy ahead of schedule, much of the marshals' equipment was misplaced in the shuffle, including radios, tear gas ammo, and loudspeakers.

As I nonchalantly made my bed and read the newspaper before going to sleep, the original crowd of two hundred white civilians, mostly students, swelled steadily to over one thousand, then toward two thousand whites, including many who were not Ole Miss students. Unaware of Governor Barnett's secret agreement with the Kennedys to stop the Mississippi highway patrol from blocking my entrance onto campus, the crowd was incited by the sight of the helmeted marshals with their tear-gas guns cocked skyward, who were at first an object of curiosity, which changed rapidly to anger, and hate.

The students were joined by assorted civilians and adults and students from other Mississippi schools, and the group transformed into a mob. They were now taunting and jeering the troops with profanities, racial slurs, and threats. The start of the fifteen hours of violent warfare was at hand. At 7:00 p.m., the spark that started the battle was the arrival of the first groups of news reporters from around the United States and overseas, which agitated the short tempers of the crowd. Newsmen were beaten up, cameras and other equipment smashed. Their cars were overturned and battered.

Simultaneously, the mob pressed toward the shoulder-to-shoulder barricade of marshals around the Lyceum. Rocks, bottles, and anything available were thrown at the marshals and their vehicles. With the marshals under strict orders from RFK not to retaliate by firing back or even by drawing their guns, the victory of the mob of white supremacists seemed guaranteed.

At 7:30 p.m., Governor Barnett gave a horribly confused statewide television speech strongly condemning the federal government, with which he had earlier struck the secret deal. "I urge all Mississippians to do everything in their power to preserve peace," he declared. "Surrounded on all sides by the oppressive power of the United States of America, my courage and convictions do not waver. My heart still says 'Never,' but my calm judgment abhors the bloodshed that would follow. To the officials of the federal government, you are tramping on the sovereignty of this great state. You are destroying the Constitution of this great nation. May God have mercy on your souls."

I was not aware of any of this.

In my dorm room, I read newspaper articles about myself and cracked a book.

I was in a kind of serene trance, a state of total peace and relaxation.

I felt I had accomplished my objective. I was an accomplished fact now—I was on the campus and nothing would make me leave. I had great confidence in the marshals and soldiers to fight off any attempts on my life and to guarantee my rights as an American citizen. Unlike Autherine Lucy's experience at the University of Alabama a few years earlier, when she was with no protection and chased out of school by a mob, I was there to stay.

I made my bed, lay down, closed my eyes, and went to sleep.

I slept for ten hours.

A few hundred yards away at the Lyceum, a small war erupted. Lighted torches were used to set the federal trucks and vehicles on fire. Their tires were slashed, gas tanks filled with dirt, windshields broken, and reporters were beaten.

At 8:00 p.m. a piece of heavy lead pipe spiraled through the air and knocked one marshal flat to the ground. Chief U.S. Marshal James McShane reluctantly gave the order to use the tear gas. He later said, "It was terrible, terrible. I prayed we wouldn't have to use gas. But we had no other choice."

Thus began one of the darkest nights in postwar U.S. history, the night America went to war against itself.

At the exact same time the first tear gas was fired into the mob, which soon included students from Mississippi State University and hardcore racists from all over the South, President Kennedy in the Oval Office went on national television to make an appeal to the state of Mississippi to comply with federal law:

> The orders of the court in the case of Meredith versus Fair are beginning to be carried out. Mr. James Meredith is now in residence on the campus of the University of Mississippi. This has been accomplished thus far without the use of National Guard or other troops. And it is to be hoped that the law enforcement officers of the State of Mississippi and the Federal marshals will continue to be sufficient in the future.
>
> All students, members of the faculty, and public officials in both Mississippi and the Nation will be able, it is hoped, to return to their normal activities with full confidence in the integrity of American law. This is as it should be, for our Nation is founded on the principle that observance of the law is the eternal safeguard of liberty and defiance of the law is the surest road to tyranny. The law which we obey includes the final rulings of the courts, as well as the enactments of our legislative bodies. Even among law-abiding men few laws are universally loved, but they are uniformly respected and not resisted. Americans are free, in short, to disagree with the law but not to disobey it. For in a government of laws and not of men, no man, however prominent or powerful, and no mob however unruly or boisterous, is entitled to defy a court

of law. If this country should ever reach the point where any man or group of men by force or threat of force could long defy the commands of our court and our Constitution, then no law would stand free from doubt, no judge would be sure of his writ, and no citizen would be safe from his neighbors. . . .

I deeply regret the fact that any action by the executive branch was necessary in this case, but all other avenues and alternatives, including persuasion and conciliation, had been tried and exhausted. Had the police powers of Mississippi been used to support the orders of the court, instead of deliberately and unlawfully blocking them, had the University of Mississippi fulfilled its standard of excellence by quietly admitting this applicant in conformity with what so many other southern State universities have done for so many years, a peaceable and sensible solution would have been possible without any Federal intervention. . . . I recognize that the present period of transition and adjustment in our Nation's Southland is a hard one for many people. Neither Mississippi nor any other southern State deserves to be charged with all the accumulated wrongs of the last 100 years of race relations. To the extent that there has been failure, the responsibility for that failure must be shared by us all, by every State, by every citizen. . . .

I close therefore, with this appeal to the students of the University, the people who are most concerned. You have a great tradition to uphold, a tradition of honor and courage won on the field of battle and on the gridiron as well as the University campus. You have a new opportunity to show that you are men of patriotism and integrity. For the most effective means of upholding the law is not the State policeman or the marshals or the National Guard. It is you. It lies in your courage to accept those laws with which you disagree as well as those with which you agree. The eyes of the Nation and of all the world are upon you and upon all of us, and the honor of your University and State are in the balance. I am certain that the great majority of the students will uphold that honor. There is in short no reason why the books on this case cannot now be quickly and quietly closed in the manner directed by the court. Let us preserve both the law and the peace and then healing those wounds that are within we can turn to the greater crises that are without and stand united as one people in our pledge to man's freedom. Thank you and good night.

It was a fine speech, but it was too late, as combat was already underway on the campus. The battle was fought by a mob of white civilians who launched themselves upon the outnumbered band of marshals in hand-to-hand combat, hurling rocks, bricks, bottles, acid bombs, rifle fire and small-arms fire.

As fate would have it, the wind was blowing the tear gas back on to the marshals as fast as they were shooting it. The angry mob was hardly affected by the gas. The Mississippi State Highway Patrolmen all pulled out and left for safer grounds. The mob went over to a construction site and secured bricks by the hundreds and threw them at the marshals, along with hastily made Molotov cocktails.

The chaos intensified with each passing hour. A construction bulldozer and a university fire truck were brought in and driven into the ranks of the marshals. Gunfire from shotguns and rifles filled the air. Marshals were being hit by the dozens, scores were wounded. Their backs were to the wall of the Lyceum, which became a modern-day Alamo.

At about 9:00 p.m., a British-French reporter named Paul Guihard was killed. He was a New York–based correspondent for Agence France-Presse and the *London Daily Sketch* who had been assigned to the story. In his last story filed before he was killed, he stated that it was difficult for him to believe that he was in the center of the most serious constitutional crisis ever experienced by the

United States since the war of secession, and that from his present point of observation the Civil War had never ended. Shot in the back by an unknown killer, Guihard, thirty-one, himself became a casualty of the war he wrote about. At about 11:00 p.m., a twenty-two-year-old bystander from Oxford named Ray Gunter was killed by a stray bullet while watching the battle.

Though clearly outmanned and overpowered, the federal forces did a magnificent job of holding their ground. Twice they ran out of tear gas. New supplies from the nearby Holly Springs Army Base were delivered by desperate trucks ramming through the fighting mob of rebels. Passages from the book *An American Insurrection* describe how the nightmare landscape resembled a war zone in the middle of the United States:

> Back on the front lines, the marshals had just about run out of tear gas, the only means they had to keep the rioters at bay.
>
> "We've got to have more gas," one marshal demanded of Nicholas Katzenbach [the U.S. Deputy attorney general trapped inside the Lyceum with the marshals].
>
> "We don't have any more right now, but we're working on it," was the reply.
>
> "We've got to have it now," the marshal shouted. "My men are getting slaughtered out there!"
>
> The marshals were pumping out tear gas faster than they could get reserves ready. McShane and the Justice Department officials were pleading for more tear gas to be flown down from Memphis, but the supplies were running so low there that marshals were commandeering crates of gas bombs from the 503d Military Police Battalion's supply. Two hours into the chaos, the riot was abruptly shifting into full-scale combat.
>
> The marshals could hear a shotgun blasting away in the distance, and it was soon joined by the rhythmic "pow-pow-pow" of a .22 automatic. Before long, gunfire seemed to be

coming from everywhere. "We were now alone," recalled newsman Ed Turner, "the crowd roaring louder with each barrage, the campus filling up with reinforcements from three states and no guard at the gates to stop them."

Across the region, cars and trucks full of armed and unarmed fighters were surging toward Oxford from all directions, especially from segregationist strongholds in adjacent Alabama and Louisiana. A few scattered Mississippi Highway Patrolmen were blocking potential rioters from the campus, but one patrolman was observed telling a carload of outsiders, "We can't let you in here but if you break into small groups you can sneak in across the railroad tracks."

Civilian volunteers armed with rifles and shotguns were flocking into the campus and taking turns opening fire at the Lyceum and the marshals, who now became the bull's-eye of a demented public shooting gallery. Over the next hours, snipers and muzzle flashes were reported at roofs and windows of the YMCA building, the Fulton Chapel, the Peabody Building, the Confederate statue, and scattered in the shadows around the Circle.

At 10:00 p.m., Deputy Marshal Al Butler reported to the deputy attorney general: "Mr. Katzenbach, that's not a riot out there anymore. It's an armed insurrection."

On the edge of campus, FBI agent Robin Cotten saw dozens of civilians carrying shotguns and long rifles as they jumped out of pickup trucks and ran up the hill toward the center of campus. Agent Cotten figured the campus was now swarming with Klansmen.

What Cotten was witnessing, among many other things, were the beginnings of a Ku Klux Klan rebellion, with scores of out-of-state armed Klansmen converging spontaneously on Oxford. They were acting on their own initiative without orders from their leadership. There hadn't been time for that.

A rattletrap school bus with Louisiana plates pulled in

behind the Ole Miss football stadium. Inside the bus, a sound system was playing a tune called "The Cajun Ku Klux Klan": "You niggers listen now, / I'm gonna tell you how, / To keep from being tortured, / When the Klan is on the prowl, / Stay at home at night, / Lock your doors up tight, / Don't go outside or you will find, / Them crosses aburning bright." A team of five stocky men disembarked with a beer cooler and picnic supplies. One of the men asked a student where the action was. Another announced that they had brought machine guns.

Hardy Stennis, a student who was observing the chaos, saw four armed men in cowboy hats and western wear walking toward the Lyceum. Stennis asked them, "Where are you fellows from?" The reply: "Louisiana." Stennis queried, "Well, what in the world are you doing way up here?" One gunman answered, "We come to help out!"

One sniper crouched down behind a pile of bricks near the construction site of the new Science Building. He shot his rifle three or four times, then trotted to a new position. Another shooter lay down in a flower bed close to the marshals and fired on them with a .22 automatic, squeezing out strings of twenty-five and fifty rounds from there and from a spot at the northwest corner of the YMCA building. When he blasted out a light near the Lyceum, the crowd cheered.

"We come to help kill the nigger," a pair of well-dressed men announced to a student. The men said they came from the nearby town of Batesville, and one had a light rifle shoved in his coat and a pint of booze in his pocket. He offered to share it with a rioter, asking, "Want a drink?"

One rioter clutching a shotgun climbed up a tree in front of the Lyceum and began firing at the marshals. A young man from southern Mississippi sprawled down flat on the grass fifty yards in front of the Lyceum, firing a squirrel gun.

He paused to exclaim to a nearby acquaintance: "God damn, this is war!"

At 10:00 p.m., Ted Lucas Smith, a young local stringer for the Memphis *Commercial Appeal,* noticed three acquaintances from his hometown of Oakland, Mississippi, strolling by him, each one toting a shotgun. They were about twenty-five years old, and not students. "They walked straight into the curtain of tear gas boiling around the front of the Lyceum," Smith recalled. "Their silhouettes raised the guns in union and unloaded five rounds each into the tear gas. Then they calmly turned and walked back past me, down the hill toward the football field, saying nothing."

Also in front of the Lyceum, a federal prison guard from Atlanta was holding a lit flashlight when a sniper zeroed in on him with a shotgun. He caught six pellets in the stomach and chest, and a seventh flew though his gas mask and punctured his forehead. He was patched up with the few first-aid supplies inside the Lyceum, and then he volunteered to go back outside on the firing line, where he stayed all night. Another Atlanta prison guard felt two blasts striking the right side of his head and chest. The eyepiece of his gas mask was cracked by a shotgun pellet, and another pellet pierced his chest. Yet another marshal was hit in the earlobe with double-aught buckshot, spun around like top, and fell to the ground as pellets slammed into the wall behind him.

Border Patrolman Dan Pursglove was sprawled on the Lyceum floor, bleeding from a shotgun pellet wound in his right thigh. "Damnit, Dan," he thought, "you've spent four years in the Marine Corps, a year in Korea, and ten years in the Border Patrol, now some fellow Americans are going to be your demise." As the night raged on, one thought increasingly dominated his thoughts: "I wonder if I'm going to see the light of day."

Deputy U.S. Marshal James K. Kemp was a thirty-six-year-old father of three from Nashville, Tennessee. "I was a gunners mate in the Navy," Kemp recalled soon after the riot, "and after my ship went down, I was in the Atlantic Ocean for about an hour." But the riot at Ole Miss, Kemp shuddered, "was the worst thing I've ever been in."

Nicholas Katzenbach grabbed the line to the White House, and finally pleaded for a military rescue.

"For God's sake," he said, "we need those troops!"

The first group of sixty federalized local Mississippi National Guard troops arrived at about 11:00 p.m., carrying unloaded weapons, as army commanders were afraid they might spill civilian blood or even defect to the side of the rioters. They held the line against the onslaught of rioters, but there weren't enough of them to go on the offensive. The only thing that slowed the mob down briefly was a midnight radio broadcast by Governor Barnett. The mob quieted down to listen to what Barnett had to say.

Instead of pleading for calm, Barnett rallied the troops: "I will never yield a single inch in my determination to win the fight we are engaged in. I call on Mississippians to keep the faith and courage. We will never surrender." The speech was calculated to squelch the rumors that were spreading like wildfire across the South that Barnett had capitulated to the Kennedys and agreed for me to be registered, rumors that were of course true.

At the peak of the fighting, JFK and Barnett spoke again by phone. According to Barnett's daughter Ouida, who was in the room with her father at the time, his hand was shaking so violently from stress that she had to handle the phone for him. But he still managed to beseech the president to pull me off the campus.

By now, the crisis had completely run away from both men.

PRESIDENT KENNEDY: "We can't consider moving Meredith as long as, you know, there's a riot outside, 'cause he wouldn't be safe."

The Battle Begins: In a surprise operation, the first wave of 400 Deputy U.S. Marshals seizes the Lyceum building at the center of campus on September 30, 1962, as night falls and the precursor of a homicidal mob of 2,000 white civilians begins to form. I will soon be whisked to a different position on campus, and the scene will explode into a riot and battle that lasted sixteen hours, saw hundreds injured, and forced President Kennedy to stage a lightning invasion of the state to rescue the university and city from widespread destruction. At one point, almost the entire Mississippi state police force decided to retake the campus from the federal marshals at gunpoint. *Photos courtesy of Donald Proehl*

GOVERNOR BARNETT: "Sir?"

JFK: "We couldn't consider moving Meredith if you—if we haven't been able to restore order outside. That's the problem, Governor."

BARNETT: "Well, uh, I'll tell you what I'll do, Mr. President. I'll go up there myself—"

JFK: "Well, now, how long will it take you to get there?"

BARNETT: "And I'll get a microphone and tell 'em that you have agreed for him to be removed."

JFK: "*No. No. Now, wait a minute.* How long—*Wait a minute, Governor.* Now, how long is it going to take you to get up there?"

BARNETT: "'Bout an hour."

JFK: "Now, I'll tell you what you—if you want to go up there and then you call me from up there. Then we'll decide what we're gonna do before you make any speeches about it."

BARNETT: "Well, all right."

JFK: "No sense in, uh . . ."

BARNETT: "I mean, whatever you, if you'd authorize . . ."

JFK: "You see, if we don't, we got an hour to go, and that's not, uh, we may not have an hour."

BARNETT: "Uh, this, this man—"

JFK: "Won't it take you an hour to get up there?"

BARNETT: "—this man has just died."

JFK: "Did he die?"

BARNETT: "Yes."

JFK: "Which one? State police?"

BARNETT: "A state policeman." [This was a false rumor; in fact, no policemen died that night.]

JFK: "Yeah, well, you see, we gotta get order up there, and that's what we thought we're going to have."

BARNETT: "Mr. President, please. Why don't you, uh, can't you give an order up there to remove Meredith?"

JFK: "How can I remove him, Governor, when there's a riot

in the street, and he may step out of that building and something happen to him? I can't remove him under those conditions."

BARNETT: "Uh, but, but—"

JFK: "Let's get order up there, then we can do something about Meredith."

BARNETT: "We can surround it with plenty of officials."

JFK: "Well, we've gotta get somebody up there now to get order and stop the firing and the shooting. Then when, you and I will talk on the phone about Meredith. But first we've got to get order."

BARNETT: "I'll call and tell them to get every official they can."

JFK: "That's right, then you and I will talk. When they've got order there, then you and I will talk about what's the best thing to do about Meredith."

BARNETT: "All right then."

JFK: "Well, thank you."

The two men had stepped into a nightmare together, and they were both clinging to fantasies.

The University of Mississippi was flying over the abyss into total mayhem and thousands of Americans were entering combat with other Americans, but Barnett still clung to the idea that he could throw me off the campus. That wasn't going to happen now that the federal government had committed overwhelming force.

On the other hand, JFK wanted state law enforcement officers to help stop the violence, and that damn sure wasn't going to happen either. Their sympathies were with the mob. Some Mississippi highway patrolmen were cheering on rioters and others were helping outsiders sneak past checkpoints onto the campus.

In fact, at one point the entire furious mass of over two hundred Mississippi highway patrolmen, enraged by the federal takeover and choking from the tear gas, withdrew from the battlefield, gathered at a spot just west of campus, and decided collectively to *retake the campus of the University of Mississippi from the federal marshals, with their guns blazing if necessary.* Their caravan was approaching the battle zone when they were intercepted in the middle of the road by Lieutenant Governor Paul Johnson, who in the impromptu speech of his life convinced them to break off the assault.

The battle raged on and eventually spilled into the downtown area of Oxford. The fighting was severe at times. The mob was under the muddled, sporadic command of former general Edwin Walker, who in 1957 had commanded the troops at Little Rock sent in by President Eisenhower and now was a full-time extremist rabble-rouser.

The federal marshals, ordered to stay on the front lines and not shoot back, were raked with small-arms fire from snipers hidden in the darkness.

The incident was an absolute disaster-in-progress for President Kennedy and Attorney General Kennedy, as an American city collapsed into fourteen hours of terror and mayhem. RFK later described it as the worst night of his life, and described the president as "torn between an attorney general who had botched things up and the fact that the attorney general was his brother." At one point inside the White House that night, JFK despaired, "This is the worst thing I've seen in forty-five years." At another point he mused glumly to no one in particular, "I haven't had such an interesting time since the Bay of Pigs."

Finally, after midnight, the first U.S. Army military police soldiers arrived at Oxford by helicopter, after hours of White House delays and local logistical problems. It was 2:00 a.m. when they arrived on campus, and it was, according to an eyewitness, an awe-inspiring sight. The advance squad of MPs, gas masks on and bayonets thrust forward, marched through a wall of flames ignited in a pool of gasoline as they approached the Lyceum, and they never even broke step.

Combat in the American heartland: Federal marshals wearing gas masks advance into a column of tear gas. They endured an Alamo-style assault by white rioters from across the South who were armed with rifles, pistols, shotguns, bricks, Molotov cocktails, and a hijacked bulldozer and fire truck. More than 150 marshals were injured. *Photo: Mississippi Highway Patrol Collection, Archives and Special Collections, University of Mississippi Libraries*

The remains of incinerated vehicles that formed a rebel barricade near the Lyceum on the morning the battle was won by U.S. troops and marshals, with the crucial help of the all-white Mississippi National Guard. *Photo courtesy of Donald Proehl*

Thousands of federal troops poured into Oxford by land and air, including paratroopers, infantry, military police, and national guardsmen. Multiple waves of Mississippi national guardsmen from all over the state came in to risk their lives to support the effort to save the university and city from widespread destruction. On Oxford's Courthouse Square around 4:00 a.m., a convoy of incoming regular Army MPs was set upon by members of a mob who poured human waste on the soldiers' heads from second-story windows and tried to decapitate black soldiers sitting in their jeeps with clubs.

Through all of this, I slept peacefully in my dormitory room. My battle wasn't with the angry, misled whites of Mississippi and the entire South who had heeded the call of their leaders to engage in this war against the government of the United States. My battle was with the leadership of Mississippi.

U.S. Army troops seal off the courthouse square of Oxford in the last moments of the final battle of the American Civil War, as the statue of a Confederate soldier stands guard, looking southward. *Photo courtesy of Donald Proehl*

During all the tumult of the crisis, I remained emotionally aloof. My attitude was that all the fighting was white folks' business. That was what all the fighting was about, how white folks were going to deal with black folks. As a matter of fact, Mississippi whites for the most part didn't consider me involved in the fighting. Their fight wasn't with me. It was with the United States government, the marshals and soldiers.

I was awakened a few times by the noise and shooting, but nothing stirred any alarm within me, as I knew the United States military was on my side.

For that reason, I had won the war before it even started.

At six o'clock on the morning of October 1, 1962, Mississippi and I awoke to a new era.

CHAPTER SIX

A New World

O N OCTOBER 1, 1962, THE ATMOSPHERE AT THE UNIVERsity of Mississippi was that of a devastated battlefield.

The air burned bitterly with the smell of tear gas. I looked out the window and saw columns of combat troops marching across the landscape. It was both inspiring and surreal to witness this on a university campus in America.

The last great battle of the Civil War was finally over that morning, nearly a century after General Lee surrendered the Army of Northern Virginia at the Appomattox Courthouse.

Upon learning from a few marshals of the details of the clash and its casualties, I felt very sorry, because I had become acquainted with several of the marshals who had been wounded.

Otherwise, I felt a powerful sense of fulfillment. I had waged a major battle against white supremacy and I had achieved victory.

The solid wall of racism had been cracked for the world to see. Even if I only had a toe in the door, the wall had been breached.

The American Constitution had triumphed, backed up with the force of American soldiers who were cascading toward Oxford and other points in Mississippi all night and into this morning.

The battle had climaxed in a lightning invasion of Mississippi by over twenty thousand U.S. combat troops, which was more soldiers than the United States had in Korea, and six times more soldiers than were stationed in Berlin at the time. The battle resulted in more than three hundred military and civilian casualties, some three hundred civilian arrests, and the mass federal confiscation of hundreds of privately owned firearms.

It was a symbolic turning point in American history that marked the death of white "massive resistance" to integration and was therefore a turning point in the civil rights era. It is considered by many Mississippians to be the most important event of their twentieth-century history, as it dealt a fatal blow to public school segregation and eventually ushered in a long, peaceful process of school desegregation in the state.

This day also marked a turning point in my own personal struggle to contribute what I could to the fight for human freedom and dignity. I felt a sudden release of pressure. It appeared to me that the particular steps that I had chosen to take in an effort to carry out the mandate of my divine responsibility had been proper and timely. No matter what the outcome of my endeavors at the University of Mississippi, I felt as though I had done my part to advance the cause of complete freedom, complete rights and privileges for each citizen in this democracy. I had fulfilled this task of my divine responsibility.

On this morning I put on the same blood-red tie I had worn the day before. Chief U.S. Marshal McShane asked me to choose another one. He said the red tie was provocative. The red tie was indeed provocative. I meant it to be. But I did as he asked me, out of respect for McShane and his men, who had gone through hell for the past twelve hours.

At 8:00 a.m., I wiped the glass off the seat of a marshal's car in which all the windows were broken out, and we drove to the Lyceum building. Flanked by my courageous federal escorts McShane and Doar, and surrounded by a blossoming throng of journalists and photographers from around the world, I walked to the registrar's office and registered as a political science major student at Ole Miss.

The university registrar, Robert Ellis, seemed to be in a state of shock and defiance, but he took me through the forms, including a late registration form and my GI Bill paperwork. I signed the papers, paid the fee, and became the first black American known to attend the University of Mississippi as a student. Only later did people discover that a light-skinned black New Yorker named Harry Murphy had in fact attended for a semester in 1945, without anybody else realizing he was black. And if you page through Ole Miss yearbooks before 1962, you'll see a number of white students who from their pictures seem to have at least some African blood in their family tree one way or another.

As I came out of the Lyceum to go to my first class, there was a black man standing in the hall, one of dozens of black workers on the campus who mopped floors, hauled trash, did laundry, and served food in the cafeteria.

This black man had a broom on his arm, and when I walked by him, he turned his body so the broom handle gently touched me, and he looked into my eyes. He was delivering probably one of the most important messages that I ever got at Ole Miss. The message was, "You are not alone. We are looking after you twenty-four hours a day. Every black eye is looking after you." I was not alone, and I never would be at Ole Miss.

At 9:00 a.m. I was on my way to my first class, in American colonial history. One of the twelve white students greeted me as I entered the classroom, leaving the United States deputy marshal outside the door. I remember a girl in the room crying. It might have been from the tear gas. I was crying from it, too. I attended another class that morning as well. The third class was canceled because of too much tear gas in the building.

John Doar was not only by my side at each failed attempt to enroll in Ole Miss, he was there when I actually signed the papers and when I attended my first class. He walked with me in triumph up the hill to my dormitory and listened in silence as I expressed my satisfaction at having broken the system of white supremacy, which was the first phase on the road to full, first-class citizenship for me and my kind. John Doar was truly a great American public servant.

The riot at the University of Mississippi was front-page news across the United States that day and triggered headlines around the world. More than three hundred reporters from all corners of the globe converged on Oxford, and many of their stories high-lighted the fact that the crisis revealed the best and the worst of the American character.

It was ironic that the two men who primarily made the insur-rection happen would have the harshest words of condemnation for the violence they had brought on. All records point to one clear conclusion, that the actions and words of Governor Barnett opened the door for the riot to transpire. And it was the orches-tration of William Simmons and the Citizens Council that did the most to create the atmosphere of defiance, bigotry, and insur-rection in which the violence of September 30–October 1, 1962, thrived.

In a nationally broadcast speech on that first day of my stay at Ole Miss, Governor Barnett laid the full blame at the doorstep of the White House: "The responsibility for this unwarranted breach of peace and violence in Mississippi rests directly with the president of the United States." Later, Barnett viciously assailed President Kennedy and the "trigger-happy federal marshals," as he called them, whom he criticized as "nervous" and "inexperienced." William Simmons went so far as to state that because of the Ken-nedy administration's ordeal with the Freedom Riders the previous year, it was "politically mandatory" to integrate Ole Miss, and that it was the Kennedys' unique opportunity to humiliate the state of Mississippi.

White southerners had a variety of reactions to my entrance into Ole Miss. Some of them realized that integration was inevitable now that the federal government was committed to using force and accepted that inevitability.

On the other hand, *U.S. News & World Report* interviewed leading editors from all over the South only days after the violence and the bloodshed. Their responses revealed a common perception: The clash at Ole Miss was a major detriment to race relations in the South. Several of them predicted future violence as a result of the generating "spark" at Oxford. Any further intervention by the federal government would certainly meet a strong resistance, predicted the editors. *U.S. News* concluded that the process of integration in the South was not only hampered but retarded, and federal "compulsion" left nothing but a bad taste in the mouth of the typical white southerner.

But except for the railing by Barnett and the Citizens Council and a small group of other southern politicians, the public assessment among opinion leaders of President Kennedy's handling of the crisis was relatively positive. The majority of congressmen, as quoted by the *New York Times*, were "impressed" with the president's performance in balancing "conciliation and force," and held nothing back in expressing their gratitude and praise.

Former president Harry S. Truman joined in as well, comparing Kennedy's actions with the historical decisions of Presidents Andrew Jackson and Abraham Lincoln in deploying federal troops to enforce federal law upon an individual state. Surprisingly, among the ranks of southern governors, there was also a consensus to condemn Governor Barnett as "an embarrassment to the South and to the nation as well." Only Governors Orval Faubus of Arkansas and William Patterson of Alabama were critical of the president's conduct in the crisis.

International reaction was mixed. Newspapers and officials in Egypt, Ghana, Spain, and Italy all favored President Kennedy's action to put down the rebellious segregationists, while some in Germany, Morocco, and Japan derided the insurrection as a disgrace to the leading nation of democracy and freedom, and as a devastating blow to its international prestige.

On a broader scale, the eruption of violence on the night of September 30, 1962, provided a social thermometer reading for all Americans to confront their position on full citizenship for all Americans. As my good friend Ole Miss Professor James Silver wrote in his book, *Mississippi: the Closed Society*, the riot and insurrection were "inevitable," since the United States was in a "slow, painful, and self-conscious" process of change from a "white society to a multi-racial society."

As noted by my attorney, Constance Baker Motley, the Ole Miss crisis also served as a vivid "demonstration of what the Constitution means in practical applications." As the federal court orders were constantly brushed aside by the highest officials of the state, it was clear that Mississippi and the rest of the country no longer operated on the same basic premises. Oxford had indeed become the symbol of mass resistance, and was the final gasp of the Civil War. Thus the Constitution, as Motley pointed out, "was put to the test and survived."

I cannot even begin to explain the state of mind of the black people in Mississippi during the first week I attended Ole Miss.

It was beyond the imagination of most blacks for another black to stand up and challenge white folks in Mississippi. It was something out of this world, beyond reality, to defeat them and live in what was deemed to be their world.

My victory at Ole Miss was an enormous boost to the psyche of black Americans at a critical juncture in our struggle for full citizenship rights.

Martin Luther King expressed dissatisfaction with the overall performance of the Kennedy administration. Although he was the leading advocate of nonviolence, King agreed with the use of force in face of the obstinate "color prejudice" that has been "woven into the fabric of American life."

I believed the lesson should have been learned from Eisenhower's performance during the Little Rock crisis of 1957: "If forced to intervene, then intervene with sufficient force." This allowed President Eisenhower to avoid any serious casualties or deaths. Unfortunately, President Kennedy and his staff at the Justice Department did not use this proven method until forced to do so.

All in all, most blacks seemed satisfied that the federal government had finally taken such a definite stand against the state of Mississippi. I made a statement a couple of days after the battle at Ole Miss, saying first of all that "change is a painful thing." I also acknowledged that the efforts of the Kennedy brothers were made to the best of their knowledge and ability. The main thing was that I had finally struck at the system of white supremacy and thus black Americans could count it as a triumph with an efficacy that would extend well into future generations.

To say that I was beloved to black Americans, and a hero to them, is a gross understatement. My honor and power seemed absolute. Many black women wanted to please me. Some would have done anything in the world that I asked them to do. Many black women were induced to openly flirt with me, sometimes in the presence of their own men.

For some reason, it seemed that in Mississippi, available black women outnumbered black men by seven to one. Having more than one woman was commonplace for black men. In fact, I did not know personally any black man between twenty-five and forty who did not have more than one woman.

I had been spoiled by women all my life, and since I was a baby women had always been telling me how pretty I was. They always liked to touch me, especially my face and eyelashes. When I became a figure in the news from the summer of 1961 through the summer of 1963, it was basically like a vast orgy of black female adoration for me. Whatever I wanted I could get. Whoever I wanted I could have.

My wife, Mary June, was my reality, and the only object of my physical sexual fulfillment, but other black women were constantly throwing themselves at me. And I loved the attention. The problem wasn't getting sexually involved with women. The question was how to escape giving them what they wanted and to preserve that built-up energy for more productive use. I became a master of that game.

Over the Christmas holidays of 1962, a group of white liberal benefactors, afraid that I would flunk out of the University of Mississippi and not be able to graduate, made elaborate arrangements for me to be flown to Yale University for a round of intensive tutoring by an all-star team of academics. I went along with this very reluctantly but pulled out soon after arriving, as I felt perfectly capable of earning my degree on my own.

I flew to Chicago to meet my wife, but discovered that my family was still in Mississippi. A good friend of mine and his fiancée, whom I'll call Rose, came to my hotel after midnight, which seemed a strange time to visit. The three of us talked for a while.

My friend got up and said, "Well! I'm going to run."

I said: "Okay! You all be good."

He said matter-of-factly, "Oh! She's staying."

I was perplexed. He walked to the door and said, "See you all tomorrow."

Neither one of us said anything for a long time.

Finally, Rose got up out of the chair, came over, and put her body all over mine.

"I love you," she said. "I've loved you for such a long time. I've tried so hard not to do this but I'm helpless. I can't contain myself."

I don't remember speaking a word the whole time.

The next day her fiancé, my friend, came and picked her up around noon and they drove back to Mississippi together. They stayed engaged for another three years but never married. I saw him many times over the next several years but the subject never came up. Rose continued to spend as much time with me as possible.

Years later I asked my friend about leaving his fiancée in my room in Chicago.

He said, "Man, you don't ever know what them women may do. When they make up their minds there ain't nothing you can do about it. She let me know that she had made up her mind and I didn't see any reason to let that come between us. You and I were tight before I ever got involved with her. There are plenty of women out there."

Then there were the white women.

Cleve McDowell, the next black student who enrolled at Ole Miss, and who was expelled from the school the next semester after I graduated for carrying a gun, told me that the reason he felt that he needed to carry a gun at Ole Miss was that the white girls just would not leave him alone. They would follow him everywhere.

When he got into his car and left the campus they would follow him. Often the white boys would get behind and follow the girls, and McDowell was scared of what they might try to do to him. So he packed his gun everywhere he went, on and off campus. This got him expelled from the university.

Several journalists told me of white female students at Ole Miss who admitted having their bells rung by the thrill of my presence, sometimes just by having a cup of coffee while sitting at the table across from me in the cafeteria.

One day, three visiting white coeds began to follow me around the campus.

One of them giggled, "Isn't it thrilling?"

I threw my head back and laughed: "Yeah, ain't it a thrill. You get to come up to Ole Miss and see the nigger!"

I started noticing one particular young white woman staring at me during my second week at Ole Miss.

Her name was Ann. She was a transfer sophomore from Arkansas, and a very pretty girl even by Ole Miss standards, which per capita had the most beautiful women of any college in America.

At first I thought she must have been a student "stringer" for one of the news services. Since the university had ruled that it would be too disruptive for a cadre of hundreds of news people to follow me around the campus all the time, several news agencies had hired students to keep tabs on me.

Every time I looked around I would see Ann, always looking pretty and giving me that special smile. Her mission became clear in the library one night.

I was doing a paper on southern history and was going to a particular section of the shelves and picking whatever book from that section looked like it might be interesting and taking it back to my work table. This time, when I got to my selected section, there was Miss Ann on the opposite side of the bookshelves trying to get my attention through an empty space between the books. I listened.

"I am in love with you," she whispered.

I didn't say anything.

She assured me that I would be seeing more of her.

I saw plenty more of her.

During my second week at the university, I was shocked to see that segregated groups of black U.S. Army troops were doing garbage pickup duty on the campus. Their guns and helmets had been removed, and white students were laughing at them.

I later learned that the great liberal hero Robert F. Kennedy had ordered thousands of black troops to be pulled off the front lines of the invasion, rescue, and liberation of Mississippi in September 1962. *For the first time in history, thousands of black U.S. Army soldiers were resegregated—on the orders of Robert F. Kennedy.* He did it apparently to avoid offending the delicate sensibilities of white

Mississippians, who would resent seeing black soldiers. The order was implemented in a chaotic fashion across different units, but the result was that soldiers in units of 101st Airborne Division, the 82nd Airborne Division, the Second Infantry, and the 716th Military Police Battalion had black soldiers and squad leaders stripped off the front lines.

At the Oxford Airport, in a formation of 82nd Airborne paratroopers, one proud, tough veteran black army sergeant kept standing at attention when his superior officer repeatedly ordered him to step back off the front line to be hidden away with other black troops. With tears in his eyes, he said, "I served my country in World War II and Korea. I will serve my country now. I refuse to step back, sir!" Scenes like this were replicated across the invasion force, and white officers had shouting matches with their superiors over how impossible the order was to implement. In the mobile 503rd Military Police Battalion, the order was repeatedly torn up and ignored, as the army officers knew they simply couldn't move forward in action without the black soldiers, who comprised many of the squad leaders and motor pool and communications troops. In a large infantry camp on the outskirts of Oxford, soldiers in the Second Infantry repeatedly nearly rioted.

I was furious at this public humiliation of black American soldiers.

I issued a public statement denouncing the segregation, and I told my federal escorts that I would quit the university unless the segregation stopped instantly.

In hours, President John F. Kennedy did as I ordered. He reversed the order and put black troops back on the front lines. He worked for me, not the other way around.

This was a typical day in my life as a student.

I awoke around 5:30 a.m. to the click of the steel-plated heels of the soldier walking his post in the hallway outside my dormitory apartment. I shaved and put on the sweet-smelling aftershave lotion one of my friends gave me. At seven I walked out the only way open, through the living room, as the other doors were barricaded for security purposes. A team of U.S. deputy marshals fell in behind me, we headed down the long flight of steps outside the dorm toward the sidewalk, and from there an alert squad of U.S. Army troops followed us in a jeep.

Before I reached the second step one of my watchers would yell, "Hey, nigger! There's that nigger!"

Every morning for the first ten months of my life at Ole Miss, someone yelled "nigger" at me before I made it to the bottom of the steps outside my dormitory, Baxter Hall.

"Nigger, nigger, nigger." The word was hurled at me on the campus of the University of Mississippi dozens of times a day on average, sometimes over a hundred times in a day, sometimes accompanied by cherry bombs, epithets, and broad-daylight shouted threats to kill me.

They must have had their eyes on those steps twenty-four hours a day. As I walked the two blocks down the hill to the cafeteria, I could hear the routine window-to-window comments. I would have been very frightened indeed if I had walked the whole distance without anybody saying anything. I would have known that something very drastic was about to happen.

At the cafeteria, amid the barrage of curses and threats, the Negro cooks and help always had a warm greeting for me and knew exactly how I preferred my food. I got my scrambled egg and crisp bacon and a big glass of grape juice.

Between morning classes I would stop by the campus post office and pick up mail. The post office was the only place where I had unguarded contact with other students. It was always very crowded, and sometimes a boy would stick his foot out and try to kick me. Often I would kick back. Later in the day I would stop by the library, but for a while I stopped going there because the bomb scares and evacuations were so frequent, and I hated to see the other students suffer so much inconvenience.

The worst event, and the most dishonorable, was when my reading glasses were stolen from the desk where I left them to go to the washroom. The campus police were called and everyone was questioned, but naturally no one had seen a thing. A few days later, one of the witnesses couldn't live with his conscience any longer and came over to tell me who did it. He also confessed to the marshals on condition that it would go no further. He would not testify in public. I guess I could understand his predicament.

By noon I always liked to be in a good position in the "chow" line. Usually I was accompanied by a surge of white students in my line, probably because they heard the Negro cooks made sure that every bit of food put on my line was the best. It was always a heartbreaking sight to see the young Negro boys and girls who should have been in junior high or high school wiping the tables and carrying the trays for white students.

Once, at supper, when I got on line on the right as usual, a bumpy-faced antagonist of mine got on the other line opposite mine. He was absolutely the foulest-mouthed individual that I ever met, and that is saying a lot, considering the average student at the University of Mississippi I encountered.

As always, for the first few moments, he kept up a barrage of the nastiest curse words I ever heard, calling me every manner of "son of a bitch, motherfucker, coconut-headed coon, baboon, and bastard."

I interrupted his aria, "Now, boy, you know you don't mean all of that, do you? You know you like me. Why can't we just be friends?"

He answered, "Yeah, yeah, let's be friends, nigger. By the way, are you going to Jackson this weekend?"

"Yes, I plan to go."

"Well, I'm going to fuck!" he declared. "You ever go down on Farish Street? Look, I'll meet you down on the low end of Farish

Street. I got me a couple of nigger bitches down there. Man! Them whores sure got some good ones. Yeah! Come on down. I'll turn you on to one of my nigger bitches."

About this time the lines opened up, I went to the right, and he went to the left, still yakking away.

I would walk ahead unflinching after a pistol-loud firecracker exploded at my heels. When students in the mess hall beat their trays and chanted, "Nigger go home! Nigger go home! Nigger go home!" I responded with a smile and a wave.

Bricks and stones and sticks would fly. I don't think I ever got hit with anything, but some of the marshals who were my body-guards did. There was also a lot of tripping action when I walked down the halls. I got in an awful lot of good kicks during this time. When someone tried to trip me or otherwise obstruct me, I would kick them.

Classes were a different thing. The same little white coed who might be yelling, "Why doesn't someone kill him?" would act as humane as any other person in America if she was sitting in the classroom.

I was not afraid. Fear is an emotional thing and it requires energy. I could not afford to be afraid, not in that period.

You can get used to anything. People, for example, dread the idea of prison. Once there a few days, however, most somehow adjust to it. People adjust and build a normal life almost anywhere if there is a constant pattern. Except in the classroom, the pattern at Ole Miss was hostile. In a short time, the hostility became normal for me. That was the normal relationship between the students and me.

A small group of diehards made me their business for the entire year. They found me wherever I was during the day. I remember one fellow, who was later a leading state senator in the Mississippi legislature, cursed me one to fifty times a day each and every day I was on the campus of Ole Miss.

I always knew this fellow liked me a lot. Can you imagine how much you have to like someone in order to curse him every time you see him, not to mention taking the trouble to find him to curse him? No one would ever spend that much time on anyone that he did not like.

The security around me was always very heavy. Several marshals always accompanied me on foot and in cars, in addition to three jeep loads of army soldiers that were always in sight. The U.S. Army soldiers were on a twenty-four-hour thirty-second alert: If anything happened to me, they had thirty seconds to come to my rescue, guns locked and loaded. There were plenty of troops to go around. On my second day of classes there were sixteen thousand soldiers in the immediate vicinity of Oxford, with another four-teen thousand or so standing by at various bases and posts in and around Mississippi. The army set up a permanent camp nicknamed "Camp Meredith" on the edge of the campus to house them, and the university and the city of Oxford resembled Civil War images of a conquered southern city, with vast numbers of federal troops drilling, bivouacking, and patrolling the liberated territory.

I had more than ten thousand personal bodyguards. I was more heavily guarded than the president of the United States, probably the best-guarded single individual in history. It cost the government a lot of money to pay for this protection. I always thought it was unnecessary, but one federal official told me, "If it were not for this massive armed protection, there are easily fifty to a hundred students who will kill you in a minute."

The U.S. Army soldiers who guarded me, white and black, were magnificent and inspiring in their sense of mission and their unyielding professionalism in the face of countless taunts and provocations, in a land that at times must have seemed like enemy territory to them. When one of them, a military police commander named Henry Gallagher, was rotated out of Oxford, I passed him this note:

To: Lieutenant Gallagher:

I know that your assignment over the past few weeks has been unique, if not indeed strange. I have enjoyed your presence and I hope you have not been too unhappy.

The processes of civilization are sometimes hard to understand. Yet, they must go on. In this development, sometimes we find ourselves (some of us) at the apex of a point of friction. Immediately we are harnessed with a great responsibility. We are all duty bound to carry out this responsibility to the best of our ability. This we will do.

Presently we are faced with a great and grave racial problem in our country. It points deep in many directions. I feel that it is essential that we solve this problem, if America is to hold the place among nations that it deserves. Finding a solution to this problem is my goal.

Best wishes, and lots of luck to you in your mission.
J H MEREDITH—November 1962

The performance of the army troops in the massive rescue and liberation of Oxford, Mississippi, in 1962 was so heroic, in fact, that they were supposed to be awarded combat medals and citations for their courage during the operation, including at least forty Army Commendation Medals. Their commanders recommended the troops for the medals. But the Pentagon brass cancelled them. Why? An army memo dated April 19, 1963, reads: "It is considered that the focus of additional attention on this incident would not be in the best interest of the nation. . . . Decorations should not be awarded for actions involving conflict between U.S. Army units and other Americans."

In other words, the higher-ups were afraid of bad publicity. As for the idea that decorations shouldn't be awarded for actions of conflict between Americans, they apparently forgot about the hundreds of thousands of medals awarded to American soldiers for service in the Civil War.

Masterminded by the Citizens Council, every conceivable attempt was made by the students to make my stay at Ole Miss as unpleasant as possible, with the hope of forcing me off the campus. Everything from threats, curses, and noise on my bedroom walls to rocks and firecrackers, BB guns and cherry bombs were used almost twenty-four hours a day. Even bomb threats became a common tactic, although more than a hundred other students lived in the same dormitory with me.

Students who attempted to be friendly with me or sit with me in the cafeteria were harassed and subjected to violent reprimands, and professors who tried to be sensible about the question of citizenship rights were severely punished by the opposition. During the year I was at the university, more than fifty professors left the campus. Many were literally forced from the state.

How I was able to cope and maintain my constant casual air of Zenlike serenity and indifference was baffling to most observers. A *Newsweek* reporter who was assigned to cover me at Ole Miss wrote, "One can't help but be impressed by the vast personal dignity of this man. He is neither cocky nor egotistical, yet he seems to possess some fantastic inner strength and discipline. He is completely dedicated; when he makes up his mind of a thing that should be done, he does it with a sense of firmness that surprises most people."

I understood that the Negro's fear of the white man was a fear that existed only in his imagination and not from a real condition. I knew that in a man-to-man encounter there were few men in the world that I could not subdue, both mentally and physically. At twelve years of age I could strike a match with a .22 rifle. I had had nine years of training in military service, I studied martial arts, and felt that few men possessed greater potential for doing bodily harm than myself. Why then should

I fear any man? My belief in my supernatural or superhuman powers was another important factor. Whether it was true or not, I had always felt that I could stop a mob with the uplifting of a hand.

And finally, I believe in the immortality of ideas and in the immortality of those who manifest them. Because of my divine responsibility to advance human civilization, I could not die. If one places society above self, and I did, life never ends. Everything that I did, I did because I must; and everything that I must do, I did.

Through it all, the most intolerable thing was the campaign to ostracize me. It did not harm me directly. I was a seasoned U.S. military veteran, and at twenty-nine years old I was a decade older than some of the students who were trying to torment me, so their threats had little effect on me. If anyone didn't want to associate with me, I was sure that the feeling was at least mutual. I didn't think anyone should be forced to enter into association with anyone else unless they choose to do so.

However, the ostracizers also assumed the right to see that no one else associated with me. If a white student sat down and drank a cup of coffee with me or walked with me across the campus, he was subjected to unhampered intimidation and harassment. I had been denied my privileges all along, but these whites had not been. Now they had lost a simple freedom. This was a setback for the Negro, because any time there is a move backward, the person already down suffers more. This campaign, which was openly tolerated by the university officials, really resulted in a reduction of everybody's rights.

People have always wanted to know what I thought and how I felt during the first few weeks at the University of Mississippi, what was being said to me and how I reacted. In addition to countless death threats, I received thousands of letters and telegrams from around the world, most of them expressions of support.

One guy sent me a piece of singed rope, and another sent a

poem, "Roses are red, violets are blue; I've killed me one nigger and might as well make it two."

But many other letters and telegrams supported me, and some of them were really touching—letters from ten- and eleven-year-olds who thought I was right and offered me their help.

Most Ole Miss students were courteous, as were all of the faculty members.

When I heard the jeers and the catcalls like, "We'll get you, nigger," I didn't consider it personal. I figured people were just having a little fun. It was a tragic kind of fun to be sure, but many of these students were children of the men who led Mississippi, and I would not expect them to act any other way. They were programmed to act the way they did.

One day a white fellow from my hometown sat down at my table in the cafeteria. "If you're here to get an education, I'm for you," he said. "If you're here to cause trouble, I'm against you."

That seemed fair enough to me.

The scene outside my window on an average night in early October 1962 was described by reporter Charles Whaley of the *Louisville Courier-Journal*: "As the evening wears on, the crowd of boys drifting from Meredith's dormitory and those nearby to the street outside grows bigger. From one of the rooms a phonograph record at its loudest pitch blares "Dixie" over and over. The boys on the street mill about, gaily cursing and shouting at Meredith. A rather effeminate cheerleader in shorts and Ole Miss sweater goes through a pep-rally yell with his cohorts and adds his own coda. His eyes are bright with hate. "What happens to Meredith when the troops leave" he shouts and then spells it out: "D-E-A-D." Everyone roars approval. Other boys in rooms above look out their windows and join in the shouting. The only silent ones are the federal troops guarding Meredith's dormitory in the glare of Army-installed floodlights."

While I was having dinner in the cafeteria on the night of October 8, a rock came crashing through the window and sprinkled glass on my table. On other occasions, firecrackers were thrown toward me, a dead raccoon was placed on top of my car, and my tires were flattened.

On October 24, I visited the Student Union Grill and was soon enveloped in a crowd of screaming students. My bodyguard, a deputy U.S. marshal, had to elbow and shoulder his way through the scrimmage to create a path for us to leave the room.

On the night of October 29, a miniriot broke out as I ate dinner in the cafeteria. Outside, a mob of some two hundred students harassed my U.S. Army escorts with bottles, eggs, high-powered firecrackers, and at least one Molotov cocktail. A marshal and soldier burst out to chase students around the campus but couldn't catch them. Students in my dormitory used slingshots to fire cherry bombs at the soldiers. One soldier reportedly opened fire on a student who was throwing cherry bombs from the window of another dorm, but no one was hurt.

Two nights later, after an airborne cherry bomb detonated near the face of a soldier guarding my dormitory building, U.S. Army military police with fixed bayonets burst into neighboring Lester Hall to search for weapons and firecrackers. They found two dismantled guns, a machete, a tear gas grenade, and fireworks.

One ice-cold December day, I was walking across campus with a marshal pacing along thirty feet behind me.

A white man, seeing me approach, stepped aside to allow me to pass.

Until now in Mississippi it had been customary instead for blacks to step aside for whites.

I said, "Thank you."

He glared at me.

"Fuck you, nigger," was his reply.

"What are you mad at me for?" I asked, "What have I ever done to you?"

"To me? Aw, nothing," he said, and sulked away.

I seldom paid any attention to the curses and yells. The thing

I did notice was the language the white students used, including the women students. I had often heard it said that blacks use bad language, but few blacks could match the creativity and vileness of the words many white students yelled. And the part that was most difficult for me to understand was that they did not care who was listening; they did not show any respect for their women, or any instructor or parent. This to me indicated that our state had degenerated to an extremely low level.

In the years that followed, you'd often hear white Mississippians blame "outsiders" for the chaos that accompanied my enrollment. Don't you believe it. It's a load of bull.

The state was shoved directly into a state of anarchy and physical rebellion by the governor and lieutenant governor of the state of Mississippi, Mississippi state officials, the Mississippi Citizens Councils, much of the state media, much of the Mississippi state legislature and the white community leaders of many towns across the state of Mississippi, some of whom organized road caravans of volunteers to travel to Oxford to blockade me and the federals from entering. At one point in the fighting, almost the entire Mississippi State Highway Patrol force decided to retake the university from the federals with their guns blazing.

While it is true that many outsiders from Mississippi and other states entered Oxford and joined the mob after the fighting started after sundown on September 30, 1962, and nonstudents formed the vast majority of those arrested, many Mississippians were arrested, and there were at least dozens of students engaged in provoking the riot and in doing some of the fiercest fighting. They later proudly called themselves the "brick-and-bottle brigades." And believe me, the people who tried to insult, torment, and eject me for months after my enrollment were all Ole Miss students, albeit a fairly small minority.

The political leadership of our state was, in my opinion, most responsible for what has gone on in Mississippi. They had the strongest hand. Where they have led, the people nearly always followed. That these leaders chose to make a showdown fight over integration at the college level seemed to me to be completely illogical.

With the state government taking the position that it did, the students had no choice but to act as they did. I talked with many, and they almost convinced me that most of them really believed that their position was right. Just as a matter of maintaining their pride, and backing up their families, who were the leaders of the state, they had to take a position similar to the one taken by the state of Mississippi.

I noticed that all kind of bumper stickers appeared. For instance, the symbol of Ole Miss was a kind of Confederate rebel colonel, and they invented a new colonel with his face painted black, and the bottom of the sticker was printed, "Kennedy's colonel."

About a month after I moved into Baxter Hall, somebody put a sign up over the water fountain in the hallway that read "White Only." It wasn't long before somebody else changed a couple of letters and it read "White Phoneys." In one classroom, if the light was not on, I would turn it on. Some of students would get up and turn the light out. Of course, no one else could see any better than I could.

Around the campus, if I happened to hold a door open for the student behind me, he might stop and not come in. Or, if one of them happened to be holding a door open, he might look up and see me and just turn the door loose. Tricks such as these did not distract me any more than they did the other students, and many students told me so. If you slammed a door or threw a bottle anywhere in our dormitory, it sounded all over the building. Whether they liked it or not, we were in it together.

The U.S. marshals were wonderful fellows. The living room of my apartment in Baxter Hall was used as the headquarters for the soldiers and marshals, complete with sleeping cots and communications equipment. There were always five or six soldiers and four or five marshals present. Armed troops guarded the building's doors.

Not that this was what I would consider an ideal college surrounding; nevertheless, it was a surrounding. Many people wrote and said that they knew that I must be very lonely. As a matter of fact, one of the hardest things for me to do was to find a way to be alone.

Every time I moved out of the building, the marshals and soldiers were reporting over their radios in code. A marshal who walked with me had a radio in his pocket hooked up to his ear like a hearing aid. The simple radio code for the soldiers was "Peanut," and a number.

They had code names for me: for the marshals, I was "the package," for the army, I was "cargo." "Hear this! Hear this! Peanut Six, this is Peanut Two proceeding from building 80 [cafeteria] to building 46 [Baxter Hall] with cargo."

People were always saying to me, "You are in the University of Mississippi, and that's the important thing." But so many unusual and unique circumstances were a part of my stay there that I seriously doubted that I was in a true sense a student of the university. I was inclined to go along with the diehard segregationists on this point. Just having a black in residence did not mean that the university had been integrated. Most of the time, I was perhaps the most segregated Negro in the world.

The only time I choked up was when a newsman remarked how hard it is for a white man to understand a black man, and I said, "You're right. But no black person understands me, either."

On March 23, 1963, my friend James Allen, Jr., came to visit me. He was the first black person to join me for dinner at the campus dining hall. He came to visit on the day a big football game was played. The game drew many visitors to the campus, and there was quite a commotion when we entered the cafeteria.

I had by now become a familiar, if widely hated, solitary image on campus, but the spectacle of not one, but two black men sitting down for a bite to eat in the university cafeteria like normal human beings was enough to cause total shock and confusion in the all-white crowd.

The managers rushed around like chickens with their heads cut off. All the black workers appeared from the kitchens and store-rooms to get a cautious view of the scene. They offered me discreet smiles and nods of approval and encouragement.

The campus police acted as if they wanted to do something, but didn't know what.

"Fuck you, niggers, get out of here or we'll kill you!" Students shouted all kinds of threats and obscenities, and beat on the tables with knives, forks, and plates, in full view of several legislators and members of the board of trustees who were in the crowded cafeteria at the time.

My friend and I finished our meal and went back to Baxter Hall.

"How in God's name do you put up with this?" he asked me.

"Oh, that's nothing." I smiled. "You should see them when they're really riled up!"

Another visitor was my cousin James C. Meredith, a captain in the air force. He came and stayed three or four days with me on the campus, and he was the only one to spend the night in my apartment. His visit really upset the military command. They first asked him not to wear his uniform. Then they asked him to stay at the military camp.

He understood the problems the army faced, especially if some-thing were to happen to him, and he tried in every way to cooper-ate, so long as it did not interfere with his visit with me. While on the campus, he used my Volkswagen, and unaccustomed to driving one, he had some difficulty at first in getting it started. The marshals thought his conduct was superb when a large crowd of students, shouting insults at him, gathered around the car. When it started, he simply nodded and smiled politely at them.

The hostility did not bother me, or affect my studies. As it turned out, my grades were good. I have always been a good stu-dent, and the University of Mississippi was no exception. I found it more difficult to study there than I did anywhere else, because now I was suddenly the man in the news. This was the real pressure for me at the University of Mississippi, learning to live as a public figure in the national spotlight.

People always asked me, "Did any of the students ever make a gesture of friendship toward you?" I replied, "What do people think Mississippians are? They are human, too. Everywhere I have ever been I have had friends and friendship. The University of Mississippi was no exception."

One might get the impression that I was defending Mississippi whites by taking this position. But my purpose was not to defend Mississippi. Rather, it was to place all white Americans in the same basic category with the Mississippians. It is only in this perspective that we can ever begin to comprehend the nature of the racial and social problems facing the United States then and today.

There was never a moment at the University of Mississippi that I did not have more friends than I could accommodate. Friendship is always expressed in relative terms. There are no exclusive acts, words, or deeds than can be used to judge the quantity any more than the quality of friendliness. A straight face when everyone else is sneering may be worth more than a pat on the back when everyone else is screaming that they want to kill you.

The students showed their position in practically every way. There were many, many students who visited my room in the evenings, until a clandestine group of segregationist students called the "Rebel Underground" started taking names and publishing the list.

Whenever a student got up and moved as I sat down in the dining hall, other white students would always fill the table around me in a defensive bubble of courtesy, even though there were empty tables nearby. The classes, except the first- and second-year courses that I had to take, were generally congenial. Some students were talkative and friendly in each of my regular classes. Many spoke on the streets and sidewalks, probably more than they would normally.

The second week that I was on the campus a pretty little freshman girl came up to me in the Student Union as I turned away from my mailbox and, with hundreds of dumbfounded students looking on, introduced herself by name, and said in the sweetest, thickest southern tones, "I C-O-M-E from AR-Kan-sas and I just wanted to tel-l y-o-u how proud we are to have you he-r-e."

I was completely surprised, almost shocked.

In my first weeks at Ole Miss, I started periodically jotting diary-type notes in a journal, a habit I continued for the next fifty years, creating the basis for the book you're now holding in your hands. One of the earliest entries reads: "The decision is made to keep the marshals and troops on the campus until I complete my course, it is all right with me, but I hope that will not be necessary. I think the marshals have been superb. They have upheld an image of America, that the law must be obeyed, no matter what they may think of it or what anybody else may think of it. But they are certainly a distraction on the campus. The thing that grieves me most about all this is that the students are not getting the best college results because they are spending too much time looking on at these various events involving me. I did not get much studying done that first week, and I don't think anybody else did."

Many little comical, and sometimes annoying, incidents occurred around the campus during the first two months. For example, I had dinner one day with a professor who had eaten with me several times. After dinner, one of the students in the dining hall said to him, "Say, Doctor, who are you going to be having dinner with when your nigger friend leaves?" The professor laughed. "Well," he said, "it looks as if I'm going to have to start eating with you."

By early 1963, a coordinated campaign of terror and harassment was underway at the University of Mississippi, aimed at white students and faculty who dared treat me as a fellow American citizen. Professors who were friendly to me received obscene phone calls and death threats delivered by letter. The little daughter of a professor who had invited me to dinner was given a black doll at a party with a card that read "nigger lover."

After having dinner with me, one white student was the target of a weeks-long campaign of constant threats, including live cherry bombs rolled into his toilet stall. Several white students were run out of the university by the threats, and other students and faculty left in disgust at the poisoned atmosphere on the campus.

I loved to play golf.

And I wasn't going to let the fact that I was the most heavily guarded man at the center of a virtual combat zone interfere with my plans to play golf.

The University of Mississippi had a good, rugged golf course.

I had learned to play the game at the age of fourteen, as a caddy. For some typical Mississippi reason the Kosciusko Golf Course had adopted a rule that barred the use of white caddies. Even the use of a player's own son was discouraged. As a result the forty cents for nine holes and seventy-five cents for eighteen holes was reserved for the Negro boys of the area. The caddies were permitted to play on the course on Sunday mornings as long as no white players were using the course.

I had planned to use the golf course as my major recreation on the campus, but during the first semester I simply did not have the time. History professor Dr. Jim Silver, remembering his promise to do something to make life more wholesome for me at the university during the second semester, asked me to play a game of golf with him. I had planned to go off campus, but I told him that I would come by his office after lunch if I didn't. I don't know if I really had a choice, because the security arrangements had been made for me to play golf. As soon as I returned from lunch and lay down for a short rest, the chief marshal came in to inquire if I had forgotten about my golf game. The army command and the campus police wanted to know the exact program.

I put on my crepe-soled shoes, since I didn't have my golf equipment with me. Professor Silver was waiting for me at his office. We walked the block to the clubhouse to pay our green fees. The club manager was expecting me, of course, and was as friendly as one could imagine. I bought a couple of used balls, some tees, and a season's ticket, entitling me to unlimited play on the course for the complete school year.

I was just a black guy playing golf in Mississippi on a Saturday morning, but this simple idea created a spectacle.

The course was crowded with players, although it was very windy and cold. This could have been because it was Valentine's Day, but a part of the large crowd can definitely be credited to my being on the course. The campus police were out in full force. Eisenhower probably never had as many Secret Service men guarding his golf games as I had United States marshals watching me play my first game at the University of Mississippi. The army was also out in force, including two helicopters that circled the field of play constantly.

The very first drive I hit sent a contingent of soldiers scurrying for safety in the graveyard of the Confederate soldiers killed a hundred years before. The ball was lost in the cemetery and I never found it. We moved slowly over the hilly course: The marshals were tense and apprehensive, and Silver seemed to be wondering whether he would live long enough to get out of it. I was really out of practice, since I had not played regularly for two years or more, but I was warming up as the game progressed.

When we reached the number 3 green, which was close to the road and directly in front of the veterans' apartments, there was a large crowd of spectators. The campus police and soldiers kept them across the street, but they didn't keep them from shouting and making remarks. My game suddenly improved. I was about 150 yards out on what appeared to be my third shot (actually it was my fourth, because I had completely missed one shot on the other side of the hill), with everybody watching the Negro play golf.

This was one of the first times in history, maybe the first time, that a black man and a white man ever played golf together as equals in Mississippi.

More jeeps and trucks full of soldiers appeared. Many of them probably were off duty and just wanted to see. The main army camp was very close to this hole. I swung and had no idea where the ball was going, but it headed straight for the flag and landed on the front edge of the green, stopping dead about twenty-five or thirty feet from the pin.

Everything got quiet.

The others approached the green and we readied for the putt. I hadn't come within two feet of the hole all day with a putt, and in addition, I was using Silver's putter. I approached the ball, lined the putt up with professional-like care, gave it a hard tap, and watched. To my great surprise it went straight toward the hole, stopping only a half inch away. We waited a couple of minutes to see if it would drop, but it didn't. The hecklers were at a loss for words.

The number 4 tee was just as much in view of our audience. I teed up my ball for the demonstration shot. My first drive had gone into the cemetery, another had gone into the woods, one had dribbled off the tee in front of me, none had gone down the fairway all day.

I used my old, but never understood by anyone, long-ball-hitting form from the days when I could hit a ball 250 yards in the air, although I was only five feet six inches tall and weighed 120 pounds. It was a fast, long backswing and a swift, hard downswing, which resulted in both my feet rising off the ground.

After reading a few golf books, I concluded that it is a mystery that I ever hit the ball in the first place. Anyhow, I swung, and it was straight down the middle and with a strong wind directly behind it; it turned out to be the longest ball that I ever hit on the University of Mississippi golf course. I never came within fifty feet of the distance again on the same hole, and I saw few drives that ever went farther during the many rounds that I was to play later.

It took us more than two and a half hours to play seven holes. Professor Silver appeared quite relieved and jumped at my suggestion that we go home at this time. I think he had had second thoughts about endeavoring to change Mississippi's social patterns in such an exposed arena.

I didn't play again for over a month, but after I started to play in the spring, I played fairly regularly. The security measures varied slightly from game to game. The second time they used only one helicopter for air cover. And the first time they decided not to use the helicopter, the most fantastic security precautions were taken. Soldiers on foot completely surrounded the golf course.

The professor who became my regular playing partner seemed the most inappropriate possible. As far as I know, he had never lifted his voice in defense or defiance of anything. He was nervous and fearful. All he did was perform his duties as head of his department during the school year and spend every summer in a villa in France. The professor just turned up one day and we played golf. Unlike the rest of the vanguard at the university, such as Jim Silver, who played with me occasionally to fulfill some sort of obligation that they felt they had, the professor played with me because he liked the game. We didn't fight any wars, we just played golf.

There were many side incidents to my golfing experiences at the university. It was not unusual for my ball to disappear from the fairway when there were other players in the area. Occasionally, someone would hit a ball into our midst. The first time that I drove my own car to the clubhouse all four tires were flat when I returned. The club manager said, "I thought I heard a funny noise outside." It happened on three subsequent occasions. Strangely, they never cut the tires, but just removed the valve stem. A couple of fraternity houses overlooked the golf course, and the boys inside always kept up a barrage of shouts and curses. I am sure that they must have been responsible for the flat tires as well.

My greatest concern was for the protection of my family; in my own case there was little danger of physical harm. I was constantly assured by the federal officers around me that I was more heavily guarded than the president of the United States. The Mississippi press even checked the record and determined to its biased satisfaction that I was the best-guarded individual in history.

Also, the press corps had a completely free run of the campus and kept their cameras, mikes, and pens ever ready and watching for any hostile move. I knew that the opposition would probably turn its attention to my family, since it was virtually impossible to get at me without getting caught.

"Some son of a bitch tried to kill me!"

My youngest sister, Willie Lou, was on the phone, in a state of shock.

"What's going on? What happened?" I pleaded, feeling powerless to help her as I was hundreds of miles away in Chicago.

"Some son of a bitch tried to shoot me, but I jumped behind the refrigerator."

"Let me talk to Cap." My father came on the line. "Cap, what happened?"

"They shot up the house," he said. "They missed Willie Lou by an inch. We're all right. The local police offered to stand guard, but I turned them down, because that would just give the shooters a better chance. We all know that they were involved in the shooting."

It was December 23, 1962, and the beast of white supremacy had lashed out in homicidal rage in the dead of night, not at me but at my family. At the University of Mississippi I was surrounded by a small army of armed federal bodyguards. But my family was utterly defenseless and alone, living in a house in the countryside, the easiest of targets.

My sister was only a sophomore in high school. She had just opened the refrigerator door when a carefully aimed blast of buckshot from a deer rifle, clearly aimed at her, crashed through a window into the kitchen, followed by blasts that shattered all the front windows of the house.

My son, John, and my mother and father offer me moral support by phone from my parents' house, spring of 1963. This house was shredded by gunfire from white supremacists a few weeks before, and the buckshot missed my sister's head by a few inches. *Photo courtesy of the James Meredith collection*

Ordinarily the white supremacists were not as cruel to black females as to black men, perhaps because so many white men were raised by black nannies. But my status as the black man who first shattered the crucible of segregation in Mississippi was more than sufficient grounds for my whole family to be put to death.

A car loaded with some of Kosciusko's leading white citizens was seen parked about fifty yards down the street with the motor running. It pulled up in front of our house and its occupants shot the house up with buckshot. The shots not only broke out all the front windows, but were of such size and power that they split or broke the wooden beams. The holes were from an inch to an inch and a half in diameter. Any of the slugs would have killed a human being.

My parents were asleep in the back room and were not hit by the gunfire. Luckily, my sister dove behind the refrigerator and was not struck by the gunfire.

But she began to die that night, as she was seized by a crippling depression and frustration from which she never recovered until she died a few years later.

For the first time, I felt afraid for my family. I told my parents that I might not return to Ole Miss. It was too dangerous, and the white supremacists had made their point. My father said nothing, but my mother insisted that I go back to school.

Everyone in town, of course, knew who the attackers were. The blacks in the neighborhood saw the car parked there for some time. Not only was it a leading white citizen who led the attack and did some of the shooting, but he was also a law enforcement officer. Other members of the gang included officers of the local police department.

If the attack had taken place at any point before my enrollment, I am sure that I would never have gone through with it. But it was too late now. It would not have made sense to drop out at this point. Medgar Evers told me that he could not get a single person to go with him to Kosciusko to investigate the incident. They were all afraid.

The day after the shooting, I went to Kosciusko. My father said, "Get in the truck. Let's go downtown. We've got to show the niggers and the white folks that you ain't scared."

"I ain't scared!" I exclaimed to my father.

"Yeah," he replied, "I know that, and you know that, but *they* don't know that."

So we drove downtown and he told me to park in front of the police station. We walked all around the downtown square, shaking hands with everybody, going into some of the stores, shaking hands with everybody, black and white. Then we went back to the truck and drove home.

My father thought it was crucial to demonstrate that we had an attitude of total confidence and strength.

I pleaded with the federal government to give my family some physical protection, but Bobby Kennedy's Justice Department refused, saying that was the job of local police. They, of course, were the people who tried to kill my family.

I stayed away from my family for a long while. I wanted the

enemy to think only of killing me. I publicly ignored the incident to give the impression to the enemy that I was unmoved by such tactics. It worked. There were no further shootings at close range, though there were several incidents of long-range rifle fire in the next few weeks following the attack.

My sister Willie Lou left Mississippi after finishing high school and disappeared. I eventually found her living as a live-in maid in California. Later, she came to New York where I was attending law school and lived with me for a while. Then she went to Milwaukee to make it on her own.

I never saw her again.

She had called me in New York a couple of weeks before she was found dead and said that she wanted me to come to Milwaukee to see her. I had a speaking engagement in Illinois less than a hundred miles away and promised her I would come see her after the speech.

Ordinarily, I always do whatever I promise. But for some reason, I did not go to Milwaukee to see my sister. I didn't even call and say that I was not coming. Instead, I got in touch with some old schoolmates and stayed in Chicago.

After my sister's death, I learned that she had made the most elaborate plans of her entire life for my visit. She had spent days organizing a celebration for her big brother. My mother spent the rest of her life grieving for her.

I have always tried to live a life without regrets. One of the few things in almost eighty years of living that I cannot positively say that I have no regrets about is the death of my sister. I have never recovered from it.

She never recovered from the shock of the experience of that night of the shooting, and from the turmoil of our family's experiences with the University of Mississippi affair. It shook her faith in mankind. Why shouldn't it?

Since her death, I have been painfully aware of the minutest feelings of other people, especially young people.

My baby sister Willie Lou was found hanging from a rope in the basement of a dreary apartment building in Milwaukee, Wisconsin.

She was twenty-five.

For a while, I wasn't sure if I should stay at the University of Mississippi.

I looked back over the past months at Ole Miss with a bittersweet taste and a pressing uncertainty about registering for the spring semester. Was all the fanfare worth it? Constant harassment, constant military escorts, constant cameras, mikes, and reporters. More important, fear for the safety of my family had become a pressing concern.

My stay there had become a kind of media circus, and I had trouble managing the stresses of being a kind of global celebrity and symbol for an oppressed people, while trying to finish my degree. I began to contemplate what it would mean if I didn't return in January 1963 for my final courses.

The real question we were facing then was whether black Americans would have access to the education that their states offered. This was the basic issue—the right of access. The right to fail is just as important as the right to succeed.

The great purpose I felt was to make way for the "average Negro." Black progress until then had been on the basis of selection, the selection of a "talented tenth" or token star Negroes to be treated as American citizens. Great efforts have always been made to get the superior, the above-average Negro the right to certain things. This was a philosophy I always thought was very dangerous. To make way for the above-average can, of course, be only token progress. But if we can make way for the average, the above average will always find their place. If getting a degree from the University of Mississippi were all I ever did with my life, I would have done very little.

Throughout the first semester I received about two hundred letters a day. Most of the people who wrote, particularly the Negroes, said that they had great admiration for me. They were praying and hoping that I would make it. Their basic attitude alarmed me. The letter that alarmed me most came from students at Alabama State College, a Negro school. The major message conveyed in this letter was that they had committed themselves to God and to me, to prove to the world that Negroes are somebody. The letter was alarming, because they had relieved themselves of all responsibility. They thought there was nothing more that they had to do. I felt that every young Negro must make his personal contribution toward the accomplishment of his freedom. No one man can fight alone. You can't confine the struggle for human freedom and dignity to one place or to one man. To free the right arm and cut the left arm off—this is not progress.

I told my friends that they could pat me on the back and tell me how great I am, they could pile all the adjectives they wanted to on my name—that still made me no less human. I had the problem of resolving whether my staying at the university was worth the intimidation and harassment that my family had to endure. My father was seventy-one years old, worked hard all his life, lived a good life, paid all his debts, never was in trouble, was a good citizen—but he couldn't sleep in peace without the danger of someone attacking him violently.

He had not gone to the University of Mississippi. Yet, one night, they fired into his house with shotguns. Our system of laws allowed such a thing to happen, and it was tragic that the opposition had degenerated to that level.

In early January I issued a statement to reporters that reflected the stakes as I saw them: "We are engaged in a bitter war for the equality of our citizens. The enemy is determined, resourceful, and unprincipled. There are no rules of war for which he has respect."

The most realistic understanding of what my family and I were going through came in letters from people in foreign countries. But the letters from this country, especially from Negroes, often did not even acknowledge that I had any right to be concerned about the welfare of my family. For a long time, not one in a hundred seemed to have understood at all. This pointed out to me the unrealistic hopes that the Negroes hold about the future. In their future to conceive of all the costs, both physical and mental, they showed that they were failing to realize the real price that they would themselves someday have to pay if they were to do their part. They more or less seemed to expect a solution to their problem from some lofty development, or from a leader like Dr. King or a "chosen one" like myself. They were still looking for some miracle to save them.

It was still clear to me that everybody was seeking to lighten or lessen the tension, not to change or correct things in a basic sense. That's just like putting salve on a wound when the blood has been poisoned. It's treating the symptom, rather than the cause.

The first step in countering this move by the opposition was to attack the age-old idea that the Negro was duty-bound to succeed whenever he was given an opportunity and that he was not entitled to equality of opportunity, which included the possibility of failing, in the first place.

It appeared to me that "the right to fail" in a publicly supported institution was just as important as "the right to pass." The general feeling seemed to be that the Negro did not have this basic right, although the whites were granted it. I can never accept a double standard. There is no right or privilege that I would concede solely to the white American, not even for a minute.

Then, on a Sunday just after New Year's, I had an experience that convinced me that, unless something could be done, we would get less in advantages than we would lose in disadvantages. An old gentleman who had been the first Negro to visit me at the university called to ask if I would go with him to a funeral in Oxford. A lot of people there wanted to meet me. After the funeral was over, all the people came and shook hands with me, from the relatives of the deceased down to the Boy Scout who had been directing traffic.

Several insisted that I stop by the house. I did, and then I decided to go visit one of my ex-classmates from Jackson State College, who is a high-school teacher in Oxford.

The old gentleman and I went up to my former classmate's door. His wife answered, but she wouldn't let us in. So we left and went back to the house of the sister of the lady who had been buried that day. You know how Negroes are at a funeral. They had every kind of food and every kind of pie laid out. The only thing expected was that you get a plate. So I did. And in came this fellow who had been my classmate.

He said he wanted to see me a minute *privately*, and I told him to wait a minute and I'd get through eating. He acted a little apprehensive, and I said, are you in a hurry? He said no, no, not particularly. We went back to an empty room.

He said, "*Please* don't come to see me anymore."

For the first time in my life, someone invited me not to visit him. He requested that I not come to town to see him anymore. He said he'd been informed by his principal, in the local Negro school, that any teacher who had anything to do with me would lose his job. He was a very pitiful sight. He begged me for understanding and mercy. He even gave me another reason for not wanting to associate with me. He was afraid his father-in-law would lose *his* job. His father-in-law was a street cleaner in Oxford, probably not making more than twenty-five dollars a week. Here was a man who would not only give up his rights and privileges and liberty, but give up his soul. And for what?

This incident played a decisive part in making me focus on the situation. I realized that I had to think out what steps I should take. In my bedroom, I wrote out a statement for the press. I pointed out that no major issues had been decided, legally or officially, illegally or unofficially, and that the enemy still observed no rules of war. Some standard must be established, I said, so that those who are fighting for equality of opportunity and those who are fighting for the right to oppress can clash without disaster falling upon either side. I knew that there was no use registering for a second semester unless some changes could be made in both the local situation and the broad one.

The rumors that I might not stay produced a most heartening change in the mail that came to me. The president of the student body in a Negro school out in Texas wrote a letter signed by a number of the students. Of course, they hoped that I would find my way clear to remain at the University of Mississippi. But this was a minor point. The main point was that they realized their obligation to move forward and were prepared to work hard for their aims, regardless of what happened in Mississippi. This was a manifestation that I had long looked for, and the same trend soon began to appear in a strong majority of the letters from Negroes, especially those under thirty-five.

I had many Negroes tell me that they'd been so involved in my struggle that they couldn't sleep at night. One of my good friends put it this way: Every Negro in America is in college.

Citizenship by bayonet was no citizenship at all. The white power structure had not changed except in a direct relationship to the presence of force. However, I was as determined as ever to break the system of white supremacy.

On January 7, 1963, I arose early in the morning and wrote a short statement for the press. I called my wife to inform her that I was about to make a statement so that she would know what it was all about when she heard it over the radio.

It was now six o'clock in the morning. I sat down at my portable typewriter and made copies of the statement. I shaved and went through my morning routine. At seven I called one of my classmates, who had been enrolled as a student in one of my classes by a leading newspaper syndicate to keep tabs on me, and told him that I would be releasing a statement at eight o'clock at my dormitory.

In the largest news conference of my life, more than a thousand people came to witness my decision, including the world-famous black author James Baldwin, the author of *The Fire Next Time.*

I made the following statement: "After listening to all arguments, evaluations, and positions and weighing all this against my personal possibilities and circumstances, I have concluded that the black man should not return to the University of Mississippi. The prospects for him are too unpromising." The crowd gasped. Some Mississippi characters in the audience exploded in expressions of joy.

Then I added a surprise twist: "However, I have decided that I, J. H. Meredith, will register for the second semester at the University of Mississippi."

In other words, I would not return as a "black man." I would return first and foremost as myself, as an American citizen, not as the Negro star of a media circus. I would return on my own terms and force the situation to become as "normal" as possible.

I registered for my final term without interference, and in a symbolic gesture, the United States military moved their camp from the campus to a location off campus.

And in fact, the spring semester manifested a definite improvement for me at Ole Miss. Petty annoyances persisted throughout, such as flattened tires and obscene phone calls, but for the most part the overt threat of violence declined with the passage of time. Still, I remained perhaps the most segregated black in the world. Every weekend I went to Jackson to visit my wife and son. Only two weekends were spent on campus during my eleven-month stay. That was one weekend more than most of the students, as Ole Miss was, and is, a "country club" school.

After that statement on January 7, some conditions did begin to change. Before, I had never noticed the campus police around where I was, only the U.S. marshals and the soldiers. But when I came from my first class after the statement, the campus police were there as I came out.

My wife, Mary June, stayed in college in Jackson, working toward her degree at Jackson State. Our son, John Howard, who turned three in January, was living with my parents in Kosciusko. This was nothing new to my wife. We spent most of our courtship discussing my plan to come back to Mississippi someday, and I guess you could say her understanding that I would try to do this sometime was almost part of the marriage contract. She was truly marvelous through all of it. I called her after I entered the university, and she picked up the phone and was so calm you would have thought she had just won a card game.

My entire crusade at Ole Miss, you see, was a love story.

It is a story about my love for America and my love for Mississippi. It is a story about the love my father and mother blessed me with. And it is the story of how I was comforted, sustained, and inspired by the love of my wife, Mary June. She was a remarkable woman.

Here are passages from her letters to me during my ordeal at Ole Miss:

> Dear My Man, How are things with you? Do you know that I love you very much? When I get lonesome I think of the wonderful years we have spent together. I think of Japan, Tokyo, San Francisco, Canada, Mexico, Taiwan, Okinawa, where we have loved and have been very, very happy. I am sorry I acted so foolish this weekend. If you left me I don't know what I would do. I will feel like running down the aisle to get my degree. Most of all, I want to see you get yours from Ole Miss. Oh James, I am proud of you. To think you are my husband. You, the Man of the Year. Oh, I love you; don't ever leave me. No one can love you like I do. No one!!! I wish you were here. Then I would enjoy the rain. You are indeed what one calls "the perfect husband." You are, James, and believe me, I love you for it. Darling, I love you. I can't wait until I am in your arms

again. Be sure to think of me always. Your wife, June
Meredith. P.S. Write often, it helps ease the pain. Telephone
bill—$5.86, Light bill last month—$7.86.

My mother and father sent me a letter on January 12, 1963,
that shows you their attitude: "Jesus Christ had to suffer and he
was the Son of God. God is with us at all times. Don't you worry.
Try to learn all you can and no one can take that away from you. I
know you can do it. With so many praying for you, you can't fail."

By January 1963, the number of soldiers had dropped to 350.
I thought they should have all been long gone. There had been no
major outbreaks of violence since October 1962, despite several
close calls.

Death was a constant traveling companion to black Americans
in the South who had achieved notoriety in asserting our rights.
In those days, the possibility of death was a fact of life. We talked
about it casually.

"I know something is going to happen to me," Medgar Evers
told me one day in early June 1963, as he and the NAACP led a
series of sit-ins and marches in the state capital of Jackson.

"We are applying too much pressure for there not to be a reaction," Medgar predicted. "Retaliation is inevitable."

The NAACP national headquarters in New York was behind
most of the campaign. It was anxious to try to get into the ball-
game with Dr. Martin Luther King, Jr., and his Southern Christian
Leadership Conference, which had been staging mass demonstrations in major cities throughout the South.

Medgar was not afraid. He was a good soldier and a good organization man, but he asked his New York headquarters office to let
a little air out of the Jackson campaign. The national office wanted
to keep pressing, because the headlines were good.

Medgar was extremely conscious of the prospect of his being killed.

His murder by a white sniper and Citizens Council member on June 12, 1963, a week after we spoke, had a most profound effect on me both publicly and privately. Since I had been considered the most likely target of assassination in Mississippi, it took time for me to absorb the reality of his death. A few minutes after he was shot, my wife telephoned the news to me from Jackson, even before it was known that he was dead. I went back to bed but I could not sleep. I felt shattered.

By midmorning on the day after Medgar was killed, I released a statement on his death and the removal of the soldiers from the campus of the University of Mississippi. Many considered this statement to be the most bitter that I had ever made.

> At this crucial moment, following the death of one of my best friends, one of America's greatest fighters for freedom and most trustworthy leaders, as well as the person perhaps most responsible for my admission to the University of Mississippi, I felt obligated to take my stand, to take the steps that my best judgment leads me to believe will most advance our cause.
>
> Early this morning, one of America's leading young men, Mr. Medgar Evers, was shot in the back under the cover of darkness, and killed. Without warning and without cause, he was murdered. A Negro's life is not worth the air it requires to keep it alive in Mississippi.
>
> Medgar Evers was one of my best and most beloved friends. He served his country with the pledge of his life during World War II. For the next eighteen years he devoted his life to making America truly the land of the free. We must not fail him now. We must continue to march toward his life's goal.
>
> This system under which we live in Mississippi, and

throughout the South, must be changed at any cost . . . I want to point out that if you hear anyone placing the blame on some insignificant person, extremist, or radical individual, he is just trying to deceive you and the public. The blame clearly rests with the governors of the southern states and their defiant and provocative actions; it rests with the blind courts and prejudiced juries. It is known both by blacks and whites that no white man will be punished for any crime against a Negro. Look at what happened to the guilty parties in the University of Mississippi riots. Nothing!

I was consumed with the idea of death for many years.

When I enrolled at the University of Mississippi I was aware that it was possible I could die. But in my own psychology, I was already a dead man. Did I wish to die? I honestly don't know. I do know that I was prepared to die for what I believed in. I also know that I have always considered myself a good soldier, and a good soldier is one who is always around to fight. I never believed that a dead soldier was a good soldier.

On August 18, 1963, I prepared to graduate from the University of Mississippi.

I was fairly impressed and surprised that this day had come, as I'd expected to be dead by then. I was surprised that I actually survived fighting the system of white supremacy. Survival was the most remarkable achievement of my last three years in Mississippi.

I had fully expected to be killed.

Many of my friends and relatives were looking forward to my graduation day. Mrs. Kenny Smith had vowed many times that she was going to "that graduation if it is the last thing in the world that I ever do." I didn't really think that she would go, because she

rarely left Jackson and seldom went anywhere except to work and to church, but she stuck by her pledge and came.

There were so many blacks going to Oxford that we formed an unplanned caravan, which included a beefed-up force of U.S. marshals.

You need to understand the context of this time to begin to comprehend how earth-shattering an event this was. A caravan of black Americans was heading for the campus of the University of Mississippi to celebrate a black man getting his diploma. This was to be a day that practically cut Mississippi history in half. Before this day, I was an experiment, a fluke, an outlier, and a walking target with a bull's-eye on my head.

But if I managed to live through this day, I would be a marker in American history, a precedent, and a definitive statement of accomplished fact. Not only would education in Mississippi and the crucible of the Deepest South be "desegregated," but the previously rebellious state itself would enshrine this fact with a gold seal on a piece of paper declaring that I had earned a bachelor's degree in political science from the state university.

That morning I drove my wife and son from our house in Jackson to Kosciusko, where we stopped at my parents' home and enjoyed a meal that my mother had proudly prepared. The caravan was joined here by several carloads of relatives and hometown friends. Some of them had come from thousands of miles away to attend my graduation.

In addition to the general excitement of the two-hundred-mile trip, the atmosphere was filled with tension, and the fear that we might be attacked along the route. From Kosciusko, we drove north on the Natchez Trace Parkway, a federal government project, where the facilities were not officially segregated. Just before we turned off the parkway onto a Mississippi highway, we stopped at a gas station to use the restrooms, because they were not segregated.

I was very concerned that something might happen at the

outdoor ceremony itself. The Citizens Council had promised to disrupt the affair. Both my young son and my now-elderly father would be there along with my friends and family, and we would be highly conspicuous in a multitude of white faces. I prayed that no violence or disrespect would come to them.

Ironically, the graduation was to take place in the same place where the battle of Ole Miss had taken place in September 1962.

In another move to deliver a symbolic message, I wore the exact same clothes I had worn the first day I registered on October 1, 1962: dark suit, white shirt, blood-red necktie, and black shoes. The only notable difference was a button I had on. It was Governor Barnett's famous campaign slogan: "NEVER! NEVER!" I wore it upside down inside my graduation robe.

Surprisingly, there was no opposition to being my marching mate. My marching partner in the first lineup was a young lady, and I heard some of the other graduates asking her how she was so lucky to get all of that "free publicity," assuming that she would be in the papers and on television with me. She appeared disappointed when a student came in late and the lineup had to be changed. No unpleasant remarks were made by the students, at least none that I could hear.

On our march to the Grove we passed through the Lyceum Building where the U.S. government had set up its headquarters on September 30, 1962, the day I came to the campus. As I passed, I took I special notice of the bullet marks that were still there, a consequence of the fighting between the state of Mississippi and the federal government of the United States. I had looked at these bullet marks many times during my days as a student. They were still there fifty years later.

We marched on past the statue of the Confederate soldier, the symbol of the blood that had been shed one hundred years ago in defense of the system of white supremacy. It was at the foot of this statue that General Walker had harangued the mob on the night of the revolt of the state of Mississippi.

We ended our march in the Grove, where the graduation exercises were being held in the open air. This was near the Circle where most of the riot had taken place on September 30. To one who knows the realities of life in Mississippi, the most striking thing about the Grove was the Negroes scattered throughout the audience. They were there in large numbers. Frankly, I was very surprised to see so many Negroes, but very pleased indeed.

The ceremony was routine. The speeches were rather mild, and only one speaker referred to the controversial issues. He mentioned something about the encroachment upon Mississippi's prerogatives by the federal government. The chancellor handed the diplomas to the graduates as their names were called and they passed across the stage. When my name was called, the chancellor handed me my diploma, shook my hand, and mumbled some remark of congratulations in the fading afternoon light. It was 5:12 p.m.

The marshals braced themselves and the cameras recorded the event. I noticed two familiar faces. One was my old Negro friend from Oxford, who had been so faithful in his support of me even when so much pressure was being applied to him. He kept his distance, standing about fifty yards away at the corner of a building. He had to live there after I was gone. The other was that of James Allen, Jr., the only black face among the many marshals, news reporters, and cameramen standing very near the stage. His boldness had placed him in a position to get the closest in all photographs taken of the chancellor handing me my diploma.

I looked out at the curious and staring audience. Cameras were clicking in every direction.

There in the audience was my father, Moses Arthur Meredith. He was sitting right up front to witness the whole event.

This was the first time I ever saw him sit in an audience with white Mississippians on a nonsegregated basis. Throughout his life he had given his all in an effort to make Mississippi and the world free for his children and his children's children. He had lived to see the day that he had always longed for but had never really expected to see. At age seventy-two, after a lifetime of planning and working to break the system of white supremacy in Mississippi, months after his home had been shredded by the bullets of the enemy, he had lived to witness this event.

He was born in 1890, the same year Mississippi adopted the constitution that made white supremacy the official and legal way of life in Mississippi. He had lived through it all, every day of it, seventy-two years of segregation and discrimination. The terror, the lynchings, the humiliations, the dread of being treated as sub-human.

Sitting on my father's knee was my three-year-old son, not yet aware of the existence of a wounded but still-vibrant culture of white supremacy that would seek in every possible way to render him less than human. He seemed quite amused by the events. My gratification came from the hope that my son might be a future governor or president.

The crowd seemed stunned into total silence.

Nothing unusual happened. I was amazed, and greatly relieved.

As I walked down from the stage, I had a smile on my face. I felt that I had finally begun to fulfill my "divine responsibility," my mission from God.

Black Americans in Mississippi could no longer be held down by the directives of the most cherished and sanctified institution of white supremacy. As noted by my attorney, Constance Baker Motley, the Ole Miss crisis also served as a vivid "demonstration of what the Constitution means in practical applications." Oxford had indeed become the symbol of mass resistance, and was the final gasp of the Civil War. Thus the Constitution, as Motley pointed out, "was put to the test and survived."

David Sansing, a longtime University of Mississippi history professor, told a reporter years later, "This event at the University of Mississippi, I think, was a major turning point in the civil rights movement because here it was decided how far a state would go in defiance of a federal court order and it was decided how far the federal government would go in enforcing that court order." He added, "I think the ultimate conclusion of the civil rights movement was drawn right here. And I think James Howard Meredith was the individual who shaped these circumstances, and he achieved exactly what he wanted to achieve."

The credit for the outcome at Ole Miss in 1962 belonged to the Founding Fathers of the United States, who created in the Constitution the principle that all citizens are equal and should be treated as equal. And the credit belonged to the executive branch of the federal government, which made the decision to use physical force to insure the rights of citizenship for a single American.

But I did not see this day as a major triumph or victory. The whole episode at Ole Miss was an insult to me and my family. The thought of having to go through all of this hassle to be able to enjoy a simple right of citizenship that was mine by birth was offensive to me, as it should be for all Americans.

After the ceremony, we marched back to the campus to discard our caps and gowns.

Just as I stepped outside the building two young white boys rushed up to me; one of them grabbed my hand, gave it a very hard squeeze, and said, "I just wanted to congratulate you!" The two boys identified themselves as the grandsons of an English teacher at the University of Mississippi.

I had visited Robert F. Kennedy in his Justice Department office in Washington, D.C., a few months after I enrolled, and he told me something that said a lot about him, and about America, and summed up my campaign to attend Ole Miss.

"In this society," he said, "people only get what they're willing to fight for."

His father, Joe Kennedy, got to a position of tremendous power and wealth by fighting hard, every step of the way. He was a ruthless, sometimes vicious bare-knuckle Irish fighter, and a lot of that rubbed off on his son Bobby. John Kennedy may have appeared super-cool and controlled, but he, too, was a tough political prizefighter. I respected that about the Kennedy brothers. They were, until 1961, lifelong collaborators with white supremacy, but when forced to confront it, they eventually recognized black Americans as full American citizens, because black people were fighting.

You only get what you're willing to fight for. And as my father often said to me, "You can get anything you want, if you go about it the right way."

In other words, life in America is combat, and you can't rely on the government or a handout to achieve success. You've got to work your butt off for it, outwork and out-think your opponents, and demand what's rightfully yours.

That's what I did at Ole Miss.

After the graduation ceremony, I invited all of the black attendees to come to Baxter Hall to see the place where I'd lived while a student at Ole Miss. Captain Meredith walked along beside me from the campus center to the dormitory.

This was a classic, typical, American scene—a parent walking across a university campus with his child. But for two black men to enact this scene at that time and place was nothing less than a cultural earthquake. It was revolutionary. It had never happened before in the history of my state. I cannot put into words the emotions I felt then and feel now about that moment.

Later that day, my father got me away from the crowd for a private talk.

He wanted to express his satisfaction at having lived to see this day. As he evaluated the University of Mississippi ordeal and the graduation exercises, he told me his surprising conclusion about the Mississippi whites.

He said, "These people can be decent."

He had watched the whites at the graduation ceremony. He

knew these people, he had lived with them all his life. For seventy-two years he had seen the meanness and contempt in their looks. Now he had witnessed a fading in this meanness. The all-pervading hatred that accompanied every contact between the whites and blacks in Mississippi, at least for one day, had been missing from their faces.

"These people can be decent."

To my father's amazement, the look of hatred was missing from the white faces.

He was a man who never let up. He always kept the pressure on. When I was a boy, he used to always tell me that I would "never amount to a hill of beans." If you grew up in the hill country of central Mississippi with its bare clay hills, you knew what that meant. You can plant all the beans that you want to. You will get a bean stalk, but you rarely ever get a bean to grow on the stalk.

My father said to me after the graduation, "You know, I am seventy-two years old and I have ten children and I was always afraid that I would not have a single one who was as good a man as I am. But you have a chance."

I left Mississippi immediately after the graduation ceremony, more or less at the request of the United States government. During the entire time I had been at the university they had been providing soldiers and marshals to protect me, an operation that the government later said cost over $55 million from beginning to end.

That day, the day I graduated from the university, was the last time I ever saw my father.

Over the next two years, his health deteriorated with each passing day. He ate less every day and grew weaker and thinner until the man who had once weighed over two hundred pounds was reduced to mostly skin and bones.

Moses Arthur "Captain" Meredith died of natural causes at age seventy-three in July 1965. He was buried in the black section of the City of Kosciusko cemetery.

His last hope was to see his son James once again before he left this world. He was bedridden for a long time and he wanted me to come visit him before he died.

But I would not visit my father on his deathbed. I sent my wife and children.

I never wanted to see my father in a weak condition.

I only wanted to see him strong.

CHAPTER SEVEN

To Conquer Fear

MARTIN LUTHER KING, JR., STOOD AT THE FOOT OF MY bed.

"James, may we speak with you for a while?"

It was June 7, 1966, the day after I was shot on the highway south of Hernando, Mississippi.

I was groggy, but very happy to see King at my bedside.

"How are you feeling?" he asked.

"I'm stiff," I replied, "but otherwise I'm as well as I've ever been."

I was in room 511B of the Bowld Hospital in Memphis, Tennessee, and the civil rights leaders of America were flocking to my bedside. One of the first to get there was Martin Luther King.

The shooting had transformed me into an icon, and a martyr in effect if not in fact, and the civil rights movement was galvanized.

Martin Luther King and I were about to unleash a chain of events that would transform my one-man walk against fear into the biggest and last great march of the civil rights era in the South—and an event that catalyzed the disintegration of the civil rights movement itself.

I had tried to call my wife at Columbia University Law School. She was in a state of shock, since she had heard the media reports that I was dead. I assured her I was all right. I tried to call my sixty-two-year-old mother in Kosciusko. She had broken down when she heard the reports of my death and was under sedation. It would be two more days before she could be told that I was alive.

My back, head, and neck were covered in gauze and bandages, and my body was peppered with scores of shotgun pellets, most of which had settled not far inside my skin, where some of them would remain for the next forty-five years. Luckily they were small birdshot pellets and they had not entered any major blood vessels or internal organs.

The doctors said if the shooter had been a few yards closer, I'd be dead.

The day before, after I got shot, I had lain on the side of Highway 51 for a good long while.

A reporter answering the phone at a Memphis news desk had misunderstood the words "shot in the head" for "shot dead," and news of my assassination ricocheted around the world.

But I could hear voices, and people moving around me. Then I felt someone opening my shirt and yelling for an ambulance. It was, I suppose, as close as I had ever come to getting killed. And at that moment I knew what millions of people listening to radios and watching television were not to know for at least an hour.

I knew that I was alive.

The story was corrected about an hour later, and news outlets scrambled to update the news.

Leaders across America rushed to put out statements condemning the attack, including President Lyndon B. Johnson, and "the Little General" Paul Johnson, Jr., now Ross Barnett's successor as governor of Mississippi, who stressed that the shooter was not from Mississippi. "I'm particularly pleased it was not a Mississippian," he announced. "We are going to see it is the last time some outsider comes in and does something like this." He added, "This is the kind of thing you pray won't happen, and when we were just doing so good."

Under Paul Johnson's low-key leadership, in fact, Mississippi had begun to quietly comply with federal civil rights legislation. Not that the state had much choice, of course. The last time state officials openly defied federal law, over my enrollment at the state university, they got run over by thirty thousand American combat troops. But many blacks in Mississippi and elsewhere still had not registered to vote. They were afraid to.

My shooting was front-page news in the U.K., West Germany, France, and Argentina. A Spanish newspaper headline read, "U.S.A. Great in Space, Shamed on Earth." The Soviet Union's government newspaper contended that "the tragedy in Mississippi has shown once again that proclamations of American propaganda about 'justice' and 'equality' are nothing but idle chatter."

Seven U.S. congressmen flew to Memphis to express their solidarity with me. Many experts predicted the shooting would help pass the federal Civil Rights Act of 1966 then pending in Congress, which called for faster school desegregation, protections for civil rights workers, and fair jury selection and housing.

In Harlem, blacks gathered at 125th Street and Seventh Avenue to express rage over the attack. "What the hell are we fighting in Vietnam for?" said one. Others said, "I'm sick and tired of turning the other cheek," "Let's get some guns and go down there and retaliate," "We have to kill one of them every time they kill one of us."

A black New York City bus driver who had won the Bronze Star in World War II heard about my shooting and went out and burned an American flag in front of his house. In Washington,

D.C., protesters appeared at the White House, calling out, "Freedom, Meredith! Freedom, Meredith!"

In London, seventeen thousand people prayed for my recovery in a service led by Reverend Billy Graham. The *Philadelphia Inquirer* editorialized, "The blood stain on Meredith's back is another stain on the honor of Mississippi, another mark of the revulsion that civilized people must feel at conditions that permit and encourage such cowardly acts of lawlessness."

On hearing the news, President Johnson instantly ordered Attorney General Nicholas Katzenbach to "spare no effort" to bring the guilty to justice. Aubrey Norvell was charged with shooting me. He later pled guilty, there was therefore no trial, and he was given two years in the Mississippi State Penitentiary at Parchman for assault and battery with intent to kill, the first time a white man had ever been sent to prison for shooting a black man in Mississippi. This was possible because he was not from Mississippi. He was from Tennessee.

My shooting was an echo of Oxford in 1962 and Birmingham and Selma in 1963, of the killings of Medgar Evers and Viola Liuzzo and the killing of the three civil rights workers by the Ku Klux Klan in Philadelphia, Mississippi, in 1964. All served as fiendish reminders that there were still places in America where a black man took his life in his hands by asserting his right to live. And the civil rights movement was energized as it never would be again.

Congress moved into high gear; my shooting gave new impetus to the section of Lyndon B. Johnson's 1966 Civil Rights bill broadening federal powers to prosecute racist terrorism. The House Judiciary Committee chairman, Emanuel Celler, said it best when he said: "There are times when the civil rights movement has no greater friend than its enemy. It is the enemy of civil rights who again and again produces the evidence that we cannot afford to stand still."

There was a huge outpouring of sympathy and support for me. Historian Aram Goudsouzian wrote, "Citizens sent letters to

Meredith. They wrote him poems. They responded with joy upon hearing that he was not dead, and they volunteered to march with him upon his recovery. Schoolteachers used his example to teach about tolerance. Children wished him well. Teenagers conveyed repugnance for his attacker. Politicians admired his embodiment of American principles." A man wrote a letter to the *Washington Post*: "Thank God for brave men like James Meredith. Mr. Meredith displayed his love of human dignity and good will."

Soon, many people were wondering, "What in God's name was Meredith trying to prove? Didn't he know that if he ventured out alone on an open highway in Mississippi someone would try to kill him? Didn't he know that his reputation as the first Negro ever to be admitted to the University of Mississippi would precede him, and that old simmering hatreds would come to a boil?"

Of course I understood those dangers: I was, after all, a black American, born and reared in Mississippi, and I knew a lot about the dark side of human nature.

But there are some things a man must do in his life, actions that answer the callings of conscience. There are some feelings that cannot be explained with mere words. Fear is one of them. It was fear, and its consequences for this country, that brought me to Mississippi. It was the fear of millions of black Americans that prevented them from voting, that most basic expression of citizenhood.

I chose Highway 51 because it was the classic route of the Mississippi Negro, a concrete river leading away from home. Going north, the road led to hope; going south it led to despair. I wanted to conquer that fear and replace it with hope.

In person, Martin Luther King was shorter than you might expect, a commanding, forceful, but gentle personality, quick with a laugh but obviously carrying the stresses and pressures of history on his shoulders. To me, he seemed the living incarnation of the crusading, triumphal modern black man.

But to me he had one flaw, and it was an enormous one: his devotion to nonviolence. By taking the option of legal, armed self-defense off the table, I felt he and other civil rights leaders had demeaned and emasculated the black race, and all Americans, especially myself.

"Who the hell ever said I was nonviolent?" I said at one point to a reporter in the hospital. "I spent nine years in the military and the rest of my life in Mississippi!" By now, of course, I was obviously losing this particular argument, to say the least. Outside of the late Malcolm X and a few black armed self-defense groups, the idea of nonviolence still held strong public sway over the movement.

King was the pre-eminent civil rights leader in the nation, but at this moment, in the technical sense he was the leader only of the Southern Christian Leadership Conference (SCLC), just one of a number of competing organizations that often feuded over money, tactics, and media coverage.

Floyd McKissick, the voluble, tightly wound theoretician and national director of the Congress of Racial Equality (CORE) stood beside King in my hospital room.

I had met McKissick at the White House Conference on Civil Rights the week before the shooting. Cooling his heels in the next room was the brilliant young firebrand Stokely Carmichael, chairman of the Student Nonviolent Coordinating Committee (SNCC), who would join the discussion later. He was at this moment considered somewhat junior to the others, and he was letting King start talking with me first, out of deference to him, but Carmichael was on the verge of being thrust into the national spotlight like a rocket.

The night before, immediately after I was shot, McKissick had announced that his organization would take up my march from the spot where I was attacked. When he rendezvoused with Martin Luther King in Atlanta he discovered that everyone else in the civil rights movement had precisely the same idea.

Hours after my shooting, three adjacent rooms in the Memphis hospital were commandeered for use by local police, the FBI, and telephone operators. Reporters were flocking to the scene.

I had about one hundred pellets of birdshot scattered in my

body, and the doctors decided that cutting out all the pellets would cause more damage than leaving them alone. Some worked their way out in a few weeks, others I carried with me for the rest of my life.

I slept fitfully through the first night. When I woke up, a huge bouquet rested on a shelf across the room. It was from the comedian and human rights activist Dick Gregory, an old friend, who had flown in the night before with his wife and children. He was my first visitor, other than those who had been with me on the march.

Dick had left home thinking I was dead. He also had vowed that if nothing else were done, he would pick up the walk from the spot where I had been shot. Now, he said, he was going out to Highway 51, to the place where I was shot, to start a return walk north, back to Memphis.

Over the next hours, a bizarre scene unfolded in and around my hospital room as I lay in the bed in medical pajamas.

For a fleeting moment I became a senior ranking leader of the American civil rights movement, something I never dreamed of wanting to do, at the exact moment in American history that the movement began to fall apart. At this moment I tried to keep peace between the feuding factions of the movement and steer everything toward some positive outcome.

My overriding goal was clear and simple—to continue my mission from God, by inspiring black Americans in the South to overcome their fear and register to vote. That's all I cared about; nothing else mattered.

For those hours my hospital room became the crisis command post of the civil rights movement, as its leaders swarmed to my bedside for consultations and my approval as I drifted in and out of fitful sleep as medication and exhaustion came and went. Civil rights legends, reporters, police, doctors, nurses, and telegrams swirled around the room. Telephone and telegraph cables were humming with coast-to-coast calls for volunteers.

Sentiment was quickly building for a mass march that would continue the one I had started. But a mass march was never what I wanted. My march was designed to evoke the exact opposite image—a lone American marching along a highway to express his citizenship by encouraging his brother and sister Americans to register to vote.

King and McKissick explained to me why the march had to go national, but they needed my approval.

"It's your march," King's top lieutenant, Hosea Williams, kept saying.

I kept telling them that they could do anything they pleased and whatever they decided to do was their thing. "No! We do what you say," said McKissick. "We're ready to go on today."

I wondered if the movement really knew what it was getting into. But I agreed to make whatever statement they thought necessary to let the march go on.

Always competitive for followers and dollars, the major civil rights groups had managed to submerge their differences in the big parades of the past, like the 1963 March on Washington and in 1965 the Selma-to-Montgomery March. But lately, with their great common legislative goals largely won, they had drifted even farther apart on the basic questions, most notably when SNCC elected the brilliant, fiery Carmichael chairman in May 1966 and veered in the process toward a go-it-alone black nationalism. This time the seams threatened to split wide open on the Mississippi highway. The only point of unanimous agreement was that the show must go on. However, it could not go on without my public approval.

King and McKissick apparently did not know that Dick Gregory had already left to start his own walk back from the spot where I was shot. And when I told them about it they seemed upset. I could understand their frustration: If anything were to be done, it probably should not have been done in a haphazard way.

But I wanted to make sure they knew what they were getting

into. King had never lived in Mississippi. I knew Mississippi much better than he did.

I told King, "I'm not going to try to tell you what to do, but I'm concerned that in the heat of emotion you'll attempt something logistically that you can't do.

"I've studied the route a long time," I explained to Dr. King and McKissick. "I know that 225 miles is a long way, four times longer than Selma to Montgomery. I don't feel you appreciate the hazards of a mass march through Mississippi. It's not the same as a walk between two large cities like Selma and Montgomery. This isn't as simple as Selma.

"I don't want any innocent people getting hurt. I've spent nine years in the air force, and I am very concerned with discipline and order. I'm concerned about the logistics of any large march. You are in enemy territory. You're going to have huge problems of housing and feeding a large number of people.

"I don't want the march turned into a publicity stunt or fund-raising contest among civil rights organizations. It is a march to inspire blacks to conquer their fear and register to vote."

I was trying to serve as a mediator or peacemaker, and draw all the civil rights groups together so that there would be no friction on the march. My projected role as a peacemaker or coordinator struck some as oddly uncharacteristic of the person that most people had come to perceive me as when I was absolutely alone at the University of Mississippi in 1962, and very proud of it.

Then I made a demand that went against one of the central tenets of their movement—their insistence on putting women and children in the line of fire. To me, this seemed like using human shields. It was both ridiculous and dangerous. The tactic created noble photo opportunities for the movement's propaganda purposes, but I was always very concerned about women and children getting hurt or killed. There was no room for women and children in this war.

"I don't want you putting women and children out on that

highway," I said. "You are in enemy territory. You are going into the belly of the beast. People are likely to get wounded and killed. Their blood will be on your hands. It should be a march for men, period." King and McKissick had no response to this.

"We've got to continue the march, James," said King. "Support is coming in from all over the nation. It is essential that what you started should be completed. The integrity of the movement is at stake. If we don't go forward, it will signal a reversal of the progress that the movement is making."

"Dr. King, anything you want to do will be all right with me," I told him. "Whatever you feel you have to do, I am for you. A man has to satisfy his conscience. All I ask is for you to remember your responsibilities to the Negroes of Mississippi. Whatever you decide to do, don't do anything that will be detrimental to those million human beings who will still be here when the march is over."

They agreed with this, and told me they would try to determine the logistics of continuing and would return to see me at four that afternoon. They assured me that they would not cross the point where I was shot before letting me know their plans.

I did not hear from the leaders again until eight-thirty that night, when one of Dr. King's aides told me what "we" had decided, what "we" were going to do. I was disturbed by this, as it looked as if they were making decisions in my name.

Charles Evers came to see me thirty minutes later. I could never talk to Charles without thinking of his murdered brother Medgar, who was one of my closest friends and allies during the tumultuous events of 1961–63. After Medgar's assassination, Charles took over his brother's role as the leader of the NAACP in Mississippi, and in his own way became a hard-working, effective leader. On this night he seemed as upset as I was, and as we talked freely about my uneasiness, his depression seemed to magnify.

Evers later released a statement to the press attacking the march leaders. "I don't want this to turn into another Selma where everyone goes home with the TV cameramen and leaves us holding the bag." He added further that he would rejoin the march only if I did, and if the outsiders promised to stay on and not merely "exploit the state for money and publicity."

Meanwhile, King, Carmichael, and McKissick had returned that afternoon to exactly where I was shot south of Hernando, and they started walking in the road, headed south, as cameras whirred.

The formation ran into three former Ole Miss football linemen, now wearing the uniform of the Mississippi State Highway Patrol.

"Get off this highway," commanded one patrolman. "You can march on the side of the road, you hear, but you get off of this highway right now."

Martin Luther King said: "We marched on the pavement from Selma to Montgomery."

The lawman countered, "I don't care if you march to China as long as you march on the side of the road."

Another state trooper started shoving the leaders off the highway. Carmichael fell into the dust. King fell on top of him.

Carmichael got up on one skinny knee and launched himself at the trooper. King grabbed him and held him back. They stopped to hold a press conference and soon resumed the march, this time marching on the side of the road in the grass.

Governor Paul Johnson quickly increased the size of the state police force and gave them clear orders to treat the marchers with courtesy and to keep potential white troublemakers off the highway.

This remarkable order seemed to indicate that Mississippi might be changing, and rather suddenly. Johnson was a "new-breed segregationist," smart enough to know that the best national image for Mississippi was a tactic of nonviolent response to Martin Luther King's nonviolent strategy. He was absolutely determined not to further damage Mississippi's image by fighting the marchers with state power.

The next morning King and McKissick came to my bedside and explained why they couldn't come back as they had promised the day before. They had decided that the march had to be resumed immediately, even before the logistical problems were settled. They felt the larger purpose was important enough to risk uncertainties and unforeseen difficulties. They did not come to see me because they were marching; in fact, they were scuffling with Mississippi highway patrolmen at almost the moment of the appointment. I found this perfectly acceptable.

My one-man "March Against Fear" now became the mass-movement "Meredith March," a march that was not of my own making.

The new march was launched with deep problems. The leaders drove back to Memphis for the night deeply divided. The question was what the march was all about. The youthful SNNC was preaching black political power. Stokely Carmichael was saying that the march ought to "put the president on the spot" over a wide range of grievances.

At the other extreme were Roy Wilkins of the NAACP and Whitney Young of the Urban League. They had flown down from New York to make sure that the march didn't turn into a demonstration for "black power." Martin Luther King held the middle ground. His talk sometimes sounded radical, but his mere presence was a symbolic bridge between the younger firebrands and the black moderates.

Each leader got his chance to make his pitch at a mass meeting that night at a local black church.

Roy Wilkins of the NAACP said, "If you start hating all white men, you're going to waste your energies."

Whitney Young of the Urban League implored the audience to "be mad at people who don't register and vote, who don't march to the libraries and PTA meetings, who don't go to school and stay in school."

Floyd McKissick of CORE spoke of the Statue of Liberty and suggested that they "break the young lady's leg and throw her in the Mississippi River."

Stokely Carmichael of SNCC declared: "We got to tell the federal government about all those lies they have been telling us. When they needed James Meredith they sent in federal troops, but when they didn't need him, he was just another nigger in the cotton patch!

"We need power!" Carmichael declared.

Martin Luther King spoke last: "We have power! And it isn't in bricks and guns. We have another weapon, nonviolence."

Whitney Young and Roy Wilkins came to see me. They seemed troubled by the church speeches. The NAACP and the Urban League saw education, voting, and legislation as the keys to black freedom. Martin Luther King's SCLC seemed to agree, and championed the principle of nonviolence. Stokely Carmichael's SNCC talked increasingly of black power and had among its membership young men who were no longer prepared to turn the other cheek. CORE was somewhere in between. Apparently Wilkins and Young felt that the more militant leaders were going to take over the march.

The real battle came later that night when the five leaders met to draft a statement outlining the goals of the march. Wilkins and Young argued for limiting the purpose to the single goal of getting a version of the civil rights bill passed. Apparently, they also felt that it was antiadministration, and too unrealistic in its demand that six hundred federal registrars be sent into Mississippi.

However, Carmichael's SNCC produced a strong statement attacking President Johnson and ignoring the proposed civil rights bill altogether. The debate went on until early the next morning. When the final version of the "Meredith March manifesto" was delivered to the press, it was addressed to the president.

It demanded that he put federal voter registrars in six hundred southern counties; it called for a multi-billion-dollar "freedom budget" to involve the black poor in "the making of their own destinies," and it called for sweeping amendments to the civil rights bill. It read, "This march will be a massive public indictment and protest of the failure of American society, the government of the United States, and the state of Mississippi to 'fulfill these rights.'"

King and the other leaders wanted me to approve the manifesto. I told the leaders, "The manifesto makes no difference to me. It is acceptable if it is written the way Roy Wilkins and Whitney Young want it, or the way Carmichael wants it." They read it to me, and that was that. I declined to sign it, since it wasn't my march anymore, but I had no problem with their putting the statement out.

King, Carmichael, and McKissick signed the statement. Wilkins and Young refused.

A delegation was sent to seek my decision on three deadlocked issues.

The number-one issue was which of the five leaders would be considered the leader and chief spokesperson to the world. My decision was immediate and unequivocal. "That's Dr. King's spot," I said.

On June 6, 1966, I was shot by a white man while I was leading a march to inspire Americans to register to vote. This photo won the photographer, Jack Thornell, a Pulitzer Prize. "That man shot me like a God-dammed rabbit," I was thinking. "He took his own good time about it. If I'd had a gun I could have got that guy." My "death" was the lead story of the network evening news. *Photo by Jack Thornell, Associated Press*

After I recovered from my wounds, Martin Luther King, Jr., came to help me finish my March Against Fear, an event that helped catalyze the collapse of the civil rights movement. He and I disagreed sharply over the tactic of nonviolence, as I believed both in the validity of armed self-defense and in the need for the federal government to enforce the rights of citizenship with overwhelming physical force delivered by combat troops, a tactic I provoked at the Battle of Oxford. But there is no American in history who better embodied the ideals of America's Founding Fathers than King. At my insistence, there are black men with hidden guns providing armed security for us, a few feet away. *Photo: Flip Schulke, Corbis*

The number-two issue was whether Stokely Carmichael could use the term "black power" in his statements and speeches. He had recently started experimenting with the phrase in his statements and speeches, and though it hadn't been picked up by the media yet, it was provoking a huge amount of discussion and concern among more "moderate" civil rights activists. It sounded too much like violent revolution to them.

I said, "Stokely Carmichael can do anything he wants to." Black power was fine with me. To me it was just a slogan. But it did capture a growing attitude among many blacks at the time, both of assertion of political strength and of frustration with nonviolence, and I wasn't going to try to stop it.

The last decision I made was simple.

I wanted guns on the march.

I wanted guns in the hands of black Americans.

I had no hesitation in approving the proposal that the Deacons for Defense, an armed black self-defense group, be allowed to provide discreet perimeter protection for the march, with radio links and carbines in the backseats of their cars.

The Deacons were well-trained, well-disciplined veterans, hunters, and farmers who carried pistols, rifles, and shotguns in full compliance with the law. They showed up at the hospital to offer their services, and their presence caused a major commotion behind the scenes. The moderates were adamantly opposed to any cooperation with the Deacons.

I thought it was a fine idea, a perfect expression of American citizenship rights under the Second Amendment.

When my three decisions were relayed to Roy Wilkins of the NAACP and Whitney Young of the Urban League, they immediately bolted from the hospital and caught the next plane back to New York, abandoning any participation in the march. They explained their refusal to sign the statement, telling the press, "We couldn't even go along with the title 'manifesto' because we were afraid it might remind people of Marx's Communist Manifesto." Whitney Young later came back to rejoin the march at the very end.

And so the march went forward, heading south toward unforeseen dangers lurking in the heart of Mississippi, still a tottering empire of white supremacy. The march was a swirling, chaotic affair, racked by disorganization, severe internal feuding, and eventually a historic and fatal split in the civil rights movement.

But the march went ahead without me.

People joined in from all over the nation, including Mississippi, where thousands of black people finally put aside the fear that had oppressed them and joined the cause.

And scores of black Americans in Mississippi started registering to vote for the first time in their lives. Organizers fanned out laterally from the highway and canvassed blacks to register to vote at their local courthouses.

The march was ragged and impromptu at first. There were no tents to sleep in or places to pitch them; no mobile canteens or portable toilets. King suggested that the group get started and talk about that while they walked. There was no time to sit down and talk about goals. There was only momentum, and the discord between King's idea of nonviolence and everyone working together, and Carmichael's theme of blacks taking control of their own affairs. The most important thing for them now was getting the march back on the highway.

Bit by bit, the logistics began to fall into place. Food relays ran fast-food lunches to the marchers. King's men rented four big circus tents that were trucked in from Atlanta. As the marchers reached their first overnight campsite in Batesville, Mississippi, a black churchyard, the white locals got restless for action. A dump-truck driver tried to run the marchers over and they escaped only by jumping into the ditches. Groups of whites cursed and hollered through the streets. One white woman proclaimed: "I wish I had a machine gun. I'd mow all the black bastards down." One white man caught a black boy by himself and punched him in the eye. The marchers posted unarmed guards around the tents.

Martin Luther King was the attraction that drew both the press and the blacks along the route. The call went out, "He's here, he's right here, the Reverend King is here and we want you to march with him!"

People joined in all along the route.

Elderly black women emerged from nursing homes and joined in for a few blocks.

Young black men dropped what they were doing and walked for dozens of miles.

One black mother and her daughter dressed in their Sunday best, held on to each other's arms and, to the cheers of onlookers, stepped into the march, gingerly at first, then with their heads held high in the Mississippi sunshine, broad smiles on their faces.

Like me, they were on a mission from God.

They were going to become Americans.

The moment I fell in the dust on Highway 51, the march had moved beyond me. Had my original purpose been wholly lost? No, and I was pleased at the sight of Ida May Jackson on national television sitting in her front yard near Senatobia, smiling in her old age at the carloads of young marchers shuttling back and forth to Memphis. "When they come by singing, why, we lit right in an' went to singing, too!" she said. "An' then some whites came by afterward, why, my husband, he told us all to stand up tall so's we wouldn't look like we was afraid." She fingered the fraying edge of her blouse. "Yes," she said, "Lord knows we tired of bein' low down. We want some freedom."

It was the chord of courage that I had hoped to strike. But it might well be lost in the clamor of the competing ambitions and ideologies of the moment.

It was hot in Mississippi. Every day the temperature ranged between ninety and one hundred degrees. The march leaders looked for ways to rally the crowds. Floyd McKissick cried out, "Uhuru!" That means freedom in Africa. It was a new rhetoric; it struck a chord, and King, ever attuned to a crowd, tried it out. "We want some black sheriffs in Mississippi," he shouted. The crowd whooped and hollered, and Stokely Carmichael, the advocate of black power politics, smiled a knowing smile. The march moved on, growing in the towns and falling off to the regulars in the countryside.

At eight-thirty on the morning of June 8, I was told by my attending doctor that he would keep me until the next day, and possibly until the day after. He said that I seemed to be all right. Then at about ten-thirty the security chief told me that I was going to be discharged. My lawyer, the only Negro in the Tennessee legislature, questioned a hospital procedure in which policemen notified patients of their discharge.

Martin Luther King went out and told waiting reporters that I was being evicted on five minutes' notice.

At ten-fifty-five the hospital administrator came in and made it official. He said that my doctor had signed my discharge papers, and they expected me to leave by the 11:00 a.m. checkout time, in five minutes. He said I could not see the doctor who had been treating me but that he did have the names of two Negro doctors who might see me. His attitude was so nasty that I said, "All right, give me the papers." I signed them, got dressed, and left.

The hospital officials insisted that I was ready to leave. I confirmed their report. Both positions were indeed true. I was ready to leave the hospital. But I had not asked to be released. They were still arguing through the media when I appeared before the press with my own statement for the press. The press had been waiting for two days to interview me. I had prepared a written statement, five pages long, and was on the fourth page when the accumulation of lights, weakness, and tension caught up with me. Television lights blazed. Newsmen crowded around. I began sweating heavily, and I became unsteady on my feet. And suddenly my hand went to my face; my voice gave out; my eyes shed tears down my cheeks, and I fainted.

Quickly revived by an intern, I was taken in a wheelchair to a waiting car that I knew nothing about.

That night I was on a plane back to New York.

Meanwhile, the march approached the Mississippi Delta, only a few miles from the Tallahatchie River where Emmett Till's thirteen-year-old body had been dumped after he was lynched for allegedly whistling at a white woman. Dr. King and Floyd McKissick were becoming very uncomfortable. But Stokely Carmichael's smile grew bigger with each mile. This was SNCC territory. They had been working this area very hard for a number of years. They knew every inch of this country and everybody in it, good and bad, white and black.

"We have all the cards now," said Carmichael. Perhaps true, but it seemed Martin Luther King's presence alone was likely to dominate and control the tone of the three-week, 225-mile march. He attracted the most attention. His marching along together with Carmichael was a running debate between the two, and the dialogue was an education for both men.

The marchers slowly wound down the highway, past cotton fields and ramshackle shacks housing desperately poor black Americans who had never been allowed to vote, and were now too fearful to do so.

Some black Mississippians, seeing the column of marchers, froze in their tracks. In the cotton fields, sharecroppers dropped what they were doing and came over to cheer the marchers on. Some people joined the march and stayed with it right to the center of Mississippi towns, where they lined up at the voting registrar's office. In Batesville, a 106-year-old man named Ed Fondern registered to vote. He was born when the Civil War started. And over a century later, he finally became a true American citizen. When he came out of the courthouse, he was hoisted up on the shoulders of a crowd of marchers.

Over the next two weeks, the march slowly wound south through Mississippi in groups that swelled to as large as three thousand marchers, as King commuted back and forth to Chicago, where he was leading a campaign against housing discrimination.

At the town of Grenada, a stunning breakthrough occurred when marchers demanded, and got, black voting registrars appointed by local officials. In hours, seven hundred blacks registered to vote.

King led the marchers to the courthouse steps and encountered the county sheriff, who vainly tried to shoo reporters away. The sheriff, looking like a man facing down an oncoming tidal wave, told King, "Bring 'em in, I'll see that you bring 'em in and get registered." The tables of Mississippi history were turning right-side up.

King addressed the crowd from the courthouse steps with the sheriff standing behind him. "We are here because we are tired of being beaten, we are tired of being murdered, we are tired of being shot down."

One June 16, after Greenwood city officials denied the marchers a permit to camp and the state police protective escort was reduced from twenty cruisers to four, a furious Stokely Carmichael mounted a speaker's platform, grabbed a microphone, and told the crowd that "every courthouse in Mississippi should be burned down tomorrow so we can get rid of the dirt." Then he and the crowd began publicly chanting the phrase that would soon be picked up by the media and become nationally controversial: "We want black power! We want black power! We want black power!"

Soon, SNCC activists were chanting "Black power!" and "Honkey's got to go!" along the march route, causing extreme alarm among the moderate civil rights organizers.

On June 21, King and 250 marchers detoured into the very Heart of Darkness—Philadelphia, Mississippi, headquarters of the gang of Klansmen and law enforcement officers who had kidnapped and murdered civil rights workers Andrew Goodman, James Earl Chaney, and Michael H. Schwerner two years earlier.

On the steps of the Neshoba County Courthouse, King came face to face with one of the gang members, Deputy Sheriff Cecil Price, who blocked King from ascending the steps.

King asked, "You're the one who had Schwerner and those fellows in jail?"

"Yes, sir," said Price.

King turned his back to Price and addressed the crowd in prayer, saying, "I believe in my heart that the murderers of the three young men are around me at this moment."

Someone called out, "They're right behind you!" The white mob roared with laughter and Cecil Price smirked.

"They ought to search their hearts," King said. "I want them to know that we are not afraid. If they kill three of us, they will have to kill all of us." He added, "I am not afraid of any man, whether he is in Mississippi or Michigan, whether he is in Birmingham or Boston. I am not afraid of any man!"

As the marchers withdrew, whites attacked them in a gauntlet of bottles, firecrackers, clubs, and fists. "I've never seen such a terrible town in my life," said King, vowing to return. He never did.

While all this was happening, I was recuperating in New York, watching events unfold through the newspapers and TV. By June 23, I felt well enough to return to complete the last few miles of the march into the capital city of Jackson, Mississippi, planned for Sunday, June 26.

I arrived in Canton, Mississippi, the night after the brave troops of the Mississippi State Highway Patrol had tear-gassed, charged, and beaten a crowd of unarmed civilians, including women and children, whose crime was to try to erect a tent in a Negro schoolyard. There was great bitterness and the potential for outright violence in response.

The march leaders, under the influence of Dr. King, had decided that to stay in Canton was to risk another attack. They had learned that in Mississippi the law was not designed to protect a citizen as a citizen but to protect the system of white supremacy. In most places in the South the local white supremacists had given in at least a little bit; in most parts of Mississippi they had not yet given an inch. The leaders decided to send an advance party on to Tougaloo, pitch the tents, and make the last walk to Jackson from there.

But I had promised many people that I would walk from Canton to Jackson, or at least that I would try. Then, that Friday, I was told there would be no marching on Saturday, and the last lap would be held up until the grand finale on Sunday. I decided to go ahead and do what I had said I would do. On Saturday morning I was in Canton, with three friends, to make the last lap.

And it was here that one of the small, hidden, but truly significant events of the march took place. The Mississippi State Highway Patrol had refused to offer me any protection whatsoever. So I asked to see the sheriff of Madison County, Jack Cauthen.

The sheriff came over, invited me into his office, and proceeded to astonish me.

We sat there, he and I, talking the way human beings talk. He said he had been up for twenty-four hours, and agreed to give me protection at least to the city limits. When we went outside, he told the people waiting that I was a gentleman, that we had made an agreement, and then he proceeded to carry out the agreement. We marched to the city limits, the four of us growing into more than five hundred, and we were protected by local law enforcement officers, as citizens should be protected. The police were not surly, there was no cursing, no bad manners, no "nigger-calling."

For the first time in history that I had ever heard of, local law enforcement officials in Mississippi were protecting from harm Negroes who were demonstrating for their rights. They were doing it with some grace, and without conditions. In its way, that was the most significant part of the march.

That gesture by a Mississippi sheriff was symbolic of what was beginning to happen in the South. He might not have liked me, he might even have hated me; but he treated me as an American citizen. He knew that change was coming.

I entered Jackson on June 26 in triumph, on foot, wearing my white pith helmet and carrying my ivory-tipped walking cane.

Behind me were more than twelve thousand American citizens.

At one point, marchers began singing freedom songs.

"Shut up," I snapped.

I didn't like music on my marches.

What had started in obscurity 220 miles earlier with myself, one white minister, and a couple of followers and reporters was now ending in a blaze of global attention with thousands of people taking part.

The march had been greatly altered from the concept I had in mind when I started, but the work of Dr. King, Floyd McKissick, Stokely Carmichael, and an army of volunteers in moving a big force through Mississippi and registering new voters served to speed the process of shedding the fear that was a real part of the lives of all black people in America.

My march became one of the largest marches and demonstrations ever conducted in the former American Confederacy until that point.

My formation linked up with a group led by Martin Luther King. He said to me, "I hope this is what you hoped for." I told him, "This is the most beautiful thing I have seen in a long time."

I put my arm around Dr. King and we walked beside each other into the city.

At my request, and with Dr. King's knowledge, a Deacons for Defense bodyguard paced along right behind us, alert for trouble, a big pistol shoved in his pocket, out of sight.

We gathered at the side of the Mississippi State Capitol Building for speeches that were broadcast on national television. I sat beside the lectern in the sweltering heat.

Stokely Carmichael declared that black Americans had to accumulate enough political power to bring white Americans "to their knees every time they mess with us."

Floyd McKissick said, "Let 1966 be the year that we decided that we would develop our own culture. That we would be proud of being *black people*. That we would no longer accept the use of the word Negro, but we would become mature and we would regard ourselves as black men—*black men in America!*"

Intense squabbling among various march organizers almost

prevented Dr. King from speaking, but I demanded that he be allowed to speak.

"I have a dream that even here in Mississippi, justice will come to all of God's children," King said. This day, he predicted, would "go down in history as the greatest demonstration for freedom ever held in the state of Mississippi."

I took the lectern, proudly introduced my mother, Miss Roxie, to the multitude, and spoke extemporaneously.

"Every inch of this country is controlled by the system of white supremacy," I announced. The purpose of the march, I explained, was to challenge white supremacy "at its base—fear."

As I looked at the cheering waves of people, and the looks of confidence, hope, joy, and victory on their faces, I felt that another crucial part of my mission from God had been fulfilled.

I concluded by pointing my walking stick over the crowd and declaring, "We are here today as witnesses to the fact that the system of white supremacy is over!"

What none of us realized at the time was that the civil rights movement itself was coming to an end. The era of black consciousness had begun.

Three months later, the Civil Rights Bill of 1966 died on the floor of the U.S. Senate, the victim in part of white northern backlash and resistance to the bill's fair-housing provisions.

Over the next two years, the American civil rights movement collapsed under the weight of internal divisions that were catalyzed on the march I started, and with the massive diversion of popular attention and energy toward the Vietnam War.

During the march in June 1966, however, some six thousand black Mississippians registered to vote. Federal voting registrars followed in force. And there was no turning back—from that point forward, the floodgates of free voter registration were open forever to all Mississippians.

The beast of fear had been slain.

Sherwood Ross was a reporter who volunteered to be my

spokesperson during the march in 1966. Reflecting on the event in 2011, he described its impact this way: "The upshot of his sacrifice was to pry open the state's voting rolls to blacks as once again federal officials were sent into the state, this time to register black voters who had been denied the franchise. Their votes sounded the death knell for white demagogues who henceforth had to squelch their racist remarks, or face defeat at the hands of angry black voters. Together with the integration of Ole Miss, Meredith's second strategic strike against the denial of voting rights literally marked the beginning of the end of Mississippi despotism—and by extension the end of Jim Crow everywhere in the South."

To this day, Aubrey Norvell has never explained publicly why he shot me forty-six years ago, and he has led a quiet life ever since being released from prison in June 1968.

"He has given me a reason, but that is in confidence," his attorney Edward Whitten once said. "He did have a personal reason for what he did. A reason that probably no one has thought of."

Contacted in 2011, Aubrey Norvell declined to discuss his motivation in 1966, saying, "I just want to get it all behind me."

I can hardly blame him.

I don't think he left home that morning intending to kill me.

I think he probably just got caught up in the emotions of the day.

CHAPTER EIGHT

Our Great Mission from God

I AM AN OLD MAN.

I have spent almost eighty years on this Earth.

I hit the gym and take power walks almost every day, always wearing my Ole Miss baseball cap, and I've survived prostate cancer and many of the travails of old age.

Shotgun pellets still dot my body, lying just under the skin like a harmless but abiding reminder of the sniper's blast on that Mississippi roadside. Sometimes the pellets cause me considerable discomfort and occasionally they decide to just pop out of my body.

I have seen cherished friends like Medgar Evers and Martin Luther King, Jr., get murdered by the beast of white supremacy. I have seen most of the lions of the civil rights era grow old and die, along with many friends and relatives. I have seen politicians and great political movements come and go. I was born into an empire of racial terror, and I have seen a black man become president of the United States.

And somehow, I'm still here walking the Earth.

In the years that followed my graduation from the University of Mississippi, people sometimes asked me, "Was it worth it?" Was the crisis I triggered in 1962 worth the deaths, the hundreds of injuries, the thirty thousand troops, the cost of millions of dollars, and all the agony and turmoil?

Yes, in spite of it all, I have learned that as my father said, "These people can be decent." People who wanted me dead in 1962 have transformed into different people, or maybe they found something in themselves they didn't know was there before.

One day, my car broke down on the Natchez Trace Parkway, sixty miles from Jackson. The third car that came along passed by like the other two, then stopped and backed up and took me to Jackson. The white lawyer behind the wheel said, "I thought I recognized you. I was an undergraduate student at Ole Miss when you were there. I was in the crowd throwing rocks and cussing as loud as the rest. I know it may sound funny coming from me, but I always wanted to get your autograph. Would you please sign one for me?"

I once walked into the post office in Jackson, Mississippi, to pick up a package. The clerk looked up and said, "Are you 'the' James Meredith? I've been wanting to meet you for a long time. Now, don't get me wrong. Back when you were trying to go to Ole Miss, I was with all the other whites in Mississippi and I probably would have shot you if I had got the chance. But, now I want to thank you and tell you that I think you did a great thing. Look at Barkum up at Mississippi State (referring to the black football quarterback). He would never be there today if you hadn't done what you did. My kids all go to school now with black kids and we have never had a bit of trouble."

This kind of thing happens to me all the time in Mississippi. It happens almost every day. Older white folks will stop me on the street or in the supermarket to introduce themselves, thank me and tell me how different they feel today. I'm kind of a walking, one-man truth and reconciliation commission, dispensing absolution and good feelings.

I am a big Ole Miss football fan, and I attend home games in Oxford whenever I can. You should see how people treat me. It's unbelievable. I'm like a rock star. I can barely make it out of the stadium on the way to the tailgate parties in the Grove before I'm mobbed by well-wishers and autograph seekers. I was kind of disappointed a few years back when the university stopped using "Colonel Reb" as the school mascot out of political correctness. He didn't seem overtly Confederate to me, he was a friendly looking cartoon character in a white plantation outfit and bow-tie and straw hat, the kind of get-up I often wear myself. I figured I had already beaten the little guy in 1962 and made him my own. He belonged to me.

One day I stopped dead in my tracks at the sight of dozens of beautiful black girls lining up on the campus, acting not only like they belonged there, but like they owned the place! It seemed like 1962 was only yesterday, yet here I was seeing the real Ole Miss before my eyes, maybe the Ole Miss of my hopes and dreams, the Ole Miss my father would have been proud of. I never really realized the magnitude of the change that Mississippi has seen until I saw their faces. We have a very long way yet to travel in Mississippi and at the University of Mississippi, there is much wrong that needs to be made right, but we have come light-years together.

It is not an easy thing to descend from the heights.

My descent occurred a long time ago.

In 1966, I was the most admired black man in America after Dr. King, a man who triggered global headlines. In the years that followed, I fell into obscurity, periodically reappearing in often perplexing ways, having many adventures and misadventures along the way.

After graduating from Ole Miss in August 1963, I spent time on the speaking circuit. At an NAACP convention in Chicago that year, I made a speech calling for black self-sufficiency and criticizing the quality of young black leadership. I off-handedly referred to blacks in the audience as "burr-heads," a comment meant to reflect the low expectations they faced from racists. No offense was intended but huge offense was taken, from the audience and from the professional civil rights elite. The remarks triggered a firestorm of criticism of me.

In 1964 and 1965, I traveled to Africa for graduate study at Ibadan University by special invitation of the government of Nigeria. I was given luxury accommodations and a staff of seven servants. The Nigerian government offered me a scholarship, but I was there several months and they still hadn't provided me with any spending money. I was short on funds, and I didn't know how I was going to make it in this strange land.

That was when a woman came on campus looking for me. I didn't know her, but she found me. She was a white woman. She endorsed thirty-six hundred British pounds to me in traveler's checks. She had a knapsack on her back. She left and I never heard from her again. I never knew her name and to this day have no idea who she was.

Over Christmas of 1964, the president of the African nation of Dahomey (now called Benin) invited me to visit his country. I drove two hundred miles north from the African coast to meet him. Then I kept driving deep into the African countryside, because I knew a piece of my soul might dwell there.

According to my family's oral history, our black ancestors were kidnapped in Dahomey by African slave traders and sold into slavery to the French. They and their descendants were brought to Canada, then down the Mississippi to a settlement called French Camp in present-day Mississippi, fifteen miles from Kosciusko, the place where I grew up.

Deep in the interior of Dahomey, I met a local king who was descended from the royalty who ruled the area where the kidnapping took place hundreds of years earlier. I was astonished to learn that he had heard the story the same way I had heard it all my life from my father. The legend he and his people had heard passed down the generations of losing part of the family was the same legend I had heard.

After all those generations, they still missed their kidnapped children as if it was only yesterday. They were still weeping for their lost children.

In that moment, I became a child of Africa.

I entered Columbia University Law School in New York City in 1965 and earned my law degree in 1968. I never took the bar exam. I never intended to practice law; just studying it was what I was after.

With my son, John, in Dahomey, Christmas 1964. *Photo courtesy of the James Meredith collection*

In 1966, Bobby Kennedy asked me to a summit meeting at his New York City apartment. He was now a U.S. senator from New York. After I was shot, I was a hot political commodity, and RFK wanted to team up with me.

I took the elevator to Kennedy's six-room pied-à-terre on the fourteenth floor of the exclusive United Nations Plaza apartments in Midtown Manhattan, home to such luminaries as Walter Cronkite, Truman Capote, and Johnny Carson. RFK greeted me at the door and ushered me to a cream-colored sofa, where the two of us spent the morning sipping coffee and talking about politics. He was building a political machine in New York, and he wanted to know if I would be a part of it.

Bobby Kennedy made two things clear to me. First, I could choose pretty much any political office I wanted and he would back me. Second, he let me know in so many words that he and his people would be boss, not me. He was very charming about it all, but I knew the game he was playing. Pure, blood-sport politics. I declined his offer, but I told him he could call me up whenever he needed a favor. He called a few weeks later and asked if I would campaign for his hand-picked candidate for a New York state judgeship in the surrogate court, a powerful patronage position. I did, and RFK's man won. That was the last time I ever saw or heard from Bobby Kennedy.

In 1967, I shocked many people when I endorsed former governor Ross Barnett for re-election as governor of Mississippi. Some people thought I did it as an act of sadistic humor intended to sabotage his chances. But all his opponents that year believed in white supremacy as strongly as he did, and I thought he was simply the better man. Barnett, you see, was a good man, despite the infamy he earned during the 1962 crisis. My family knew him very well as a young man. In fact my youngest uncle played and hunted with Ross Barnett as a boy, and he knew Ross Barnett much better than he did any of his own older brothers and sisters.

After he left office in 1964, if I was in Mississippi and in serious trouble, I guarantee you I would have called up to get Ross Barnett to be my lawyer. In private practice, he did more to bring equal justice to blacks in trouble with the law in Mississippi than any other man in Mississippi for the last fifty years. Was he a bigot? No more than millions of other Americans. And I've always preferred bigotry to be out in the open where I can confront it.

Ross Barnett got clobbered in the election, coming in sixth in a field of seven.

Also in 1967, I decided to dethrone the most powerful black man in Congress, Democratic Representative Adam Clayton Powell, Jr., from the Harlem congressional seat he had held for more than twenty years. The Eighteenth U.S. Congressional District seat had been carved out for Powell during World War II as part of a Roosevelt administration plan to keep blacks pacified and loyal while the country devoted its energies to fighting the Germans and the Japanese. Two seats were created, one for Powell, who was to represent blacks east of the Mississippi River, the other in Chicago for William Dawson, who was to represent blacks west of the Mississippi River. As it turned out, Powell's brilliance and charisma meant he actually became the political spokesman for a whole nation of blacks. Any black GI, no matter where he was from, who wanted to write to his congressman would write to Adam Clayton Powell.

His fellow congressmen accused Powell of various infractions and barred him both from his leadership posts and from returning to Congress until the results of a special election to be held in 1967. But what drove Powell from power was that for more than twenty years he had gone along with a philosophy and method of tokenism and then, for reasons that I can certainly understand, he served notice he was not going to go along any more. That was what triggered his destruction.

Representative Powell began to lose his power after he sponsored a black power–type conference held in his congressional offices in 1965. Going along with a system of tokenism for twenty years and then deciding to rebel is something that you just don't do under the system and survive. Two years later, Powell was ousted from Congress and the special election was ordered in New York to fill his seat.

The Republican party bosses of New York state asked me if I would run against Powell for his seat in Congress. I said yes. Once again, I was thrust into the global headlines. An intensely chaotic few days followed, during which most members of the American black elite leadership called me or visited me to beg, plead, and beseech me not to run against Powell, who to them symbolized a fallen hero fighting for his political life, which he was.

I pulled out of the race. The reason wasn't any sympathy for Powell. The reason was I wanted to run the campaign my way and I wanted proper funding from the Republican party bosses. Instead they promised me the opposite: minimal funding and maximum interference. I went back to being a student at Columbia University Law School and Adam Clayton Powell was re-elected.

I was called to the dean's office one day and given a message to call a certain lawyer. He instructed me to come to his office. Upon arrival he informed me that I was the beneficiary of an anonymous gift. He said I could never know who the donor was, only that he was a white relative whose roots were the same as mine, Attala County, Mississippi. He handed me a check for $150,000. The check was good. I later surmised the gift came from a cousin and fellow descendant of my great grandfather J.A.P. Campbell, one of the founders of white supremacy in Mississippi.

Using the money as a down payment, I bought a whole city block in New York City, consisting of fifty-four apartment units and nine commercial business outlets. It was in an all-white area of the Bronx. No black had ever lived in my block before I bought it. I tried to negotiate rent increases to pay for improvements necessary to keep the buildings from collapsing from disrepair. In 1969, the tenants rebelled and sued. I was accused of harassing them. That wasn't my intention, and I argued my innocence, but the judge felt otherwise. He sentenced me to two days in jail and the press called me a slumlord who harassed his tenants.

In 1971, I returned to Mississippi. I settled in Jackson, and, in time, got into a variety of entrepreneurial ventures, including the entertainment business, running nightclubs like the Chimneyville Lounge. In 1979, my first wife, Mary June, died at age thirty-nine of a massive coronary, leaving me with three young sons to raise. Losing my wife caused the greatest change in me. I cried a lot, and I couldn't remember ever doing that. My father used to say, "No use crying when somebody dies."

I ran for Congress in 1974 and surprised everyone by winning the most votes in the Democratic primary against four candidates. Then I pulled out of the Democratic run-off contest. Then I campaigned as an independent. Then I pulled out altogether. My goal wasn't to win the election. It was to add many voters to the voting rolls, which I did.

In 1984, after applying in vain to get a college teaching job in

Mississippi, including an application to Ole Miss, the University of Cincinnati offered me a year-long contract to serve as a visiting lecturer. I looked forward to the assignment with a renewed sense of mission. I moved to Ohio with my new wife, television reporter Judy Alsobrooks, and two of our children. Judy is a brilliant, wonderful woman, a source of tremendous strength and support to me, and one of only two women I ever met who could tolerate me. I bought a three-story house and office building, which I named the James H. Meredith Office Building, across from the University of Cincinnati campus. My contract was not renewed after I spoke of Cincinnati's role in promoting slavery, denounced integration as "a sham" and "the biggest con job every pulled on any people," and denounced the university's abysmal record in graduating black students.

On one occasion the police were called to the University Nautilus Club, of which I was a member, to remove me from the premises. The club management said I looked like a regular walk-in off the street. The incident hit the press and the response from the black men of Cincinnati was unbelievable. I was a greater hero to them than I ever was in the Ole Miss affair. They all said that they were treated that way all the time and there was no one to complain to. A few years later, I issued pronouncements that were fiercely critical of national black leaders, claiming, among other things, that some of them were using drugs or otherwise connected to the drug culture.

In 1988, I wrote to a number of U.S. congressmen and senators, pitching myself for a job on their staff. The only one who replied was Senator Jesse Helms, and he offered me a job at thirty thousand dollars a year as his domestic policy advisor and research assistant focusing on urban, education, and family issues. My wife, Judy, was based in San Diego, so we had a commuter marriage for that time. I spent most of the following eighteen months researching black family issues at various think tanks and archives.

It was hard for most Americans of all persuasions to imagine an odder couple than conservative senator Jesse Helms, Republican of North Carolina and former segregationist, and me, the civil rights pioneer who integrated Ole Miss, one of the heroes of the black movement of the 1960s. But to me he was a kindred spirit. We both believed that liberal welfare programs helped destroy the black family. Much was made in the press about the fact that I was the first black ever to serve on Senator Helms's staff in his eighteen years in the Senate. No one ever mentioned the fact that I was one of only a microscopic handful of blacks working in the United States Senate in significant staff-level positions. The rest of the senators, Republican and Democrat, had abysmal records in hiring black staff.

I left Senator Helms's staff in 1991. He was too liberal for my tastes.

I am the American Don Quixote. Over the years I've led countless one-man marches across different stretches of Mississippi, announced my campaigns for offices ranging from mayor of Jackson, Mississippi, to president of the United States, briefly started my own church, sold Amway products, and lectured to many audiences. Sometimes I lecture to large audiences and sometimes I lecture to empty rooms. Still I keep on moving.

I think I have survived all of it. Now, instead of being James Meredith the celebrity, the honored one, I find I can be just James Meredith, the grandfather, the civilian, the citizen, the idiosyncratic American who is free to shoot his mouth off on anything he feels like talking about.

The greatest moment of my life came ten years ago, on a summer day in Mississippi.

It was the day I saw my son Joseph receive his doctorate in business administration at the University of Mississippi, graduating at the top of his class.

I sat in the audience with his six-year-old daughter, Jasmine, my granddaughter, bouncing on my knee, watching him receive his diploma, steps away from where I received mine in 1962.

My son had not only already graduated from Harvard University with excellent marks and lined up a professorship at a college in North Carolina, but on this day he won the 2002 Outstanding Doctoral Student Achievement Award at the University of Mississippi's School of Business Administration.

This was the day I felt the most pride, the most gratitude to God, and the most pure, unbounded joy of my whole life.

This was the vindication of my entire life, and particularly my goal of breaking the system of white supremacy. My goal forty years earlier was to break the legal and official system of white supremacy in Mississippi so that black Americans could become anything that we were capable of being in this country. And now my son had proved to be the best in his field in my lifetime. I remembered my father's words at my graduation two generations earlier: "These people can be decent." How right he was.

This was the vindication of all the struggles I'd been through. I was never proud of going to Ole Miss until the day my son Joseph graduated. Until then, I felt the entire episode was a grotesque insult and a humiliation for me, for black Americans, and for all Americans to have one citizen's rights so flagrantly violated in a spectacle for the world to see.

But when I saw my son receive his doctorate that day at Ole Miss, I felt an important part of my mission from God was now complete. He died of lupus at age thirty-nine.

Other days have come very close to the glory of that day, like the day my twin sons graduated from Philips Academy at Andover, Massachusetts, and the days my sons received their master's degrees, and the recent day when my wife, Judy, received her doctorate from Mississippi State University. They were days defined by what always has been the most important subject of my life, education.

For me, the hardest thing I've ever experienced was growing old.

I feel like I'm thirty-eight, but I look in the mirror and I see a guy cruising into his eighties.

These days I keep my name on the edge of the news. I am not in the page-one headlines much anymore, but occasionally you'll find me on the inside pages. I am often invited to give speeches. My speeches are sometimes sharp, sometimes broad and desultory, and often vague. Sometimes I am just plain wrong.

I'm still managing to confound people and defy expectations, like the day in 1997 when I donated my personal papers to Ole Miss. Rather than give a boilerplate "civil rights speech," I chose to discuss my Choctaw Indian heritage and announce a quixotic candidacy to run for mayor of Jackson, Mississippi. The audience was totally befuddled. One former University of Mississippi official in the audience offered his opinion of me. "He is a man of incredible courage," he said. "He is also, in some ways, nutty as a fruitcake. A very strange man. But he has more guts than a violin factory."

People are constantly ascribing great courage to me in my campaign to enter Ole Miss fifty years ago. I totally disagree. As a black male living in Mississippi in 1960, I was already a walking dead man. I had no rights, other than the right to be treated as a subhuman, and the right to be beaten, and the right to have my house burned down or shredded by gunfire, and the right to be murdered on the whim of any white citizen or lawman.

As a dead man, I had nothing to lose by walking around with a bull's-eye target on my chest before the cameras of the world media. It takes no great courage for a dead man to want to live.

Right now there is a five-hundred-pound bronze statue of me on the campus of the University of Mississippi, a few yards from the Lyceum building, the epicenter of the insurrection in 1962, and one hundred yards from the statue of a Confederate soldier that stands guard at the eastern entrance to the Circle, the center of campus.

I have become a piece of art, a tourist attraction, a soothing image on the civil rights tour of the South, a public relations tool for the powers that be at Ole Miss, and a feel-good icon of brotherly love and racial reconciliation, frozen in gentle docility.

The statue must be destroyed.

My sons, John Meredith, Joseph Meredith, and James
Meredith and I pose at the James Meredith statue
on the campus of Ole Miss at its dedication in 2006.
I have asked the university to destroy the statue, as it
is a false idol and a violation of God's law, the Second
Commandment. *Photo courtesy of the James Meredith
collection*

I repeat that: *The statue must be destroyed.* And it must be destroyed immediately. The statue is a likeness of me walking alone
toward a seventeen-foot-tall circular limestone portal inscribed
with four banal generalities: "Courage," "Perseverance," "Opportunity," and "Knowledge."

There is a marker nearby, featuring a butchered, out-of-context
quotation from my 1966 book *Three Years in Mississippi* expressing
my love for the land of Mississippi but making no mention of my
hatred of its ruling system of white supremacy.

It also makes no mention of my war against white supremacy;
no mention of the state of Mississippi's illegal, official, and popular insurrection against the United States in 1962; no mention of
the violent upheaval that disgraced the university and the state;
no mention of the fact many hundreds of Americans engaged in
combat with one another around that very spot; no mention of
the fact that hundreds of armed federal marshals were required

to physically force me onto the campus or that they were nearly overrun and wiped out by a homicidal mob of two thousand white civilians; no mention of the fact that two innocent white men, Paul Guihard and Ray Gunter, were killed that night; and no mention of the fact that thirty thousand federal soldiers and Mississippi National Guardsmen were mobilized to rescue the school and city from widespread death and destruction.

In a supreme insult to me personally, the statue of me and the portal are together known as the "Civil Rights Monument," which ties my name to a phrase I find highly objectionable. The whole thing is, from my perspective, a hideous presentation.

I would have pointed all this out to anyone at the university who was interested, if anybody had bothered to ask for my approval or consult me on any of this before they put the statue up. Actually, I take that back. I did get a phone call one day from then chancellor Robert Khayat asking me if a statue should feature me in a suit or casual clothes. I told him I usually wore a suit on campus. That was the extent of the consultation.

The statue and the monument had a tortured, controversial history that spanned eleven years. It started off having nothing to do with me. In 1995, a group of Ole Miss students launched an effort to honor the civil rights movement by putting up a monument. The monument would be a counterpoint to some of the Confederate imagery that lingered on the campus. The students specifically did not want it to be a monument to me. Then over the next decade, plans and designs were debated, tempers flared and cooled, and a design was settled on. But then Chancellor Khayat and university officials stepped in, hijacked the process, and vetoed the original design, in part because it included the word "fear," which they didn't feel was appropriate, and the statue of me resembling a gentle, solitary supplicant was added late in the process.

Well, if they don't understand that the word "fear" is at the heart of any hope of understanding Mississippi history or civil rights history, then they know nothing about history.

The James Meredith statue was dedicated in 2006, at a ceremony I was invited to and reluctantly attended. There was a crowd of fifteen hundred people, plus lots of reporters. My son was invited to make remarks. Civil rights hero and U.S. Representative John Lewis, a man I did not know and had never met before, was invited as the keynote speaker. He gave a rip-roaring "civil rights speech" that brought the cheering audience to its feet.

"This is a day to rejoice!" exclaimed Lewis. "With the unveiling of this monument, we free ourselves from the chains of a difficult past. Today we can celebrate a new day, a new beginning, the birth of a new South and a new America that is more free, more fair, and more just than ever before!"

I had no idea what he was talking about.

When Congressman Lewis claimed, "This is a monument to the power of peace to overcome violence," I thought, "No, actually this should more accurately be described as a monument to the threat of organized violence in the hands of U.S. combat troops to crush a state-sponsored popular insurrection."

The Mississippi-born actor Morgan Freeman, another man I did not know and had never met before, was invited to give a speech, too. "A lesser man might have given up, but James persevered," Freeman declared. "By breaking down the barriers of segregation he liberated all Mississippians." He asserted, "Mississippi is a much better state today because of James Meredith, and this is a much better university. Thank you, Mr. Meredith." I enjoy Mr. Freeman's movies but I'm still not quite sure what he was doing there.

Former Mississippi governor William Winter told the press, "Let the word go out, there is a new birth of freedom here . . . Ole Miss is a place where racial reconciliation has found a home." When he said this, I thought to myself, "Talking about 'racial reconciliation' may make some people feel good about themselves, but the only meaningful racial reconciliation that ever occurred in America was the reconciliation between white southerners and white northerners after the Civil War."

Chancellor Khayat apparently saw great public relations potential in my statue. He told a reporter, "The perception of Mississippi and Ole Miss has changed, for the better, because of James Meredith and so many others. This monument will inspire hope for generations to come and show that one person can make a difference."

I sat up there on the lectern in the scorching heat and I sat through all of the speeches.

I was the man of the hour, all right.

But they wouldn't let me say a word.

Before the ceremony started, as I held my speech in my hand, Ole Miss officials told me I couldn't speak at the dedication ceremony of a statue of myself. Not enough time, they said.

They scampered around frantically as if they were walking on eggshells, horrified that I might actually get near the lectern and say something anyway. I played along because I didn't want to cause a ruckus. I half-expected something like this might happen, so I handed out copies of the speech I had planned to give. I guess they figured they'd better not try to handcuff me, so I got away with it.

When I saw the details of the monument in person that day, I was deeply depressed. The idea that people involved in the process had good intentions didn't make the statue and marker any less unacceptable to me. I held my tongue out of courtesy that day, and I've held it for the past six years as the statue stood on the campus of my university. This was a mistake. I'm an older man now, and I feel free to speak the unvarnished truth, even if I hurt people's feelings.

The statue must be torn down.

I'll say it again: *The statue of me on the campus of the University of Mississippi must be torn down immediately.*

On the day this book is published, I am asking the chancellor of the University of Mississippi to destroy the statue. I don't want them to move the statue or put it in a less conspicuous place, or put it in storage, which would be horrible ideas, since the thing could be displayed prominently again someday.

I am asking the chancellor to destroy the statue no later than October 1, 2012, the fiftieth anniversary of my registering as a student at the University of Mississippi. I make this demand not based on any artistic opinion of the statue itself, of which I have none. I make this demand not out of any ungratefulness or false modesty, either.

Any other objections to the statue pale beneath the most important one of all: It is a violation of God's law, "Thou shalt not make unto thee any graven image," which is known as the Second Commandment.

The James Meredith statue is a false idol.

It must be destroyed and ground to dust.

———

Not long ago, I stuffed all of the important notes, diaries, booklets, letters, and other writings I had produced over my adult life into a suitcase, flew to Los Angeles, and boarded a nonstop flight to Tokyo.

I wanted to travel back to Japan, the land where I became a man, the place where I first embarked on my mission from God.

I thought that I could clear my mind there, away from all distractions, to reflect on my life's journey and begin to pull together the pieces of my life into the book you are now reading. The last time I took the trip, in 1957, I flew on a propeller plane and had to stop in Hawaii and Guam. It took me three days to make the trip. This time the flight was ten hours and thirty-seven minutes.

I must have been quite a sight, a black senior citizen in a leather bomber jacket and an Ole Miss baseball cap, dragging a giant suitcase filled with paper and weighing over one hundred pounds through the streets of Japan. I struggled up and down long staircases and made many detours and wrong turns in train stations, since I couldn't always figure out where I was. Being the loner I usually am, I traveled solo and pressed on with great determination.

I was in search of something, and not sure of what it was.

On my first day in Japan since 1960, I got up at 7:30 a.m. and caught the train to Nishi-Tachikawa, the city west of Tokyo that once hosted the long-gone U.S. Air Force base I was posted at during my three years in Japan. I checked into the "Authentic Hotel," and got a room facing east that every morning afforded me a spectacular view of the sunrise. I learned from experience why Japan is called the Land of the Rising Sun. No sight have I ever seen was more beautiful and aesthetic. You cannot explain it. It can only be experienced. I never remembered seeing the sunrise as beautiful in the whole previous three years I was in Japan, as it probably never happened during that time. The whole atmosphere has to be perfect between your spot of view and the rising sun.

For several weeks I banged away at my writing in the local library, fortified by breakfasts of Japanese green tea, bananas, and Kellogg's Corn Flakes, and rice and beef curry for dinner. I settled into the rythms of Japanese neighborhood life and felt completely at peace and at home. I drank beers with salarymen at the local noodle shop and bantered with shopkeepers trying out their English on me. I spent hours wandering around trying to find the old house where I had lived decades earlier, only to realize it had been replaced by miles and miles of high-rise buildings.

I once looked up from my library desk, and everyone seemed ultrafocused, studying for some serious purpose. I walked downstairs and the kids were hard at work in the children's section of the library. They too were dead serious. They were sealed in total concentration to the books that they were studying. Nothing seemed to distract them. Although no one said a word to me all day or even acted as if they noticed I was there, upon leaving most of them came by to say good-bye to me, and the ones who have gotten their English together told me they wanted to go to America for vacation or told me that they spoke a little English or asked what state

I was from. What a strange country. I am eternally fascinated by it.

It is very easy to lose your perspective in life. Many people throughout my life have reminded me of my good fortune to have been privileged to live "the Good Life," and the Japanese people I met during this trip made the point to me most clearly. I have never had to really work a day in my life in order to make a living. I've never had a "real job." Yet God somehow always takes care of me. Many times I would not know where it was going to come from but every time it would just be there.

The only time I ever experienced any difficulty was when I lost faith and failed to believe in my divine responsibility. During these brief periods I felt stress and discomfort, sometimes even a little depression. But something would always happen to reinstill the fire in my heart.

One day during my trip to Japan I took an excursion that re-awakened my sense of my mission from God.

I witnessed the most beautiful scene that I had ever seen in my life.

Mount Takao is a nearly two-thousand-foot mountain, home to a lush array of wildlife and breathtaking views of the staggering Mount Fuji. It is a wilderness paradise that is only an hour from one of the most densely populated cities in the world, Tokyo.

I have traveled to more than fifty nations all over the world, seen the Swiss mountains and valleys, the vineyards of France, and many beautiful places in America and the Canadian Rockies, but never had I seen a view to compare to the hamlet of Takao-Sanguchi and the countryside leading to the peak of Mount Takao. I cannot describe the beauty.

Elsewhere in Japan, the cherry blossoms had come and gone, but here in the mountains they were in their glory. All along the stream were planted cherry trees, one pink, one white, as far as you could see. Up the mountainsides, going straight up like the skyscrapers of Manhattan, was a dazzling symphony of greenery of every shade and color.

The view of Mount Fuji from Mount Takao, west of Tokyo. When I returned
to Japan, the land from where I embarked on my mission from God,
something happened to me on Mount Takao that revealed what the final
chapter of my destiny would be.

I stopped and took a close look. There was a whole section of
loblolly pine trees that looked like they were right from the heart
of Mississippi. They really looked strange growing straight up the
side of that mountain. I looked at them and thought of the 140
acres of pine trees in Mississippi that I started planting in 1960 on
my daddy's farm.

I heard a very familiar sound, "Caw! Caw! Caw! Caw!" I looked
up. It was a speaking crow. Sounded just exactly like the crows in
Mississippi. Suddenly I missed Mississippi terribly. I crossed the
first bridge where two small streams came together to form a bigger stream.

I did not miss Mississippi now.

I was in Mississippi and I was ten years old.

My daddy always told me that if a stream runs in Mississippi, the water is fit to drink. If it didn't run, you'd better not drink it. I followed his advice but really never bothered to figure out why it was true. Now, I saw the stream coming out of the mountain in Japan just like I used to see them come out of the rocky hills of our farm in Attala County, Mississippi. The water was crystal-clear like I had remembered it in Mississippi and I knew it was sweet, soft, good-tasting, spring water as we called it. I knew I could safely drink as much as I wanted.

I finally reached the top of Mount Takao and savored the glorious view.

When I sat down on a bench to have a sandwich and relax my legs, some Japanese schoolchildren slowly approached and started trying out their English on me.

Other children joined in, and before long I was an old sage on a mountaintop surrounded by a flock of children asking questions about me, my life, my family, and my home. It seemed like we were there for hours.

"What is it like in Mississippi?" one girl asked.

For once in my life I was stumped for words.

I could only smile at her.

"As a matter of fact," I said, "it's a lot like right here."

In the days that followed, I thought of my time on top of that mountain and I thought of those Japanese schoolchildren and the energy, joy, and curiosity they exuded. I thought of the children back home in Mississippi, including my then thirteen-year-old daughter, Jessica.

Before long, I realized what my final destiny would be.

I could see the final chapter of my mission from God.

I decided to dedicate the rest of my life to trying to improve the education of our children. And I want you to join me.

I think I've finally figured out what old men are supposed to do. They are supposed to finish things they haven't finished, and teach things they have learned to young people. Everybody talks about Moses leading children out of Egypt, but people forget how many times he tried before he succeeded. He only succeeded as an old man.

For much of my life I thought God and I were partners, and I was the senior partner. I freely admit that I have a colossal ego, and I have been so convinced that I am literally on a mission from God that I have often acted like a man with a messiah complex. I now realize I am not a messiah, far from it.

When I reached my peace with God a few years ago, I heard him tell me, "James Meredith, you talk too much."

To tell you the truth, over the last ten to fifteen years I've been trying to figure out why in the world God let me stay alive this long. Now I know why. I'm going to use all my energy to do what I think God sent me here to do.

He wants me to be a messenger.

The message he wants me to deliver is that *you and I have a divine responsibility to transform America to make it a better place for our children and our grandchildren, through the power of our love.*

It is not an option for us to love our fellow Americans in this way. It is not a choice, it is not an option and it is not a gift.

It is our absolute, ironclad moral responsibility. It is our destiny. It is the mission established for us by God, Abraham, Christ, Buddha, Mohammed, and all the gods and prophets of the ages.

This is the reason you and I were born.

I have learned one great lesson in my life.

It is the truth revealed by Leo Tolstoy in his short story "What Men Live By": "And the angel said: I have learnt that all men live not by care for themselves, but by love. It was not given to the mother to know what her children needed for their life. Nor was it given to the rich man to know what he himself needed. Nor is it given to any man to know whether, when evening comes, he will need boots for his body or slippers for his corpse. I remained alive when I was a man, not by care of myself, but because love was present in a passer-by, and because he and his wife pitied and loved me.

The orphans remained alive, not because of their mother's care, but because there was love in the heart of a woman a stranger to them, who pitied and loved them. And all men live not by the thought they spend on their own welfare, but because love exists in man."

People ask me how I felt to see a black man become president of the United States. They ask if I ever could have dreamed of such a thing in 1962.

I'll tell you the truth. I didn't feel much one way or another. Personally, Barack Obama strikes me as a very intelligent man and effective campaigner. But when I saw a black man being sworn in as the president on TV, two simple thoughts crossed my mind: "I knew it would happen someday. Should have happened a long time ago."

People often ask me if we are living in a postracial society, especially now that a black man is president. I have to stifle my impulse to laugh when I hear this. Of course not. It almost strikes me as an irrelevant question. I'm not even sure we should live in a postracial society, whatever that means. What's wrong with living in a society where different races are celebrated, acknowledged, recognized, and honored? But does a postracial society mean we all are treated equally as full American citizens? Then we aren't there yet.

The much more important question is: Has the psychology of white supremacy been destroyed in America? Not by a long shot. This will only happen when we are honest about our history and honest about ourselves, and honest about our problems and failures.

As I look back on my life, I have some strong regrets.

I wish I could have done more to advance the cause of Mississippians, white and black, who are blessed to live in one of the most beautiful lands on Earth, the state with the highest proportion of black citizens, and a state that has in many ways set the highest, most advanced standard in dealing with issues of race and racism in America. But it is a state that has been cursed by fate.

I live in a devastated land.

My homeland of Mississippi today is the dead-last poorest state in the nation, the state with the highest portion of people living in poverty, arguably the worst educational system of any American state, the most illiterate citizens, the highest infant mortality, and the unhealthiest citizens, with the highest proportion of people dying of largely self-inflicted lifestyle diseases like type 2 diabetes, obesity, and heart disease, victims of ignorance, suicidally unhealthy eating habits, and a lack of regular physical activity.

I wish I could have provided stronger leadership on the issues I care about most, and I wish I could have communicated my messages of triumphant American citizenship, black advancement, and black self-transformation much more forcefully and clearly. So far, I have failed completely in doing so.

My greatest regret in life so far is that I have not done nearly enough to help America's poor, and especially its poorest black citizens.

The American civil rights movement, which I alternately criticized and cooperated with but was never a part of, achieved most of its limited goals, such as removing voting barriers and desegregating public facilities.

But it failed utterly in uplifting America's poor. Despite the entry of blacks into positions of political power and the rise of a large black middle class, millions of black Americans are still imprisoned in chains of abject poverty and ignorance. The well-intentioned, misguided liberal social policies of the 1960s created generations of dependency and failure for a huge portion of black America. The result today is that the appalling economic and educational conditions of America's poor black underclass have created a national security emergency and a moral crisis of colossal proportions.

The human condition of poor blacks in America is far beyond a failure or a disaster, it has become a real-life, flesh-and-blood horror movie. Some blacks have a tendency to blame everything on somebody else. Well, I'm going to tell you the real problems of the black race these days are mainly our own fault. It isn't what somebody else did to us anymore. It's what we have not done for us.

But if you don't think that the impact of white supremacy continues today, or you don't understand the scale of the massively disadvantaged position many black Americans find themselves in today, consider these shameful facts.

The black family, the traditional backbone of the black race, has completely disintegrated for an alarming number of our brothers and sisters. A half century of the welfare system, which helped run black men out of their homes, abandoning their women and babies, combined with our surrender to the culture of dependency, has created a situation today in which more than 70 percent of all black children are born to single women. Most people think blacks were freed in 1865, but in 1965 they were re-enslaved by the welfare system. Until the 1950s, nearly 80 percent of black children lived with two parents, compared with today's 35 percent. Believe it or not, a black child had a higher chance of being raised by two parents in the days of slavery than he or she has in America today.

In America today, blacks are unemployed at a rate almost twice the overall rate. Young black men murder each other at a rate nine times the rate of white youths. Blacks are 13 percent of the U.S. population but comprise 38 percent of prison or jail inmates. Blacks commit 52 percent of all murders and make up 49 percent of all murder victims—90 percent of them are killed by other blacks. For millions of black young people, a culture of crime, drugs, promiscuity, school violence, and contempt for education has become the social norm.

At the root of many of our problems as a nation is the fact that our public education system is an unmitigated disaster for many of our poor white, Latino, Native American, and black youths. By the time they reach twelfth grade, black students are four years behind their white peers in English, math, and science, and score two hundred points lower average SAT scores than white students.

America ranks forty-eighth in math and science education among the world's nations, according to the World Economic Forum.

Almost 80 percent of white students in America complete high school, compared to about 56 percent of black students. If black students get to college, they're half as likely to graduate as whites. Millions of young black Americans cannot be competitive in the new global information economy because of their inability to read, write, and spell proper English.

In Mississippi, there is desperation, particularly in the Mississippi Delta, where conditions haven't changed much for the better in decades. Only 10 percent of high-school students in the Delta are ready for college in math, science, and language.

After public schools in Mississippi desegregated in earnest beginning in 1970 under court order, many white families fled to better-funded white-dominated "private academies," creating a double system of schools that has devastated the population as a whole. The creation of these schools was supported in part by resources provided by the Baptist Church and local banks. The private academies became the bulwark of a new wave of de facto segregation in public education in Mississippi that endures to this day.

As is the case in many white families, our black children in America have been allowed by their elders to be overwhelmed by television and video games. But the problem for blacks is much worse. According to a recent study by the Kaiser Family Foundation, black youths spend 41 hours a week watching television, while white kids spend under 25 hours per week. When you factor in video games, social networking, and other time-destroying distractions, it gets even worse. Black and Latino children consume 4.5 more hours of total media every day than white children. Our black and Latino kids spend 30 hours less every week than white children in doing the things they should be doing—homework, exercise, reading, developing social skills, and enjoying family interaction.

Overt racism against black Americans has decreased radically since the 1960s, and blacks have made great gains in our nation, but bias remains entrenched in many sectors of society, including in the allocation of educational resources, in financial and credit markets, in hiring and promotion, in how the criminal justice system is applied, and in how Hollywood and the media portray us. All of us are responsible if we tolerate these conditions: black and white, North and South, liberal and conservative.

These trends are a national disgrace. They cannot be allowed to continue. The fate of nations used to be determined by their borders and how they could defend them. No more. The fate of nations today and into the future will be decided by the degree to which the nation practices what it preaches. If America is to hold her rightful place as leader of the world, we must come nearer to our ideal of human equality and justice—for all our citizens.

The last remaining pillar of white supremacy in America is the Myth of Innocence. We will not live in a postracial society and we will not live in a truly United States of America until this myth is confronted and destroyed.

The Myth of Innocence is the national delusion that white supremacy is no longer a powerful and destructive force in the American soul.

The Myth of Innocence is the vast national denial of responsibility for the horrific conditions of poverty and ignorance that millions of Americans live in today as a direct result of the legacy of centuries of slavery, segregation, and persistent, systemic, institutionalized white supremacy and racial discrimination, the entrenched results and shock waves of which linger to this day.

The Myth of Innocence is the belief among many white Americans that their own ancestors had little or nothing to do with creating these conditions, and the belief among many black Americans that they themselves are blameless or are powerless to change these conditions.

When black Americans admit that a culture of dependency, helplessness, irresponsibility, and failure has destroyed the lives of multitudes of our people and that we are in part responsible for creating that culture and we are primarily responsible for changing it, then America will begin moving toward a postracial society.

The biggest problem facing the black race today is the deterioration of the black family structure, which I attribute to the welfare system, and the break-up of the extended family system, the traditional backbone of the black race.

Some black people still blame whites for all our problems, when in fact black people now have their hands on the levers of power of the White House and a wide spectrum of the political apparatus in America, especially in the South and urban areas. We have got to step up to the plate and take on our responsibilities. I'll never recognize any man's ability to be unjust to me. The fact of my existence I can't deny, but I can honor no man with the credit, with the power, to blame him for my circumstances. It took five hundred years for us to get where we are today. If we do the right things, we can reach our rightful place in one generation.

When white Americans in the North and South acknowledge that the vast majority of their ancestors, with some heroic exceptions, were collaborators with white supremacy and segregation and did absolutely nothing meaningful to fight these evils, and that this collaboration directly enabled white supremacy, segregation, discrimination, and racial terror to thrive in this country for many generations, then we will move toward a postracial society.

When white Americans in the North and South, liberal and conservative, Republican and Democrat, admit that with some heroic exceptions, the racial attitudes and behavior of their ancestors, and in many cases their own parents or grandparents, in passively collaborating with or actively supporting the culture of white supremacy was wrong, un-Christian, hypocritical, and destructive, and that admitting these facts is not an act of disrespect for them but in fact the opposite, a sign of truth and our love for them, when that happens, then we will move toward a postracial society.

William Faulkner identified a great human truth when he wrote of loving all of Mississippi while having to hate some of it, because "you don't love because: you love despite; not for the virtues, but despite the faults." If we look deep in our hearts, that insight can illuminate our love for our ancestors and our love for America.

When the Democratic party admits that it was built in part on a foundation of racial terrorism in America from the Reconstruction Era into the early 1960s, then we will move toward a postracial society. When the Republican party admits that much of its ascendancy since the late 1960s has been based on race-baiting and blatantly cynical pandering to white supremacy, then we will move toward a postracial society.

When American churches, universities, and businesses in the North and South fully admit and showcase their institutional failings and guilt in collaborating with racial terror and white supremacy through American history, then we will move toward a postracial society.

When Americans of all backgrounds can teach and debate these truths fully and openly without fear of political, professional, or community suicide, then we will live in a postracial society and a truly United States of America.

Above all, when every American child has equal access to the best educational resources regardless of their background, then we will live in a postracial society.

When all these things happen, we will begin to slay the lingering beast of white supremacy that is shielded by the Myth of Innocence and we will begin to live in the America that the Founding Fathers and Mothers of America dreamed of creating.

Now it is time for our next great mission from God.

It is time for us to work together to strive to make the best possible education available to every single child in America.

Today, I'm still marching against fear. In 2008, I was invited
to attend the Obama–McCain debate at Ole Miss as an
honored guest. Instead, I joined a 170-mile walk to fight
AIDS, above. I am devoting the rest of my life to improving
the public education of America's children. *Photo by Matt
Heindl, Jackson Free Press*

MY CHALLENGE FOR AMERICA

**I challenge every American citizen to commit right now
to help children in the public schools in their community,
especially those schools with disadvantaged students.**

I am convinced in my heart and soul that those twenty-five
words, that one sentence, if acted upon by you and me and our
fellow citizens, will create a revolution of love in our country that
will transform our nation, uplift our children, and help America
lead the world.

That one sentence, if acted upon, will directly address many of
the most urgent, intractable, and interconnected problems America
faces today, including poverty, crime, drug abuse, and joblessness.

Right now there are millions of teachers, educators, and parents

across America who are devoting their lives to providing the best possible education for our children. But they need our help, because the public education system is failing many of our children.

We need parents, teachers, citizens, and religious communities to work together. We need to stop playing politics, pushing the blame game, and see what we can do together. Every responsible person has to do his or her little bit.

There are two great insights that can guide us toward solving our educational crisis in America.

The first is the saying of the biblical King Solomon: "You should train up a child in the way he should go, and when he is old, he will not depart from it." Children not only need to be taught and raised correctly from the earliest age, they need to be "trained up," which means they must be exposed to all the values and behavior that they will need to succeed for the rest of their lives, including diligence, discipline, compassion, curiosity, personal pride, humility, tolerance, respect for others, honesty, self-awareness, and interdependence.

The second insight is the African proverb, "It takes a whole village to raise a child." To me that means that only the family of God, the whole community working together, can solve the problems of our times. In Mississippi, for example, I am launching an initiative to challenge every church community in the state to keep a record and progress report of every child born in their immediate area from birth to age twenty-one. I am traveling to every county in Mississippi to spread this message.

With the publication of this book, I am launching a Facebook page for all Americans to come together to discuss ways to improve our public education system. On that Facebook page, I will tell you about good and promising ideas and groups I have heard of and I will introduce you to people across America who are leading the way toward a better educational future for our children.

There are countless ways you can help. You can walk into your local public school and offer to read to children. You can contact a mentoring group and volunteer to be a mentor to a child who desperately needs your attention and leadership. You can become involved in your community's school board. You can lobby for smarter, more effective school policies. You can educate yourself by studying a cross-section of education reform initiatives, including promising ideas like improving parental education, stronger early childhood programs, expanded preschooling and after-school programs, universal savings accounts for every child, and community schools, which build partnerships with local faith communities and nonprofits.

I recently asked one hundred of the greatest minds in America on the subject of education to give you and me their best ideas for how we and our fellow American citizens can improve our public schools. They include parents, educators, think-tank policy experts, teachers' union executives, and advocates from the liberal, conservative, and moderate viewpoints. There are ideas many of them agree on, such as the benefits of volunteering to read to children, mentoring, and getting involved in PTA efforts, and other things they disagree on, sometimes vociferously, such as the effectiveness of charter schools and vouchers.

I believe all their ideas should be heard, which is why I am posting their in-depth comments on my Facebook page so you can develop and refine your own views. Here is a sampling of the most interesting ideas this extraordinary panel is sharing with me:

> Get involved. Whether or not you are a parent you have a stake in the quality of public schools in your community. It impacts your local economy and the overall quality of life. Get involved by being a mentor or tutor. Help the school to put on events. If you can, be a guest speaker or help to beautify the school. If everyone supported the local public schools the entire country would be better off.
>
> Hold schools accountable. Ask questions about what students are learning, about academic performance, about

graduation rates. Don't accept excuses for low performance or poor behavior. There is absolutely no reason why all kids, regardless of their background, can't go to well-run, well-organized schools, that provide a sound, basic education. We must insist that they do by attending school board meetings, writing articles about the schools in local papers, and letting local educators know that we're watching what they do.

Hold parents and students accountable. Everyone must do their part to make education work. Students must go to school regularly, they must behave themselves appropriately, and they must put in their best effort. We should accept nothing less. Parents must also be involved, especially at home. They must turn the TV off, get their kids to bed on time, read to their children when they are small, and follow up with homework as they get older. Parents must be advocates for their children and they must reinforce the importance of learning at home.

I am part of a national policy effort called the Broader and Bolder Approach in education that is calling for universal access to preschool, health care for all children, and extended learning opportunities in summer and after school.

—Pedro Noguera, Professor of Education,
New York University

Organize a PTA or start attending PTA meetings at the school level or higher (PTA has "unit"—school-level—as well as council, district, state, and national levels) to learn about specific issues in the particular district and start learning how to advocate.

Learn from those sources about the school governance structure in your state—here in California, our noncharter public schools are required to have a School Site Council made up of elected school staff, parents, and community members; run for that body or attend its meetings. And/or start attending board of ed meetings, or organize a rotating group of like-minded parents/school advocates to do so.

Find out how to volunteer to help at a school—volunteers don't have to be highly educated.

PTAs are almost everywhere, so that's the obvious place to start. Other organizations vary by community. Here in San Francisco, we have an organization that recruits and supports volunteers to help out in schools.

I think community schools are one of the most promising reforms—schools that provide all types of support services for students and families to meet their needs so that students can focus on learning. I believe that if the powerful and wealthy philanthropists who claim they want to support education yet who do not even ask educators what would be effective were to change their attitude and consult with teachers, this is what they would decide to fund.

—Caroline Grannan, Founding Member,
Parents Across America

Pay attention to decisions being made on the school board. Are they putting the needs of the kids above the needs of the adults? For instance, if they are dealing with the budget crisis by cutting art and music, slashing extracurriculars, and shortening the school day or school year, you can tell that the kids' needs are not coming first. If the school board is not doing its job, show up at meetings and let them know it. Write letters to the newspaper. Donate to their challengers.

Volunteer! Well-run schools, whether they be public, private, or charter, know how to engage community volunteers. Lots of schools have tutoring programs. If that doesn't work, though, you might be able to help organize fundraisers, help coach a team, serve on a committee.

Support politicians who back education reforms. At the local, state, and federal levels, back politicians who are willing to push the system to improve and aren't afraid to take on the vested interests, like the teachers' unions.

Most promising initiatives: Reforms that seek to hold schools and educators accountable for results, that work to create additional options for parents, and that seek to "stretch the school dollar" in these challenging times.

—Michael Petrilli, Executive Vice President, Thomas B. Fordham Foundation

Three ways to improve education: parental involvement, rigor in the curriculum, adherence to high standards. Best policy initiatives: curriculums with clear and undeviating goals.

—Herb London, President Emeritus, Hudson Institute

Parental involvement is the key to educational improvement. Any education reform strategy that fails to restore parents' critical role in the education of their children will be unsustainable and inadequate.

Research demonstrates time and again the powerful role of parental involvement, so we must re-engage them. No amount of money or school program will ever be able to replace the critical role parents play in their children's education.

Improve incentives for teacher quality. Next to parental

involvement, we know that teacher quality has a significant impact on children's learning. The current structures (primarily union collective bargaining agreements) for teacher pay and evaluation fail to reward our best teachers and they also fail to push out mediocre or poor ones. School boards can adopt better incentives to recruit and retain excellent teachers, if they have community support to go against union opposition to such measures.

The best efforts are to work toward greater school choices for all parents, including public school choice, charter schools, home schools, private schools, religious schools. It is the lack of choice of parents and the lack of competition among schools that have allowed parents to abdicate their responsibilities and schools to resist reform and innovation.

Incentive-based reforms address the systemic problems of the education monopoly by giving the consumers (parents) more choices and forcing providers (schools) to compete.

By funding children, instead of systems, all schools are forced to treat parents as customers to be served rather than captive audiences. This new dynamic compels all schools to either improve or risk going out of business.

Giving more parents the ability to choose their child's school will provide the critical incentives in the system that will spur the innovation, continuous quality improvements, and economic efficiencies currently missing in the public school system.

—Matthew Brouillette, President and CEO,
Commonwealth Foundation for Public Policy Alternatives

On the policy side, the three big ideas to me are:

National academic standards, known as "Common Core," and adopted, at least nominally, by some forty-five states.

More quality choices, including but not limited to charters, magnets, vouchers, and online options, so that everyone can access a decent education that is suited to them and nobody is trapped against their will in a bad school.

More rigorous standards for teachers coupled with better compensation for the good ones!

—Chester Finn, Senior Fellow, Hoover Institution,
Stanford University

Read to your kids every day, or volunteer to read to kids.

Demand that school systems demonstrate that they're spending dollars smart before voting for new bonds or referenda.

Serve as a mentor.

I think it's less about a particular initiative and more about creating a context where educators and entrepreneurs can tap tools, talent, and technology to better serve kids. This includes finding ways for terrific teachers to serve more kids, and be compensated appropriately, to expand choice, to facilitate online learning when useful and appropriate, and recruiting more effective teachers.

—Frederick Hess, Resident Scholar and Director of
Education Policy Studies, American Enterprise Institute

There is a poisonous element to parent involvement today: attempts to influence the allocation of educational opportunities to benefit one's own child even if the preferred policies or practices harm the other children in the community. The explosion of school choice policies has facilitated or catalyzed this element.

The fundamental suggestion then is from John Dewey, not me: "What the best and wisest parent wants for his own child, that must the community want for all of its children."

Accordingly, the types of truly helpful involvement and assistance that community members can offer vary widely, but should all follow from the premise that the public schools serve a public good, and equitable provision of high-quality learning opportunities should be the ultimate goal.

Finally, I strongly believe that educational policy in a community should arise in large part by the organized, forceful voice of people in that community. So visit the local organizations; determine if they are truly grass roots; learn how they are deciding on what matters to them and how they go about advocating for children; and decide if you feel comfortable joining in.

The current policy landscape is pretty bleak, with the vast majority of initiatives focused on privatization, deregulation, and defunding. But most initiatives have kernels of potential. School choice can be framed around magnet ideas and constrained interdistrict choice that truly opens up opportunities.

Expanded (ideally universal) high-quality preschool would undoubtedly be helpful, as would sound policies to increase high-quality parent involvement of English language learner students, policies to create healthy and safe school environments (particularly for lesbian, gay, bisexual, and transgender students), and my own favorite, because it's been the subject of my research, "detracking," or abolishing the practice of grouping students into different classes by perceived ability, and instead promoting outstanding student achievement.

—Kevin Welner, Professor, University of Colorado at Boulder School of Education, Director of the National Education Policy Center

The most important elements in whether a child succeeds in school are the involvement/interest of the parents, the effectiveness of the teacher, and the quality of the curriculum. Participation in the school's PTA can inform the parents about the school and at the same time support the school. The most promising new development I have seen is the writing and adoption of common academic standards for English language arts and mathematics.

—Jack Jennings, President and CEO,
Center on Education Policy

The lay person should look at comparative data about schools and districts, and not just that reported by their own school or district. Check out websites like www.greatschools.org. Many states have excellent data systems that can also be easily accessed.

Based on the data, ask tough questions. Why are so many kids in special ed, why are there not more advanced-level courses? What happens to students after they graduate? Is there a reading program for elementary schools that is consistent across the district and what evidence is there of its effectiveness? What is being done to close racial and ethnic gaps in student performance and to what effect? Talk to current and former students about their experiences.

Get involved with education-focused citizen action groups. There are twenty-three states with such groups and countless communities. The state organizations belong to the PIE network (www.pie-network.org) and the locals to Public Education Network (www.publiceducation.org). If no such organization exists in your community, start one.

Get involved with local schools by serving as a mentor or

volunteer, but insist that it be doing substantive work, not just keeping attendance and filling out forms.

Vote in school elections, better yet, run for the school board and support effective leadership, don't micromanage or interfere with management.

Most promising policy initiatives are those that call for transparency of data at all levels and those that bring attention to the gaps between better and worse performing schools and that highlight effective practices, and initiatives that focus on better preparation of school and district leaders.

—Christopher Cross,
Education Policy Consultant

Work with community organizations in your city to train, empower, and organize parents, students, and community members to be leaders in their community and change education policy.

Volunteer your time or expertise to your local school. Because of budget cuts in so many states schools specifically in neighborhoods of color and where there are high levels of poverty, schools have had to make severe cuts to after-school programs, art, music, advanced placement classes, and other vital services that our children need.

If you're not from the community, learn the history and makeup of the schools and the students. If you are really going to help make a difference you must go into the schools with high expectations, no stereotypes, and the belief that all children can learn regardless of socioeconomic status.

—Zakiyah Ansari, Advocacy Director,
Alliance for Quality Education

Demand school choice, to give real, immediate power to the people the schools are supposed to serve. This must be done largely at the state level, but in some states local districts might be able to provide vouchers or tax credits for use with any educational option.

Be very wary of claims that your district is underfunded. Districts are often awash in resources, and will exclude huge chunks of money spent on buildings and other capital costs when telling the public what they spend.

Pay attention to school district politics. It can be time-consuming and often boring, but absent choice—which lets you quickly "vote" against a bad district with your feet—the only way to come close to balancing the power of vested interests like teachers' unions and administrators is to be actively involved.

Get involved in the fight for educational freedom. Most states have groups that are actively involved in the school choice movement, or you can go national and work with such groups as the Alliance for School Choice.

A promising policy initiative for effective education re-form: tax credit programs for people or corporations who donate to scholarship-granting organizations, such as exist in Florida and Pennsylvania. These programs are growing very quickly and give lots of people educational freedom without even the relatively limited coercion of vouchers. And the research shows clearly that such market-based education works.

—Neal P. McCluskey, Associate Director,
Center for Educational Freedom, Cato Institute

Support your local public schools, financially and in other ways. Be a positive role model for all of the young people with whom you come into contact. Treat teachers and administrators with respect.

Keep up with what is going on in education, by reading a respected newspaper like the *New York Times* or a respected broadcast outlet like National Public Radio—avoid the cable channels!

Learn from Finland, which has the most effective schools and which does just about the opposite of what we are currently doing in the United States. You can read about what Finland has accomplished in *Finnish Lessons* by Pasi Sahlberg.

—Howard Gardner, Professor of Cognition and Education,
Harvard Graduate School of Education

I think the single most important thing average citizens can do to help improve the education of children is to get involved in school board elections and state elections and support candidates who will address the economic segregation of American schools.

—Richard D. Kahlenberg, Senior Fellow,
The Century Foundation

Poverty is a root cause of low achievement.

To mitigate effects of poverty, we need high-quality early childhood education.

We need health clinics or professional nurses in every school.

We should take the billions now devoted to testing and put it into the arts, which encourage creativity and innovation and inspire children.

We need smaller class size, especially for minority children.

We need experienced educators.

Current reforms are based on belief in free market applied to schools, with carrots and sticks. There is no evidence for these strategies. The research-based ideas I suggest above are ignored in context of No Child Left Behind and Race to Top.

—Diane Ravitch, Senior Fellow,
Brookings Institution

Get involved in your local school; find out if there is a governing body like the local school councils in Chicago or advisory groups that help make policy for the school, and join in!

Join an internet news group or follow a blog or Facebook or Twitter feed of cutting-edge education advocates. Suggestions—Bridging Differences blog at Education Week, the Answer Sheet blog at the *Washington Post*, Save our Schools on Facebook.

Be very skeptical about what you are reading in the mainstream media about charter schools, turnarounds, or other public education "miracles."

Talk to your teacher friends—they will tell you what's really going on in the schools!

Promising policy initiatives: authentic assessment including student portfolios (getting away from high-stakes testing); smaller class sizes; parent involvement in school governance; integrating "the basics" with civics, history, hands-on science, arts, and sports. I also like nongraded classrooms.

—Julie Woestehoff, Executive Director, Parents
United for Responsible Education

I don't endorse any specific policy initiatives, legislation, or political viewpoints when it comes to education reform and opening the doors of quality education for all our children. What I do endorse is a great national dialogue, debate, and clash of creative ideas on improving our education that includes the perspectives of all our citizens, left and right, parents and nonparents, experts and nonexperts.

There is one thing that I am sure of: When you decide to commit to help children in the public schools in your community, especially those schools with disadvantaged students, I believe you will be carrying out our great mission from God, and you will help make America a much better place for our children and grandchildren, a place where the good life promised us by our Creator can be enjoyed by all.

Together, we can transform America.

Will you join me?

Please visit me, contribute your ideas and opinions, and join the challenge to improve the public education of our children at: www.facebook.com/jamesmeredithusa.

Acknowledgments

We thank our families for their support, and our editor, Malaika Adero; assistant editor, Todd Hunter; copy editor, Sean Devlin; and agent, Mel Berger, of William Morris Endeavor. We also thank the educators and experts who contributed their ideas to this book.